MISERICORDIA DEI

STUDIES
IN MEDIEVAL AND
REFORMATION THOUGHT

EDITED BY

HEIKO A. OBERMAN, Tübingen

IN COOPERATION WITH

E. JANE DEMPSEY DOUGLASS, Claremont, California

LEIF GRANE, Copenhagen

GUILLAUME H. M. POSTHUMUS MEYJES, Leiden

ANTON G. WEILER, Nijmegen

VOLUME IV

DAVID CURTIS STEINMETZ

MISERICORDIA DEI

LEIDEN

E. J. BRILL

1968

MISERICORDIA DEI

THE THEOLOGY OF JOHANNES VON STAUPITZ IN ITS LATE MEDIEVAL SETTING

BY

DAVID CURTIS STEINMETZ

LEIDEN
E. J. BRILL
1968

PATRI MATRIQUE
IN GRATITUDINE DEDICATUS

TABLE OF CONTENTS

PREFACE

The preface is, perhaps, the most difficult part of a book to write. It is not easy to express gratitude in the formal prose of a few brief paragraphs and make that expression sound at all convincing, either to those for whom it is intended or to the casual reader who runs his eyes over this page as he moves on quickly to the text of the book itself. And yet not to acknowledge the debts which one owes, however justifiable the hesitation, would be far worse than to acknowledge them inadequately.

The research upon which this book is based was undertaken at Harvard University and at the University of Göttingen. The project was made possible with the aid of the Pilling Traveling Fellowship from Drew University, the Westengard Traveling Fellowship from Harvard University and a Rockefeller Doctoral Fellowship. These research grants enabled me to gain access to important research collections in European libraries, to buy requisite microfilms of rare manuscripts and to discuss my project with scholars engaged in pursuing related research.

Father Reinhold Weijenborg, O.F.M., and Father Damasus Trapp, O.S.A., discussed my research with me while it was still in its early stages. Professor Hubert Jedin of Bonn reacted to my thesis when it had taken more definite shape and offered valuable criticism. To those who read and criticised the finished manuscript—Professor George H. Williams of Harvard, Dr. Maria Grossman of Andover-Harvard Library, and Professor Leif Grane of Copenhagen—I owe a special debt of gratitude.

Professor Ernst Wolf of Göttingen, whose important study, *Staupitz und Luther*, is discussed in some detail in the pages which follow, received me graciously into his home and fully and frankly discussed his own work on Staupitz with me. Though I was led finally in my own research to disagree with many of the conclusions which he defended in his earlier book on Staupitz, it was always with the greatest reluctance that I differed with him and only when my own reading of the evidence compelled me to do so.

Professor Heiko A. Oberman, now Director of the Institut für Reformationsgeschichte of the University of Tübingen, guided my research on Staupitz and subjected my results to searching criticism.

He debated page by page, paragraph by paragraph, sentence by sentence the typewritten manuscript as I submitted it to him. And having satisfied himself at last with the development of the argument in the final draft, he became as vigorous an advocate of the finished thesis as he had been a demanding critic of the manuscript. This combination of rigorous scholarship and of warm, personal encouragement stimulated my research on Staupitz and made my study of his thought a far better book than it would otherwise have been.

Finally, I should acknowledge publicly the cheerful willingness with which my wife adapted, not only to the strain of a prolonged period of graduate study and research but also to the strangeness of life in a alien culture. That adaptable spirit contributed not a little to the speedy completion of this book.

DAVID C. STEINMETZ
Lancaster Theological Seminary
Epiphany, 1968

INTRODUCTION

Johannes von Staupitz was not a speculative theologian. The fine points of metaphysics and epistemology, which fascinated many theologians in the later middle ages, excited little interest in him. His theological reflections were devoted almost exclusively to the explication of the drama of human redemption. The dialogue between heaven and earth, between the self-giving *misericordia* of God and the dire *miseria* of man is the central and perennial theme of his sermons and treatises. If the problem of the intellectual capacities of fallen angels could be used to clarify some otherwise obscure aspect of the story of God's redeeming activity among men, Staupitz was not reluctant to discuss it. If it seemed to him irrelevant, he did not hesitate to omit it. The truth of the more speculative aspects of Christian theology was never for him in question. But as a preacher and pastor he narrowed his message to fundamentals. He was, above all,—to use Luther's phrase— a preacher of grace and of the cross.[1]

The fact that Staupitz was principally a preacher and administrator does not mean that he was a slip-shod or careless theologian.[2] His early sermons on Job show evidence of his wide reading, while his later treatise on predestination demonstrates a systematic ability of a high order. Although it is true that he did not write a *Summa* or even a commentary on the *Sentences* of Peter Lombard, his grasp of theological issues was by no means superficial. The warm piety which suffuses his writings is not the antithesis of his learning, but its practical expression. The task of the theologian is the confession of the praise of God.[3] Insight into the divine mysteries is not cultivated for

---

[1] Luther uses the title to characterize the Staupitz he had known prior to the latter's entry into the monastery at Salzburg: "Vere nonnihil me contristavit ista tua submissio, et alium quendam mihi exhibuit, quam Staupitium illum gratiae et crucis praeconem." *WAB* 2, 264, Nr. 376, 47–8 (9 Feb. 1521).

[2] We reject, therefore, the position of Alfred Jeremias that "...man sollte nicht von Staupitz' Theologie sprechen, sondern von seiner christlichen Lebensanschauung." *Johannes von Staupitz, Luthers Vater und Schüler* (Leipzig, 1926), p. 75.

[3] H. A. Oberman points out the similarity between Staupitz and Luther on this point: "As for Staupitz, so for Luther, theology is not scientia nor attributio per analogiam. The theological enterprise is for both an act of thanksgiving, the imputation of the highest praise to God, confessio laudis." "'Iustitia Christi' and

its own sake. Knowledge of God finds its fruition in the praise and service of God.

The difficulty of arriving at a fair and balanced assessment of the theology of Staupitz has been complicated by his special relationship to Martin Luther. Luther once claimed in his characteristically expansive fashion that he had "received everything from Staupitz" and acknowledged his old friend to be the originator of evangelical doctrine.[1] Staupitz, for his part, in his last letter to Luther dated April 1, 1524, referred to himself as Luther's brother and pupil.[2] Even if these judgments must be tempered by dispassionate historical research, the very fact that they have been made places Staupitz in the center of concern for the student of Reformation history. Unfortunately, however, this interest in Staupitz is—more often than not—derivative, a by-product of a primary and more important interest in Luther.

The historian who succumbs to the temptation of viewing Staupitz as if his entire historical and theological importance were dependent upon his relationship to Luther, is at least partially justified in doing so. It is undeniable that whoever understands the theology of Staupitz will have in his possession a key for the better understanding of Luther's theology. But that does not mean that a historian can safely limit his investigation of Staupitz's theology to the question of Staupitz's relationship to Luther or that he can even hope to understand this relationship properly as long as he leaves unexamined the relationship between Staupitz and his medieval theological environment.

Perhaps the time is ripe now to redress the imbalance in the study of Staupitz's theology, to examine his thought within the larger framework of the theological world of the later middle ages. This first chapter will attempt to explain why this is true and, by doing so, to

---

'Iustitia Dei', Luther and the Scholastic Doctrines of Justification," *HTR* 59 (1966), 26, footnote 52.

[1] Heinrich Boehmer cites this saying of Luther's without giving a precise reference. *Martin Luther: Road to Reformation* (New York: Meridian Books, 1960), p. 105. Cf. *WATR* 1, Nr. 526 (Spring 1533): "Unser Herr Gott ist unser Herr, ille vocat nos, so mussen wirs sagen. Wer wolt sonst den hass ausstehn? Quia contemptus et ingratitudo est summa. Sed Staupicius meus dicebat: Man mus den man ansehen, der da heyst Christus. Staupicius hat die doctrinam angefangen."

[2] This letter is found in a collection appended to the book by Th. Kolde, *Die deutsche Augustiner-Congregation und Johann von Staupitz* (Gotha, 1879), pp. 446–7. The address reads: "D. Staupicius. D.M.L. amico summo et Christi servo Frater et discipulus tuus Johannes Christi servus."

indicate the reasons why this present book was undertaken. We shall begin by examining briefly Staupitz's life and writings and then proceed on to a discussion of the general state of scholarship on his theology.

I. LIFE AND WRITINGS

Johannes von Staupitz was born in the town of Motterwitz in Saxony sometime during the decade 1460–9. Staupitz's family, unlike Luther's, belonged to the nobility, and Johannes grew up as the friend and companion of Frederick the Wise, who lived in the nearby town of Grimma, and of Johannes, the future bishop of Meissen, who lived in the nearby town of Mügelentz. There was an Augustinian convent in Grimma, and it was here in all likelihood that Staupitz first became acquainted with the Order of the Hermits of St. Augustine, the order which he was later to join.[1]

The Order of the Hermits of St. Augustine had been created in 1256 by Pope Alexander IV, who united the Hermits of Tuscany, the Williamites, the Zambonini, and the Hermits of Brettino into a new mendicant order.[2] By the time Staupitz first came in contact with the Augustinians they were firmly established as one of the learned orders of the Church and had produced a series of significant theologians—men, for example, such as Giles of Rome and Gregory of Rimini—who represented the order at the University of Paris. Staupitz was attracted to the order and took his vows, according to tradition, at the cloister in Munich.[3]

He began his course of study under the faculty of arts at the University of Cologne in 1483.[4] In the summer semester of 1485 he ma-

---

[1] Biographical information about Staupitz is given by Kolde, Boehmer and Jeremias in the books just mentioned. A brief biographical survey is given by Ernst Wolf, *Staupitz und Luther, Ein Beitrag zur Theologie des Johannes von Staupitz und deren Bedeutung für Luthers theologischen Werdegang, Quellen und Forschungen zur Reformationsgeschichte*, Band IX (Leipzig, 1927), pp. 30–5, 130–8. See also the article by Wolf on Staupitz in *RGG³*, col. 342.

[2] Eelcko Ypma, *La formation des professeurs chez les ermites de Saint-Augustin* 1256 à 1324 (Paris, 1956), p. xvii.

[3] Kolde, *Augustiner-Congregation*, p. 213, footnote 4. Wolf, *Staupitz und Luther*, p. 33, suggests the possibility that Staupitz entered the unreformed cloister in Cologne, which had been incorporated in the University of Cologne since 1391. Wolf appears later to have changed his mind, *RGG³*, 342.

[4] Franz Lau indicates that the Observants laid great stress on theological study:

triculated at Leipzig. He returned to Cologne to study for the degree of master of arts and then in October, 1489, came once more to Leipzig.

In 1497 Staupitz was sent by his superiors to the Augustinian cloister at Tübingen to continue his studies at the university there.[1] Gabriel Biel, the famous disciple of William Ockham on the faculty of Tübingen, had died two years earlier.[2] His successor as the chief protagonist of nominalistic thought at Tübingen was Wendel Steinbach, under whom Staupitz may very likely have studied. The evidence available indicates that Staupitz also attended the lectures of Konrad Summenhard[3] and Paul Scriptoris. Indeed, Staupitz thought so highly of the lectures of Scriptoris on the *Sentences Commentary* of Duns Scotus that he required the entire Augustinian cloister to hear them.[4]

On October 29, 1498, Staupitz began his series of lectures as a *baccalaureus biblicus*. On the tenth of January of the following year he took the second major step in his theological education and began to lecture as a *baccalaureus sententiarius*. By July 6, 1500 (in, one must say, a remarkably brief time) Staupitz had completed the requirements for the doctorate and was granted his licentiate. A few days later the *insignia magistralia* were conferred on him.[5] It was during this period of his theological study at Tübingen that he preached thirty-four

"Among the monks of Observant monasteries theology professors had a special rank. Certain decisions could not be made without an explicit hearing of the professor's opinions. Theological zeal was alive in the Observance. Not only was study cultivated with great diligence and devotion by individuals, but the order and its Observant branches maintained formal professorships. Observant monks were appointed professors in universities, moreover, not only because they were the cheapest talent available, but above all because they were the most learned scholars." *Luther*, trans. by Robert H. Fischer (London: SCM Press, 1963), pp. 29–30.

[1] For a history of the Augustinian cloister in Tübingen see Martin Brecht, "Das Augustiner-Eremiten-Kloster zu Tübingen," *Mittelalterliches Erbe-Evangelische Verantwortung, Vorträge und Ansprachen zum Gedenken der Gründung des Tübinger Augustinerklosters* 1262 (Tübingen, 1962), pp. 45–89.

[2] Heiko A. Oberman, *The Harvest of Medieval Theology, Gabriel Biel and Late Medieval Nominalism* (Cambridge: Harvard University Press, 1963), p. 20, gives the date December 7, 1495.

[3] According to Luther, Staupitz was fond of quoting the remark of Konrad Summenhard: "Quis liberabit me ab ista rixosa theologia?" *WATR* 5, Nr. 5374 (Summer 1540).

[4] H. Hermelink, *Geschichte der Theologischen Fakultät in Tübingen vor der Reformation* 1477–1534 (Tübingen, 1906), p. 164.

[5] Wolf, *Staupitz und Luther*, pp. 33–4. Cf. Otto Scheel, *Martin Luther*, Vol. II (Tübingen, 1917), p. 193.

sermons on Job which are the earliest writings from his hand.[1] It was also during this period in 1500 that his first tractate, a legal discussion of the obligations of church attendance entitled *Decisio questionis de audiencia misse in parrochiali ecclesia dominicis et festivis diebus*, was printed in Tübingen by Johannes Othmar.[2]

Staupitz left Tübingen in 1500 and proceeded on to Munich, where he remained for two years as the prior of the Augustinian cloister in that city. His activity in Munich was called to a halt by his old childhood friend, Frederick the Wise, who had set about to establish in Wittenberg a university to rival that of neighboring Leipzig. According to the arrangements made with the Augustinian Hermits, the Augustinians were to supply two professors for the new university to fill the chair of Bible on the theological faculty and the chair of moral philosophy on the faculty of arts. Staupitz was chosen to serve as the first biblical professor and as the dean of the faculty of theology.

Staupitz's career as a theological professor was interrupted almost as soon as it began. In 1503 he was elected the vicar-general of the German Observants, a group officially known as the Reformed Congregation of the Hermits of St. Augustine.[3] The Augustinian Order in Germany was divided at that time into four provinces: Saxonia, Rheno-Suebica, Colonia and Bavaria. Each province elected its own provincial prior at a meeting of the provincial chapter held for that purpose once every three years. To be legally valid, it was necessary for this election to be confirmed shortly thereafter by the general prior in Rome. The Reformed Congregation, though still part

---

[1] *Staupitz Tübinger Predigten*, ed. Georg Buchwald and Ernst Wolf, *Quellen und Forschungen zur Reformationsgeschichte*, Band VIII (Leipzig, 1927). For a description of the sermons and a discussion of their dating cf. Wolf, *Staupitz und Luther*, pp. 16–27; *Tübinger Predigten*, pp. vii–xiv.

[2] For a description of this edition cf. Wolf, *Staupitz und Luther*, p. 11. The question was whether a layman could leave his own parish on a Sunday or feast day to hear the more learned preacher in a mendicant church. Staupitz admits that a person who transgresses without just cause the precept of the Church, requiring him to hear mass in his own local parish, shows contempt for the parish priest set over him as a father in Christ and thereby sins mortally. If, however, a just cause can be shown for going to another church, then, of course, the layman commits no sin and may in fact do something positively beneficial. In developing his case, Staupitz uses a scholastic form of argumentation which contrasts sharply with his later treatises and sermons. He shows as well a familiarity with the principal texts of canon law: Gratian, Godfrey of Trano, Hostiensis, Johann Andreae, Panormitanus. He also cites Biel, Gerson, Bonaventura, and Thomas Aquinas.

[3] For a brief history of the Augustinian Order in Germany see Ernst Wolf, "Die Augustiner-Eremiten in Deutschland bis zur Reformation," *Mittelalterliches Erbe-Evangelische Verantwortung* (Tübingen, 1962), pp. 25–44.

of the larger Order, was not divided into administrative provinces. It consisted rather of all of the Observant cloisters scattered throughout Germany, regardless of their geographical location. Late in the fifteenth century these cloisters had been drawn together into one organization by Andreas Proles, the first vicar-general of the Congregation. Their unity was not based on their proximity to one another, but on their adherence to a strict observance of the rule.

In order to safeguard a more stringent interpretation of the rule, the Reformed Congregation had sought, and to some degree obtained, an independent status within the Augustinian Order. The cloisters of the Congregation were permitted, for example, to elect their own chief administrative officer, the vicar-general. The election of this officer was not, as was the election of the provincial, subject to the confirmation of the general of the Order. Only the Holy See retained the final right of approval or rejection. However, the independence of the vicar-general was by no means absolute, since he was still expected to be obedient to the general of the Augustinians and to act in the best interests of the Order.[1]

Staupitz's elevation to the chief position within the Reformed Congregation and his acceptance of the heavy responsibilites of administration and visitation which accompanied the office insured that he could spend no more than a portion of his time in Wittenberg. Though he did not resign from the university faculty, he lectured only at infrequent intervals. In 1504 he wrote a new constitution for the Congregation, the *Constitutiones Fratrum Heremitarum sancti Augustini ad apostolicorum privilegiorum formam pro Reformatione Alemanie*, which was printed in Nuremberg.[2]

The years from 1504–1507 were filled with administrative activities of various kinds. Staupitz attempted, for example, to strengthen the position of the Observants in Germany over against the Conventuals by entering into an agreement with the Lombardian Congregation. This latter group enjoyed even greater freedom within the Augustinian Order than did the German Observants, since they were in fact completely independent of the general prior in Rome. In 1505 Staupitz succeeded in obtaining a papal bull which granted to the Congregation in Germany the privileges of the Observants in Lombardy. But the victory was short-lived. The General of the Augustinian Hermits, Augustine of Interramna, vigorously opposed the

---

[1] Th. Kolde, *Augustiner-Congregation*, pp. 226–32.
[2] For a description cf. Wolf, *Staupitz und Luther*, p. 12.

further decentralization of the Order. Taking advantage of a certain imprecision in the language of the first bull, Augustine sought to nullify the victory of the German Observants and bring them back under the control of the central administration of the Order in Rome. His strenuous opposition was rewarded on March 24, 1506, with a second bull, which explicitly took away from the Reformed Congregation what the first bull had vaguely and imperfectly granted.[1]

Shortly after the death of Augustine of Interramna in 1506, Giles Canisio of Viterbo, was elected to succeed him as the General Prior of the Augustinian Hermits.[2] Under the new general, and at least in part with his collaboration, Staupitz attempted once more to reform the organizational structure of the German Observants, this time through a proposed merger with the Saxon Province.[3] The members

---

[1] Th. Kolde, *Augustiner-Congregation*, pp. 226–32.

[2] For a bibliography of his writings cf. F. X. Martin "The Problem of Giles of Viterbo: A Historiographical Problem," *Augustiniana* 9 (1959), 357–79; 10 (1960), 43–60. See also "Giles of Viterbo and the Monastery of Lecceto: The Making of a Reformer," *Analecta Augustiniana* 25 (1962), 225–253.

[3] This history of the attempted merger and of the consequent controversy within the Augustinian Order is still much debated. The oldest works on the subject were written by Th. Kolde, "Innere Bewegungen unter den deutschen Augustinern und Luthers Romreise," *ZKG* 2 (1878), 460–80, and *Die deutsche Augustiner-Congregation und Johann von Staupitz* (Gotha, 1879). Other works are Heinrich Boehmer, *Luthers Romfahrt* (Leipzig, 1914); A. V. Müller, "Der Augustiner-Observantismus und die Kritik und Psychologie Luthers," *ARG* 18 (1921), 1–34; Hubert Jedin, "Die römischen Augustinerquellen zu Luthers Frühzeit," *ARG* 25 (1928), 256–70; W. Huempfner, O.E.S.A., "Äussere Geschichte der Augustiner-Eremiten in Deutschland," in the Festschrift, *St. Augustin* (Würzburg, 1930), 147–96; Otto Scheel, *Martin Luther, Von Katholizismus zur Reformation*, Vol. II, 3rd and 4th editions (Tübingen, 1930), pp. 480–550. In 1957 Reinhold Weijenborg, O.F.M., published a series of six documents (four of which were unknown), which, he believed, cast new light on the legal problem at the heart of the proposed merger between the Reformed Congregation and the Saxon Province. ("Neuentdeckte Dokumente im Zusammenhang mit Luthers Romreise." *Antonianum* 32 (1957), 147–202.) Weijenborg argued that Staupitz, although he knew that he had not met the terms of the New Bull, pressed ahead with his attempt to unite the Congregation and the Province. His arbitrary and illegal activity prepared the way for the Reformation. Cf. p. 202: "Auf diese Weise hat er schliesslich das Entstehen der lutherischen Reformation als Volksbewegung weitgehend vorbereitet und ermöglicht." In 1960 Franz Lau published an excellent critique of Weijenborg's contribution to Staupitz studies in "Père Reinoud und Luther: Bemerkungen zu Reinhold Weijenborgs Lutherstudien," *Luther-Jahrbuch* 27 (1960), 64–122. Lau acknowledged, quite rightly, the validity of Weijenborg's documents and accepted his thesis concerning the legal problem to which they pointed. He challenged, however, the notion that the controversy could be understood wholly in legal terms or that the union was at any time opposed by the Saxon Province. He especially deplored Weijenborg's vitriolic personal attacks upon Staupitz, which seemed to him wholly unjustified in the light of the evidence. He suggested that

of the Saxon Province, it appears, favored the proposed merger
strongly. Together with the vicar-general of the Reformed Congregation, they petitioned the German legate, Cardinal Bernhardin
Carvajal, for a bull authorizing the union of the two groups. The
Cardinal was persuaded by their arguments and in 1507 at Memmingen
issued the requisite bull. The terms of the union as set forth in the bull
were quite explicit. The province and the Congregation were granted
permission to hold a joint chapter for the purpose of electing a common superior. This jointly-elected superior was in turn authorized by
the bull to carry out the work of uniting the province and the Congregation into a single corporate unity.[1] These were the legally prescribed
stops on the road to union.

In point of fact, however, the joint chapter was never held. Instead
Staupitz was elected at—it should be noted—*separate* meetings of the
Congregation and the province to a new term as vicar-general
(Munich, 1508) and a first term as provincial (Münnerstadt, 1509).
While one may argue that the spirit of the bull was thereby preserved,
its explicit provisions concerning a joint meeting and a common
election were nevertheless clearly violated. It is evident to a legally
trained mind that the only union which had been effected by this
maneuver was not a union of the two independent corporations
(which remained legally independent) but rather a union in the person
of Johannes von Staupitz, who as vicar-general and provincial held
the chief office in each organization.[2] This legal difficulty was not
mitigated by the approval of the general prior in Rome, who had, in
any case, no authority over the election of a vicar-general and no
power to by-pass the terms of a papal bull. The resultant legal muddle
reinforced the objections which the Observants could raise against the
proposed merger. Because of the size and significance of the opposition party in the Observant family, Staupitz waited until September,
1510, before he published the bull openly. Even then, seven of the
twenty-nine monasteries of the Reformed Congregation refused to
approve the union. Among those seven were two of the largest and

---

Staupitz's role in the struggle could only be properly evaluated by historians
willing to consider the total picture of the man which emerges from his writings.
We would add that it is necessary as well to keep in mind the zeal for reform of
Giles of Viterbo. In this connection see John O'Malley, S.J., *Giles of Viterbo on
Church and Reform* (to be published in 1968 by E. J. Brill of Leiden).
   [1] Weijenborg, "Neuentdeckte Dokumente," pp. 158–61.
   [2] Weijenborg, "Neuentdeckte Dokumente," pp. 170–1.

most influential of the cloisters, Nuremberg and Erfurt—the latter the
cloister of Martin Luther.[1]

The Observants were afraid that the privileges which they had
obtained over the course of the years and the style of life which they
had developed would be lost in any merger with the Conventuals.[2] In
order to forestall such a union, the seven monasteries dispatched two
brothers to Rome to appeal directly to the pope himself. The second
of the two brothers sent on this journey was Father Martin Luther.

The appeal of the seven monasteries to Rome was unsuccessful. The
General of the Order, Giles of Viterbo, had no intention of approving
the request, though he did not wish to aggravate the controversy
further by a curt dismissal of the German representatives. Accordingly, he dispatched a representative of his own to Germany to pour oil
on the troubled waters there. Staupitz, however, was disheartened by
the turn of events and began to waver in his support of the union. In
1511 he granted concessions to the dissident cloisters which all but
eviscerated his reform program.[3] Finally in 1512 at the meeting of the
Observant chapter in Cologne he announced his intention of abandon-
ing the project altogether.

It was during the period of controversy within the Order that
Luther and Staupitz first came into real contact with one another. In
1508 Luther had been appointed at Staupitz's behest to the University
of Wittenberg to fill the Augustinian chair of moral philosophy in the
faculty of arts. It is difficult to ascertain whether the two men developed any real friendship at this time.[4] Staupitz was in Munich part of the
year and when he returned, he was involved in his heavy administrative responsibilities.

In any event, both Staupitz and Luther were in Wittenberg in 1511.
In September of that year Staupitz presented the doctor's cap to four
Augustinians. Staupitz took advantage of the occasion in order to

---

[1] The other five cloisters were Kulmbach, Konigsberg in Franken, Sanger-
hausen, Nordhausen, and Sternberg. Cf. Kolde, "Innere Bewegungen," pp. 466ff.

[2] Lau stresses a dual basis for the opposition to the merger of the Congregation
with the Saxon Province: (1) the Observants fear of coming under the control of
a Conventual Provincial and (2) the resentment of Observant cloisters in other
Provinces at the thought of coming under the control of the Saxon Province.
Luther, pp. 47–8.

[3] For the Jena Recess of July, 1511, cf. Weijenborg, "Neuentdeckte Dokumente," p. 198.

[4] In attempting to ascertain the time when Staupitz influenced Luther in his
view of predestination, Wolf was forced to leave open a span of years from ap-
proximately 1507 to the fall of 1512. Wolf, *Staupitz und Luther*, p. 222.

encourage Luther as well to become a doctor and preacher of the Order. Luther demurred, but Staupitz insisted.[1] In October, 1512, Luther received his doctorate and was assigned to take the biblical chair at Wittenberg which had formerly been occupied by Staupitz.[2]

It was during these years in Wittenberg that the relationship between the two men flowered. Luther, we know, confessed to Staupitz and sought his counsel in temptation. Staupitz, for his part, found it difficult to understand the nature of the fierce struggle for assurance which racked the soul of the younger man.[3] Nevertheless, in spite of a certain lack of empathy between them, Staupitz was able to give Luther some comfort in his temptations and to lead him away from a nominalistic view of predestination to a more genuinely Augustinian one.[4]

Staupitz was still occupied with the duties of visitation. During Lent, 1512, he preached a series of sermons at St. Peter's in Salzburg.[5] In the winter of 1512–13 he was still in the city of Nuremberg. The following year was spent in Salzburg with time out for a brief trip to Rome. In 1514 he visited the Netherlands, returning in 1515 to Wittenberg, and then proceeding to Gotha. In the summer of 1516 he was off again on another tour of the Netherlands and Belgium. In

---

[1] Luther enjoyed recounting the anecdote of his resistance to the idea of assuming the doctorate. Cf. *WATR* 5, Nr. 5371 (Summer 1540); Nr. 6422; *WATR* 4, Nr. 4091 (6–9 Nov. 1538); *WATR* 2, Nr. 2255 (18 Aug.–26 Dec. 1531).

[2] Gordon Rupp, *Luther's Progress to the Diet of Worms* (New York: Harper Torchbooks, 1964), p. 24.

[3] *WATR* 1, Nr. 22 (30 Nov.–14 Dec. 1531); Nr. 141 (14 Dec. 1531). Cf. also Heinrich Boehmer, *Martin Luther*, p. 103: "Thus Staupitz never understood Luther's affliction because he himself had never experienced anything like it, as he openly admitted, and so underestimated the peril in which the young man found himself."

[4] Wolf, *Staupitz und Luther*, p. 221: "Dass Luther bei Staupitz eine von der gabrielistischen wesentlich verschiedene Prädestinationslehre kennengelernt haben kann, ist wichtig." Wolf's explanation of this, however, is not sufficiently precise and does not take note of the points of agreement between Staupitz and Biel. H. A. Oberman has indicated two points on which further research needs to be done; namely, certitude of salvation and mystical piety. *Harvest*, p. 230, footnote 124 and p. 351, footnote 87.

[5] These Lenten sermons are preserved in the handwritten codex Hs: b V 8, St. Peter, in the library of the Benedictine foundation, St. Peter's, in Salzburg, Austria. Also in this volume are sermons from the years 1518, 1519, and 1520. There are two codices in St. Peter's and four in the Benedictine convent at Nonnberg. Of these six Salzburg codices, only three contain unprinted works of Staupitz—in this case, all sermons. They are codex Hs: b V 8, St. Peter; codex Hs: b II 11, St. Peter; and codex Hs: 23 E 16, Nonnberg. Cf. Ernst Wolf, *Staupitz und Luther*, pp. 276–9.

the midst of this strenuous activity he found time to write and in 1515 published a little treatise on the life of Christian discipleship called *Ein büchlein von der nachfolgung des willigen sterbens Christi.*[1]

In October, 1516, Staupitz returned to Munich, where he intended to spend the winter months, but the invitation of his old friend, Christoph Scheurl, to come to Nuremberg instead proved to be too enticing to resist. Nuremberg provided not only an opportunity for the renewal of old friendships, but also a chance to preach the Advent sermons in the Augustinian church of that city.

In 1517 Staupitz made a brief visitation to Koburg, returning as soon as possible to Nuremberg, where he preached a second series of sermons.[2] Fortunately, these Lenten sermons have been preserved in the notes of a listener. In the same year he published his treatise on predestination, the *Libellus de executione eterne predestinationis*, which was also issued in a German translation by Christoph Scheurl as *Ein nutzbarliches büchlein von der entlichen volziehung ewiger fürsehung.*[3]

The circle of friends in Nuremberg which surrounded Staupitz formed a *Sodalitas Staupitziana*. This *Sodalitas* numbered in its membership many of the prominent citizens of Nuremberg, such as: Anton Tucher, Jerome Eber, Caspar Nuzel, Jerome Holzschuher, Sigismund and Christophorus Furer, Lazarus Spengler, Albrecht Dürer, Wolfgang Hoffmann and, of course, Christoph Scheurl. Staupitz's tabletalk was written down by a member of this *Sodalitas* and thus preserved.[4]

In the winter of 1517 Staupitz moved on again to Munich, where he was invited to preach the Advent sermons. Using these sermons as the basis for his meditations, he again found leisure to write and

---

[1] The first edition was published in Leipzig in 1515 by Melchior Lotther. Our citations are taken from the edition prepared by J. K. F. Knaake, *Johannis Staupitii, opera quae reperiri poterunt omnia: Deutsche Schriften*, Vol. I (Potsdam, 1867). For a description cf. Wolf, *Staupitz und Luther*, p. 15.

[2] The original of these sermons is found in codex C of the *Bibliotheca Scheurlina*, fol. 168ᵃ–174ᵃ. They have been reprinted by Knaake, *Staupitii opera*, pp. 13–50. Knaake, however, erroneously refers to these as Advent sermons, whereas their content clearly shows that they were preached in the Lenten season. Cf. Wolf, *Staupitz und Luther*, p. 15.

[3] This treatise was based on the 1516 Advent sermons preached in Nuremberg, of which we have no other record. The German translation appeared on January 20, 1517; the Latin original somewhat later on February 6, 1517. Both editions were printed in Nuremberg by Federicus Peypus. The German translation is available in Knaake, pp. 137ff.

[4] According to Scheurl it was Lazarus Spengler who wrote down both the table-talk and the Lenten sermons of 1517. The original is also found in Codex C of the *Bibliotheca Scheurlina*, fol. 168ᵃ–174ᵃ, reprinted by Knaake, pp. 13–50. For a list of the members of this *Sodalitas* cf. Knaake, p. 14.

composed the treatise so highly valued by Luther, *Ein seligs newes Jar von der lieb gottes*.[1] This was not the first time Staupitz had reworked sermon material for a new publication. Indeed, his treatise on predestination had in a similar fashion been based on the Advent sermons of 1516 delivered in Nuremberg.

In 1518 Staupitz returned again to Nuremberg to preach in the Augustinian church there. It was while he was in Nuremberg that he began to receive reports of the proceedings which were being undertaken against Dr. Martin Luther. In 1515 at the meeting of the chapter in Gotha, where both Staupitz and Luther were present, Luther had been elected district vicar and placed in charge of eleven monasteries. Now Staupitz was being summoned by the turn of events to look with new eyes on his successor at the University of Wittenberg.

At the meeting of the chapter in Heidelberg in April, 1518, Staupitz acted as if nothing had happened during the course of the past year and calmly appointed Brother Martin to preside over the public disputation which was held in the great hall of the monastery.[2] Furthermore, there was no official discussion of the indulgences controversy in the chapter itself, though it can safely be assumed that the furor in Germany was the subject of many private conversations between Staupitz and Luther. Indeed, it was probably in response to a suggestion by Staupitz that Luther prepared his *Resolutions*, a copy of which was to be sent to Pope Leo X as evidence of Luther's catholicity and loyalty. Later in the same year Staupitz addressed a letter to Luther from Salzburg urging him to join Staupitz there and warning Luther that he saw only martyrdom ahead.[3]

Luther, however, instead of joining Staupitz in Salzburg, set off for Augsburg to be examined by the great Thomist scholar, Cardinal Cajetan. When Staupitz was apprised of the situation, he immediately left for Augsburg to stand by Luther in this time of testing, convinced as he was of the great danger which threatened Luther's life. Cajetan attempted to enlist Staupitz as his agent for the purpose of persuading Dr. Luther to recant his opinions. Staupitz demurred, maintaining

---

[1] The first edition was printed by Melchior Lotther in Leipzig, 1518. It is reprinted in Knaake, pp. 88–119. For Luther's judgment of its worth cf. Knaake, p. 89.

[2] For the text of the Heidelberg Disputation, *WA* 1. 353–74.

[3] This letter is number 6 in a collection of documents appended to the end of an essay by C. L. W. Grimm, "De Ioanne Staupitio eiusque in sacrorum christianorum instaurationem meritis," *Zeitschrift für historische Theologie*, ed. Illgen, N.F. 1 (1837), 58–126.

cleverly that only the great learning of the cardinal himself could avail anything.[1]

Staupitz, however, did urge Luther to write a letter to the cardinal, apologizing for some of the insolent statements which he had made against the pope, and even suggested that Brother Martin examine his conscience concerning the proposed recantation.[2] Yet this was not much of a victory for Cajetan. Staupitz was thoroughly disgusted by the cardinal's handling of Luther, and was shocked and indignant when he learned that the cardinal already had a warrant of arrest for Luther from Gabriel della Volta, who had succeeded Giles of Viterbo as the General of the Augustinians. Accordingly, Staupitz attempted to raise a loan from his friends in Augsburg in order to send Luther out of Germany, preferably to Paris. But he was unable to gather the necessary funds. Having failed in his attempt, he released Luther from his vows to the Order so that the young reformer could act without taking the Order into consideration. Then, without a word to Cajetan, he vanished from the city.[3]

Luther and Staupitz corresponded in the interim, and in July, 1519, following the Leipzig disputation with Eck, the two men conferred in person at Grimma.[4] Staupitz was still busy with his duties as vicar-general. In October he could be found in Munich. In March of the following year he was in Erfurt. Meanwhile, Staupitz had not been forgotten in Rome. There was still hope that he might be able to intercede with Luther and so bring the whole controversy to a speedy end. Acting on the basis of this hope, the pope instructed the General of the Augustinians, della Volta, to write to Staupitz and admonish him to assist in terminating the struggle with Luther.[5] This letter, however, had an unexpected effect on Staupitz; it stimulated in him a desire to resign his office as vicar-general. Thus at the meeting of the Augustinians in Eisleben in 1520 Link succeeded Staupitz as the vicar-general.[6]

Matthew Lang, the Cardinal-archbishop of Salzburg, invited Staupitz to his see to serve him as a preacher and adviser. Staupitz accepted, hoping to find peace in that city. With increasing anxiety he

---

[1] Heinrich Boehmer, *Martin Luther*, p. 239.
[2] Heinrich Boehmer, *Martin Luther*, p. 241.
[3] Heinrich Boehmer, *Martin Luther*, pp. 241–2.
[4] Heinrich Boehmer, *Martin Luther*, p. 290.
[5] Heinrich Boehmer, *Martin Luther*, p. 349.
[6] Alfred Jeremias, *Staupitz*, pp. 54–5.

watched the events building up to the Diet of Worms, fearing not only for Luther, but also for his own life.[1]

In 1521 Staupitz met with his successor, Link, in Munich during the Easter season. On April 26th in Rome a dispensation was issued, permitting Staupitz to leave the Augustinian Order and join the Benedictines. By August Staupitz received official notification of the dispensation. He immediately entered the Benedictine monastery in Salzburg. Six days later he was elected abbot, and consecrated in this office on the fifteenth of the month.[2]

Luther, of course, knew nothing of what had happened in Salzburg. He was at this time isolated in the Wartburg. In December, 1521, he wrote to Link that he had heard nothing definite about Staupitz's activities, only a rumor that he was now in Salzburg.[3] By June, 1522, he had received confirmation of the rumor and took time to write a letter to Staupitz.[4] Staupitz appears not to have attempted to answer this letter. Undeterred by the fact that he had received no response from Staupitz, Luther wrote to him again in September, 1523.[5] This letter was pointed and direct. Luther deplored Staupitz's move into the abbacy and urged his old friend to foresake his cardinal and the pope for the sake of Christ.[6] He had not forgotten that it was through Staupitz himself that the light of the gospel had once again begun to shine in the darkness.[7]

---

[1] For Staupitz's feelings at this time see especially letters 6, 8 and 10 in the collection by Grimm. Cf. above footnote 40. Jeremias feels that letter no. 6 was written after rather than before Luther's examination by Cajetan; i.e., on September 7, 1519 rather than 1518. Jeremias, *Staupitz*, p. 344. Boehmer argues on better grounds that the letter was written on September 14, 1518 and that Luther did not leave for Augsburg until after September 24th. Boehmer, *Martin Luther*, p. 229.

[2] Eight of the sermons which Staupitz preached in Salzburg have been republished in modern editions. These eight sermons are taken from the codex Hs: b II 11, St. Peter, dated 1523. Sermons 1–7 are reprinted by H. Aumüller, "Die ungedruckten Staupitz-Predigten in Salzburg," *Jahrbuch der Gesellschaft für die Geschichte des Protestantismus in Österreich* 2 (Wien, 1881), 49ff; 11 (1890), 113ff. Sermon 24, an undated Advent sermon, is reprinted by Kolde, *Augustiner-Congregation*, pp. 452ff. Our citations will be from the more recent, and relatively more accessible, editions of Aumüller and Kolde.

[3] "Patrem nostrum charissimum Staupitium nescio, ubi sit. Audio autem eum idoli Salzburgensis aulicum esse, quod homini optimo invideo. Tu eum salutabis." *WAB* 2.415. Nr. 446.34–6 (18 Dec. 1521).

[4] *WAB* 2.566–8. Nr. 512 (27 June 1522).

[5] *WAB* 3.155–7. Nr. 659 (17 Sept. 1523).

[6] "Ego plane non desinam optare et orare, quam ut alienus a Cardinale tuo et papatu fias, sicut ego sum, imo sicut et tu fuisti." *WAB* 3.156. Nr. 659.36–8 (17 Sept. 1523).

[7] "Sed nos certe etiamsi desivimus tibi grati ac placiti esse, tamen tui non decet

A half year passed before Staupitz wrote in reply to Luther. He asserted that his faith in Christ and in the gospel were unshaken that his love for Luther could only be compared with the love of David for Jonathan.[1] He disagreed with the Reformation movement, however, in its strife over *adiaphora*[2] and in its abuse of evangelical freedom.[3]

A few days after the letter was dispatched to Luther, Staupitz wrote from Braunau to Father Chilian in Salzburg that he was in poor health and was living under the supervision of a physician.[4] His health failed steadily after that and on December 28, 1524, he passed away. He was buried at St. Peter's in Salzburg.[5] A year after his death a posthumous work on faith was published, entitled *Von dem heyligen rechten Christlichen glauben*.[6] The publication of the tractate may presumably be attributed to Wenzeslaus Link. In 1559, thirty five years after his death, Staupitz's works were placed on the Index by Pope Paul IV.[7]

---

esse immemores et ingratos, per quem primum coepit euangelii lux de tenebris splendescere in cordibus nostris." *WAB* 3.155–6. Nr. 659.5–8 (17 Sept. 1523).

[1] "Ad quod ego: fides mea in Christum et euangelium integra perseuerat, tametsi oratione opus habeam, ut Christus adiuvet incredulitatem meam, detesterque humana et ecclesiam tepide amplectar. In the constantissimus mihi amor est eciam supra amorem mulierum *[2 Sam. 1:26]* semper infractus." Staupitz to Luther (1 April 1524), Kolde, *Augustiner-Congregation*, Nr. 22, p. 446.

[2] "Videmini mihi damnare multa prorsus externa, quae ad fidem et iusticiam nihil faciunt, neutra sunt, et in fide domini nostri Jhesu Christi facta minime conscienciam grauant, cur igitur turbantur Simplicium corda, et quid monachorum habitus naribus tuis odio fecit, quem plerique in sancta fide Christi gestant. Intervenit proh dolor fere in singulis humanis exerciciis abusus et rari sunt qui fide metantur omnia, sunt nihilominus aliqui, ideo non est rei substancia reprobanda propter accidens malum, quod in aliquibus est. Vota passim omnia abijcitis, in paucissimis forte uno duntaxat fundatj. Effundo itaque ad te preces, dulcissime amice, recordare paruulorum et non inquites pauidas consciencias. Que neutra sunt, et cum sincera fide stare possunt, oro ne damnes. In illis vero, que fidei aduersantur clama, ne cesses." Staupitz to Luther (1 April 1524), Kolde, *Augustiner-Congregation*, Nr. 22, pp. 446–7.

[3] "Dominus Jhesus tribuat incrementum, quatenus euangelium, quod nunc auribus percipimus, quod in ore multorum voluitur, tandem vivamus, si quidem ad libertatem carnis video innumeros abuti euangelio." Staupitz to Luther (1 April 1524), Kolde, *Augustiner-Congregation*, Nr. 22, p. 447.

[4] Staupitz to Father Chilian (14 April 1524), Kolde, *Augustiner-Congregation*, Nr. 23, p. 448.

[5] Jeremias, *Staupitz*, pp. 67–8.

[6] For a description see Wolf, *Staupitz und Luther*, pp. 14–15. It is reprinted in Knaake, pp. 121–36.

[7] Jeremias, *Staupitz*, p. 75.

II. THE STATE OF SCHOLARSHIP ON THE THEOLOGY OF STAUPITZ

Nineteenth century publications on Staupitz discussed three principal problems: the relationship of Staupitz to mysticism, to scholastic theology and to Luther. The first problem, the question of Staupitz's relationship to mysticism, evoked a certain degree of unanimity. Most scholars were agreed that Staupitz was a mystic, and that he differed with German mysticism by maintaining the metaphysical discontinuity between creature and Creator[1] and by refusing to engage in the kind of metaphysical speculation which so delighted the medieval mystical mind.[2] There was sharp disagreement about the sources of his thought. Geuder[3] and Keller[4] stressed his dependence on German mystics, whether Tauler or the so-called Friends of God. Ullmann[5] and Zeller[6] emphasized rather his similarity to Bernard and Gerson. Grimm[7] and Ritschl,[8] however, laid stress on his originality as a mystic, noting how he shunned both the pantheistic tendencies of the German, and the *subtilitas* of the Latin mystics.

There was a tendency in the nineteenth century to place a low value on Staupitz's learning and ability as a scholastic theologian.[9] While it was generally acknowledged that his writings showed evidence of his scholastic training, especially his early *Decisio*,[10] his obvious reluctance

---

[1] C. L. W. Grimm, "De Ioanne Staupitio eiusque in sacrorum Christianorum instaurationem meritis," *Zeitschrift für historische Theologie*, N.F. 1 (1837), 58–126. See especially pp. 111–15.

[2] W. Braun, *Die Bedeutung der Concupiscenz in Luthers Leben und Lehre* (Berlin, 1908), pp. 68–9.

[3] A. D. Geuder, *Vita Ioannis Staupitii*, dissertation for the University of Göttingen (1837). Cf. especially Chapter 5.

[4] Ludwig Keller, *Johann von Staupitz und die Anfänge der Reformation* (Leipzig, 1888), pp. 75–7.

[5] C. Ullman, *Reformatoren vor der Reformation*, Vol. II (Hamburg, 1842), pp. 256–278. See p. 257. For a survey of prenineteenth century research see *ibid.*, p. 256, note 2.

[6] Paul Zeller, "Johannes von Staupitz, seine religiös-dogmatischen Anschauungen," *Theologische Studien und Kritiken* 52 (1879), 7–64. See especially pp. 56–64.

[7] Grimm, "De Ioanne Staupitio," pp. 111–15.

[8] According to Ritschl, Staupitz differed from German mysticism in his doctrine of God: "Now Staupitz separates himself from the mystical theologians of the fourteenth century definitely and specifically by establishing the concrete personal idea of love as an element of our idea of God..." Albrecht Ritschl, *A Critical History of the Christian Doctrine of Justification and Reconciliation*, Vol. I, trans. by John S. Black (Edinburgh: Edmonston and Douglas, 1872), p. 109.

[9] C. Ullmann, *Reformatoren vor der Reformation*, p. 257.

[10] Kolde, *Augustiner-Congregation*, p. 219: "Staupitz ist noch ganz der Scholastiker, der keinen Stein am Wege liegen sehen kann, ohne ihn aufzuheben und ihn

to become entangled in the arguments of the schoolmen[1] and his practical turn of mind were widely interpreted as proof that one should think of him primarily as a mystic.[2] The sources of his dogmatic thought were Paul, Augustine, Anselm, Bernard, William of Auvergne, Thomas Aquinas, Gerson and John of Paltz.

Staupitz's relationship to Luther provoked, as might be expected, vigorous debate. Opinions ranged from Ullmann,[3] on the one hand, who argued for substantial agreement between the two men, to Paulus,[4] on the other, who emphasized their disagreement. The most elaborate thesis on this subject was the one worked out by Kolde,[5] who traced the development of Staupitz's ideas from the early *Decisio* of 1500, in which Staupitz showed himself to be thoroughly scholastic, to the final essay on faith of 1525, which, he felt, bore a marked resemblance to the theology of Luther. Keller,[6] and to some extent Clemen,[7] maintained that Staupitz was a representative of an evangelical movement in Germany, which was neither Roman Catholic nor Lutheran. On the whole, however, it could be said that most scholars were willing to admit that Staupitz had been influenced by Luther,

---

fortzuschleudern, oder ihn zu einem Haufen zusammenzutragen, um ihn dann Stein für Stein wieder abzutragen."

[1] Staupitz's emphasis on soteriology over theology demonstrated to Grimm "...quantum Staupitius a Scholasticorum argutiis abhorruerit." Grimm, "De Ioanne Staupitio," p. 92.

[2] This is the position taken by Geuder, *Vita*, Chapter 5; Grimm, "De Ioanne Staupitio," pp. 111–15; Ullmann, *Reformatoren vor der Reformation*, p. 258, p. 269; J. Köstlin, *Luthers Theologie* (Stuttgart, 1863), Band I, pp. 40–46; W. Braun, *Concupiscenz*, pp. 69–71. Henri Strohl, by giving his own estimation of Staupitz, summarized admirably this scholarly tradition: "Staupitz n'était pas ami des hautes spéculations ni des distinctions scolastiques. Sa piété plus simple s'en tenait à la personne du Christ s'immolant pour l'humanité pécheresse, consolant et enflammant par son amour le coeur du croyant." *Luther jusqu'en 1520*, 2nd. ed. revised (Paris, 1962), p. 71.

[3] Ullmann, *Reformatoren vor der Reformation*, p. 277: "Staupitz [nahm] im Wesentlichen schon denselben Standpunkt ein, wie Luther; Staupitz ist ein Vorbereiter und Vorläufer der Reformation."

[4] N. Paulus, "Johannes von Staupitz, seine vorgebliche protestantische Gesinnung," *Historisches Jahrbuch der Görres-Gesellschaft* 12 (1891), 309–346. For the relation of Staupitz to Luther see p. 328ff.

[5] Kolde, *Augustiner-Congregation*, pp. 219ff. passim. A. W. Dieckhoff rejected Kolde's developmental hypothesis in his article, "Die Theologie des Johannes von Staupitz," *Zeitschrift für kirchliche Wissenschaft und kirchliches Leben* 8 (Leipzig, 1887), pp. 169ff: 23ff. The late writing on faith was not fundamentally different in viewpoint from the earlier writings. Cf. *ibid.*, pp. 242–3.

[6] L. Keller, *Johann von Staupitz*, p. 4; 194ff.

[7] O. Clemen, *RE*[3] 18, 781, 58ff.

though they could not reach a consensus on the nature or degree of that influence.

All nineteenth century scholarship, though it produced many fine and important essays on Staupitz, was dependent upon a limited *corpus* of Staupitz's writings. In 1879 Kolde introduced the sermons from Codex Hs: b II 11, St. Peter, to supplement the writings available in the critical edition of Staupitz's writings published by Knaake in 1867.[1] Seven of these sermons were published by Aumüller in 1881.[2] Paulus, writing in 1891, substantiated his claim that Staupitz had ended his life as a convinced Roman Catholic by quoting two hitherto unknown *Gutachten* written by Staupitz against Agricola.[3] About this time unpublished sermons of Staupitz on Job were discovered in the library in Munich. Although Kolde, Brieger, Hauck, Hermelink, Jeremias and Scheel were aware of their existence, Scheel was the first to make use of them in his book on Luther.[4] A critical edition of them was not prepared until 1926.[5] Wolf, the editor of the critical edition, discovered still more unpublished sermons of Staupitz in Salzburg while preparing his own book on Staupitz, which was subsequently published in 1927.[6] Though he made use of these unpublished materials, he did not edit them. The drastic increase in the sources available to the historian from 1867 to 1927 has meant that nineteenth century works on Staupitz, while not without their enduring merits, must be used with some caution.

Contemporary scholarship on Staupitz began in the decade following the conclusion of the First World War. In 1925 Heinrich Boehmer published his famous study of the formative years of Luther's life, a study which dealt with Staupitz's life and thought as it influenced the development of the young Luther. Boehmer characterized Staupitz both as a Thomist and as a disciple of the *devotio moderna*. Like the

---

[1] Kolde, *Augustiner-Congregation*, pp. 336ff.

[2] See above, p. 14, footnote 2.

[3] N. Paulus, "Johannes von Staupitz," *HJ* 12 (1891) 309–46; 773–777. The position of Paulus is defended by Adolar Zumkeller, "Die Augustinerschule des Mittelalters: Vertreter und Philosophisch-Theologische Lehre," *Analecta Augustiniana* 27 (1964), 167-262. Like Paulus, Zumkeller argues that "...Staupitz in seiner Glaubenshaltung ganz auf katholischem Boden stand." *Ibid.*, p. 256.

[4] Scheel, *Martin Luther* II, pp. 364ff. For a brief story of the discovery of these sermons see Jeremias, *Johannes von Staupitz*, pp. 6–7.

[5] Ernst Wolf indicated to me in conversation in Göttingen in August, 1964, that Scheel had first drawn his attention to these unpublished sermons on Job. Wolf then decided to edit them and to write his *Habilitationsschrift* on Staupitz.

[6] For a description of these unpublished materials see Wolf, *Staupitz und Luther*, pp. 275–284.

mystics of the *devotio moderna* in the low countries, Boehmer maintained, Staupitz did not look forward to a union with the divine essence as the goal of the mystical life, but rather to a union of the will and affections which, however intimate, did not threaten the metaphysical distinction between the Creator and His creatures. This unique combination of Thomism and voluntary mysticism, Boehmer felt, bore a stronger resemblance to the thought of Loyola than it did to the thought of Luther.[1]

Boehmer did not deny, however, that Staupitz's thought exercised a creative influence on Luther. Staupitz taught Luther, for example, that penance began with the love of God rather than with the love of self (as Luther had been taught at Erfurt). Moreover, it was Staupitz who pointed Luther to the cross as the evidence of the mercy of God, when Luther suffered temptations concerning the status of his own election. This is not to say that Luther and Staupitz viewed matters in quite the same way or from quite the same perspective, but only that Staupitz gave Luther hints which he later developed in independent directions.[2]

Alfred Jeremias, writing in 1926, felt that it was not quite correct to speak of Staupitz's theology, but that in view of its loose and unsystematic form one should rather speak of his "christenlichen Lebensanschauung."[3] According to Jeremias one could easily reduce the thought of Staupitz to its bare essentials by the use of three labels: Pauline-Augustinian, biblicistic and mystical. Staupitz was Pauline-Augustinian in his treatment of grace, election and works. He was biblicistic in his placing of the Old and New Testaments on the same level, standing in the same relationship to the gospel. And, finally, he was mystical in his devotion to Christ and in his somber preoccupation with the idea of death.[4]

The single most important study of Staupitz's theology was published the following year in 1927. It was Ernst Wolf's carefully documented work, *Staupitz und Luther*. Wolf took for his province the question which previous scholarship had raised many times but had never satisfactorily settled; namely, the question of the exact nature of the influence of Staupitz's thought on the theological development of the young Luther. To answer this question he examined the

---

[1] Boehmer, *Martin Luther*, pp. 98–101.
[2] Boehmer, *Martin Luther*, pp. 102–9.
[3] Jeremias, *Johannes von Staupitz*, p. 75.
[4] Jeremias, *Johannes von Staupitz*, pp. 76–8.

statements of Staupitz and Luther themselves, written in many cases long years after the event, and assessed their validity in the light of the evidence garnered from the theological works of the two men dating from the pre-Reformation years.

There were three areas in particular in which, Wolf felt, the influence of Staupitz on Luther needed to be assessed. The first area concerned the necessity and value of temptation. Staupitz placed a generally positive valuation on the testing of faith to which the Christian is subjected during the course of his earthly pilgrimage. All temptation, he maintained, was due to the wise foreordination of God. It was decreed to teach men not to trust in themselves, but rather to flee to the mercy of God. It offered the believer an opportunity for growth in Christlikeness and an occasion for increase in merit. Moreover, it provided the neighbor of the Christian man with an edifying example of Christian fortitude. Temptation, Staupitz therefore taught, was to be embraced joyfully by the Christian man rather than fearfully shunned.

Luther likewise came to put a positive valuation on temptation, but not for quite the same reasons nor in quite the same way as Staupitz. Luther's positive valuation of temptation depended upon his fresh apprehension of the meaning of Romans 1:17 and his new understanding of the righteousness of God. It was the man who was justified by faith alone who could dare to snap his fingers in the face of the devil or be free to regard the fiercest temptation as a sign of his own election. Nevertheless, in spite of the significant difference which one is able to discover between Staupitz's theology of temptation and the *sola fide* teaching of Luther, Wolf was forced to conclude that it was impossible to deny that Luther had found comfort in Staupitz's words about the usefulness of temptation, even if his own thought subsequently developed in an independent direction.[1]

The second area of influence was the doctrine of predestination. Luther had been raised in the school of Gabriel Biel to view predestination as if it were based on foreseen merit. He was led by Staupitz to embrace a doctrine of predestination based on mercy alone, thus excluding the notion of human merit. For Staupitz predestination

---

[1] Ernst Wolf, *Staupitz und Luther*, pp. 138–68. A brief summary of Wolf's conclusions can be found in his article: "Johann von Staupitz und die theologischen Anfänge Luthers," *Luther-Jahrbuch* 9 (1929), 43–86. A study in the English language which relies heavily on the result of Wolf's investigations is U. Saarnivaara, *Luther Discovers the Gospel* (St. Louis: Concordia Publishing House, 1951), pp. 19–34.

was a decisive action on the part of God, motivated by His gracious lovingkindness alone and not a reaction on His part to the prior activity of His creatures.[1]

The third area in which Staupitz influenced Luther was in his understanding of the doctrine of penance. Luther had formulated his doctrine of penance under the influence of his nominalistic training at Erfurt with its strong emphasis on the ability of the natural powers of man, unaided by grace, to do the will of God. Against this nominalistic upbringing Staupitz opposed the conviction that true repentance is the product of God's activity. The possibility of repentance depends upon grace and not upon the volition of man.[2]

Surveying the whole body of evidence gathered before him, Wolf concluded that Staupitz should be valued by Luther scholars as an important stimulus in Luther's theological development in the period prior to the fresh apprehension of the meaning of Romans 1:17—even though Luther frequently did not understand what Staupitz had said in the way that Staupitz himself understood it and in spite of the fact that he freely accommodated what he heard to fit his own system.[3]

Wolf devoted relatively little attention to the question of the relationship of Staupitz to mysticism and to scholastic theology. He argued briefly that Staupitz was a disciple of Giles of Rome, the official doctor of the Augustinian Order, on whom he relied for the resolution of difficult questions.[4] When dealing with larger and less complicated problems, he would occasionally call on Thomas Aquinas for assistance. There was no evidence of the influence of nominalistic thought on Staupitz, except for one citation from Gerson—which

---

[1] Wolf, *Staupitz und Luther*, pp. 169–222.

[2] Wolf, *Staupitz und Luther*, pp. 223–252.

[3] Wolf, *Staupitz und Luther*, p. 261: "Wenn man in dieser Hinsicht Staupitzens Weisungen erst auf Grund der neuen Rechtfertigungsanschauung völlig verstanden werden lässt, so darf dieses 'völlig' allerdings nicht besagen, dass Luther erst dann diese Ratschläge nach dem ihnen von Staupitz beigelegten Gehalt in vollem Ausmass erfassen konnte, sondern dass er ihnen einen tieferen Sinn abzugewinnen lernt, über ihre ursprüngliche Bedeutung hinausgeht. Damit wird einerseits deutlich bezeichnet, dass Staupitz als bedeutsamer Anreger für Luthers theologische Gedankenbildung vor dessen eigener und befreiender Entdeckung des Sinnes von iustitia dei in Röm. 1,17 zu werten ist; andererseits aber wird zugleich darauf hingewiesen, dass Luthers Aussagen über diese Förderungen nicht von vornherein vollinhaltlich als Wiedergabe von Staupitzens Meinung anzusehen sind...."

[4] Wolf, *Staupitz und Luther*, pp. 28–9: "Im allgemeinen hat man den Eindruck, als ob Staupitz sich vor allem an seinen dominus Egidius halte, jedenfalls bei schwierigeren dogmatischen Fragen, während Thomas doch mehr gelegentlich herangezogen wird."

Wolf was not inclined to take seriously.[1] Indeed, Wolf went so far as
to maintain that Staupitz's mysticism was really derived from his
scholastic theology.[2] Staupitz was a mystic of the *schola Aegidiana*,
whose emphasis on conformity to the will of God had been learned,
not from reading the mystical writers suggested by the scholars of the
nineteenth century, but from his study of the *Sentences Commentary* of
Giles of Rome.[3]

III. The Necessity for a New Study

It is evident by this time—or at least it should be—that the literature
on Staupitz is fairly extensive, even if somewhat old, and, perhaps,
somewhat contradictory. The claim, therefore, that further research
on Staupitz is necessary, or even possible, requires at least some justification. There are several reasons why a fresh study is required.

1. The first, and most obvious, reason is that much of the older
scholarship on Staupitz is concerned with Staupitz's relationship to
Martin Luther. Was Staupitz, historians have asked, fundamentally on
the side of Rome or of Wittenberg? What influence or influences did
he bring to bear on Luther? How was he influenced by him? Questions such as these, while perhaps unavoidable, have dominated too
much of the research on Staupitz's thought, limiting its scope and
giving ample opportunity for the expression of party loyalties.

---

[1] Wolf, *Staupitz und Luther*, p. 27: "Erstes Ergebnis: von der via moderna findet
sich bei dem Tübinger Lektor fast keine Spur, wenn man nicht Gersons Traktate
dafür geltend machen will. Von den Zitaten aus Gerson ist jedoch nur eines bedeutsam, das (aus De vita spirituali anime) die Gnadenlehre betrifft..." Cf. pp. 27-
8: "Staupitz kennt also wichtige Schriften des Pariser Kanzlers, doch kann von
hier aus allein seine Einreihung in die via moderna nicht hinreichend begründet
werden..." Although Wolf speaks of one citation from Gerson as *bedeutsam* it does
not function in his later argument, so that its real significance is not explored.
[2] "...es sieht so aus, als ob Staupitz in ähnlicher Weise 'Mystiker' sei, 'Mystiker'
aus der Schule des Aegidius Romanus." Wolf, *Staupitz und Luther*, p. xi. According to Wolf, Staupitz has "...den conformitas-Gedanken, aus Ägidius übernommen..." Staupitz und Luther, p. 97, footnote 5. For a fuller discussion of
Wolf's views on Staupitz's mystical thought, see below, Chapter Six, Section I,
"The State of Scholarship on Staupitz's Mystical Theology."
[3] Wolf, *Staupitz und Luther*, p. 90. The position of Scheel, *Martin Luther* (Tübingen, 1921), Vol. II, pp. 364ff. and Wolf, *op. cit.*, pp. 30–35 that Staupitz stood
somewhere between Thomas and Aegidius is accepted by Gordon Rupp, *Luther's
Progress to the Diet of Worms* (New York: Harper Torchbooks, 1964), p. 20. Lau
identifies him as a Thomist (*Luther*, p. 51). Saarnivaara holds that he "...cannot be
identified with any school of theology." He adds, however, that "...he was closer
to Aquinas than Scotus or Occam..." U. Saarnivaara, *Luther Discovers the Gospel*,
p. 25, footnote 68.

Perhaps, one example may help to make this clear. Although the whole *corpus* of Staupitz's writings has been accessible since the publication of the sermons on Job in 1927, no one has as yet examined Staupitz's Mariology,[1] in spite of the fact that this doctrine has important implications for Staupitz's understanding of faith and discipleship. Wolf, who had the first opportunity to do so, did not attempt to expound the whole of Staupitz's theology. His interest in Staupitz was limited to a cluster of problems arising out of Luther research. Any doctrine which did not illumine these problems was discussed briefly, if at all. And no one in the intervening years, has attempted to continue where Wolf left off. The study of the theology of Staupitz has remained a subsidiary branch of Luther research.

2. Secondly, much of the existing scholarship assumes that, Luther apart, Staupitz is his own best interpreter. While it has focused on selected problems in the writings of Staupitz, it has discussed them in isolation without a systematic attempt to relate them to the broader medieval theological tradition. To be sure, this neglect has not been wholly intentional. The historian who wrote twenty five years ago had at his disposal a critical edition of Luther's works and a rich scholarly tradition upon which he could draw in examining the relationship between Staupitz and Luther. He was relatively less fortunate in the tools which lay at his disposal for the study of the relationship between Staupitz and his theological environment. Few of the texts of the period had been reprinted or were easily accessible, and while the period had been studied, it had been examined principally as a chapter in the history of philosophy. The historian was forced by these circumstances either to comment briefly on the relationship between Staupitz and the better known figures of the Middle Ages—such as Anselm and Bernard of Clairvaux—or not to comment at all. Nevertheless, the relative neglect of this question, however it may be explained or excused, has meant that there is a hiatus in Staupitz's scholarship, a gap which has not yet been bridged. It is the responsibility of newer scholarship, which is relatively more favored in the tools at its disposal, to bridge this chasm.

3. Thirdly, new scholarship is needed because of the errors and inadequacies in the older interpretations of the theology of Staupitz. It

---

[1] There have been occasional references to it. Jeremias, for example, notes that Staupitz's "...Marienverehrung ist stark, aber sie ist mystisch begründet, und sie verdunkelt nie die Gestalt des Heilandes." Jeremias, *Johannes von Staupitz*, p. 12. But he does not attempt to expound this doctrine any further.

is not necessary, or even appropriate, to catalogue here in the introduction all of the deficiencies in previous studies of Staupitz, since these points may be more adequately discussed in the context in which they occur. We shall restrict the discussion, rather, to one crucial issue: the relationship of Staupitz to late medieval thought.

Wolf argued that Staupitz's understanding of the Christian faith was strongly influenced by his study of the theology of Giles of Rome. God was for Giles of Rome the *paterfamilias* who directs the universe according to the good pleasure of his will.[1] According to His distributive justice He apportions to each what is due him. The God of Giles of Rome—unlike the God of Gabriel Biel—never acts arbitrarily.[2] All the acts and choices of His will are governed by His goodness.[3] Even the love of God is subordinated to His *bonitas*.[4] Staupitz, by taking over this understanding of God and His relationship to the world,[5] mediated to Martin Luther a picture of God fundamentally different from the one which Luther had received in his theological study at Erfurt.[6] God was not an arbi-

---

[1] Wolf, *Staupitz und Luther*, p. 80: "Allerdings will Staupitz, ebenso wie etwa Ägidius, mit dem Bild des Hausvaters zunächst den Weltregierer bezeichnen." Cf. Giles of Rome, I *Sent.* d.20 q.1.

[2] Wolf makes clear his conception of the nominalist doctrine of God when he writes in *Staupitz und Luther*, p. 220: "Nicht der willkürliche Despot, wie für den Nominalismus, sondern der Hausvater, den auch Aegidius nennt, ist für Staupitz das Gleichnis Gottes."

[3] Wolf, *Staupitz und Luther*, p. 80: "Der Gedanke der bonitas Gottes ist eng verbunden mit der Vorstellung von der Vollkommenheit eines Gesamtorganismus, in dem kein Glied verkürzt werden soll und, damit Gottes Zweck erreicht werde, auch nicht darf..."

[4] Wolf, *Staupitz und Luther*, p. 81: "Dieses Verhalten lässt sich in die herkömmliche Bestimmung des diligere als velle alicui bonum unschwer einfügen. Damit ist eine Verbindung zwischen der Kennzeichnung Gottes als bonitas und seiner Beschreibung als Liebe angegeben..."

[5] Wolf, *Staupitz und Luther*, p. 82: "Sucht man, um diese Gottesanschauung geschichtlich einreihen zu können, nach solchen Gottesvorstellungen, die verwandte Züge aufweisen, so bietet sich, auch was Einzelheiten anbetrifft, in besonderer Weise diejenige des Thomas an und vielleicht hinsichtlich des weitgehenden Wirkens Gottes in der Kreatur noch mehr diejenige des Ägidius. Dazu kommt, dass Staupitz sich gerade auch in dieser Beziehung auf beide beruft."

[6] Wolf, *Staupitz und Luther*, pp. 219–220: "Dennoch ist die Behauptung, Luther sei infolge der Unterredungen mit Staupitz ein 'neues Verständnis Gottes' aufgegangen nicht verfehlt. Die Qual Luthers erreicht, wie seine Angaben ersehen liessen, ihre Höhe dort, wo ihm Gott als der vollkommen frei Schaltende, Willkürliche und zugleich als der gerecht Vergeltende in Widerstreit geraten. Hier hat Staupitz gemildert; seinem Gottesbild eignen Züge undurchsichtiger, anscheinend grundloser Willkür unbeschadet des freien göttlichen Entschlusses nicht. Das Zweckvolle und vernunftgemässer Einsicht Zugängliche göttlichen Handelns, also auch der tribulationes, ist ebenso betont wie die unabänderliche Durchfüh-

trary and capricious Despot; He was a kindly and just Father.[1]

Wolf tended, however, to skirt the marked differences between Staupitz and Giles of Rome, on the one hand, and to underestimate the similarities between Staupitz and Biel, on the other. It is undeniable that Staupitz profited from his reading of Giles in discussing problems of epistemology, whether divine, human or angelic.[2] Traces of Giles' influence can be found throughout Staupitz's writings.[3] In defining *gratia gratum faciens*, however, Giles remained within the medieval tradition with which Staupitz broke. For Giles, infused grace made man pleasing to God; for Staupitz, it made God pleasing to man.[4]

The wider significance of this difference becomes clear when the distinction is placed within the context of ecclesiology. Man cannot be pleasing to God without grace—which is to say, without the sacraments. The sacraments are the possession of the Church. Therefore, concludes Giles, man the sinner must be subject to the institutional

---

rung der Vorsätze Gottes, also auch des Erwählungsbeschlusses. In der Beantwortung des cur deus homo folgt Staupitz Anselm im Unterschied von Biel." Wolf does not notice, as we shall later document, that in answering the question *cur deus homo* Staupitz agrees with Biel in his rejection of the supralapsarianism of Scotus. Staupitz also differs with Anselm by stressing the Abelardian motif of the psychological impact of the cross on fallen man and by undercutting the necessitarianism of the formula *aut poena aut satisfactio*.

[1] Gordon Rupp agrees with Wolf's description of the influence of Staupitz on Luther: "To the Nominalist philosophy with its recurring 'perhaps' and its emphasis on the power of the human will, Staupitz brought the wholesome corrective of the *via antiqua*, with its emphasis on the design of God, and work of grace within the human soul." Rupp, *Luther's Progress*, p. 31. This position is also accepted by Henri Strohl: "Connaissant le caractère de la piété de Staupitz, nous devons aussi admettre qu'au lieu d'opposer la volonté divine révélée à la volonté divine impénétrable, dans le sens dont en parlaient les occamistes, il puisait aux sources du mysticisme.... L'atmosphère de sereine piété qu'il faisait règner autour de lui ne pouvait manquer de faire du bien à l'âme de Luther, tourmentée par les spéculations auxquelles l'avait initié la théologie occamiste." Strohl, *Luther jusqu'en 1520*, p. 71.

[2] Cf. *Hiob* (1497–8) 11.85.14ff. Compare with Giles of Rome, I *Sent.* d.35 q.4; d. 38 q.1.

[3] Wolf has noted 30 citations from Giles of Rome in the 1497–8 sermons on Job. *Staupitz und Luther*, p. 23.

[4] "Per sacramenta ergo Ecclesie consequimur gratiam et fimus grati Deo." Giles of Rome, "Aegidii Romani Impugnatio Doctrinae Petri Ioannis Olivi An. 1311–12," ed. P. Leo Amorós, O.F.M., *Archivum Franciscanum Historicum* 27 (1934), p. 442. Cf. Staupitz, *Libellus* (1517) 36: "Hec est gratia gratum faciens non hominem deo sicut multi exponunt, quia hoc ipsa electio fecit, sed solum deum facit placere et gratum esse homini per charitatem...." Cf. *Libellus* (1517) 40, 86, 131, 152.

Church.[1] The lengths to which Giles was willing to carry this argument in the defence of papal supremacy do not concern us now.[2] It is sufficient to note here that the grace which makes man pleasing to God is a function of the Church.

Staupitz, however, thinks within a quite different frame of reference. A man is made pleasing to God, not through the sacraments, but through the divine decree of election. The Church and the sacraments are the means through which God awakens love in the elect. They are subordinate to the divine decree of election.[3] The visible institution is important, but it is secondary. Staupitz reverses Giles' emphasis. It is the Church itself with its sacraments which is a function of the *gratia predestinationis*.

More problematical, however, than Wolf's high estimate of the influence of Giles of Rome is his assumption that Staupitz had not been influenced by nominalistic thought. There is no question that Staupitz differed sharply with Biel on fundamental doctrinal issues. When Biel argued that fallen man could bring forth an act of love for God *super omnia* by the exercise of his own natural powers, he took a position diametrically opposed to the position held by Staupitz.[4] But that does not mean that Staupitz was wholly uninfluenced by nominalistic thought, or that he was an unshakeable defender of the *via antiqua*. In point of fact, Staupitz agreed with the nominalists on many issues.

---

[1] "Sacramentum ergo universale est baptismus omni tempore, quia si ante octavam diem moriatur infans non baptizatus, de iure communi non dicitur esse salvus. Est eciam universale hoc sacramentum omni generacioni et omni sexui, cum nullus posset consequi salutem sine eo vel in re vel in voto. Et quia sacramentum hoc datur in ecclesia, ideo ecclesia est catholica idest universalis, et est mater omnium, cum nullus possit consequi salutem, nisi sit subiectus ecclesie et nisi sit eius filius." Giles of Rome, *De Ecclesiastica Potestate*, ed. Richard Scholz (Leipzig, 1929), reprinted by Scientia Aalen, 1961, pp. 72–3.

[2] For a brief discussion of Giles' position see Brian Tierney, *The Crisis of Church and State* 1050–1300 (Englewood Cliffs, N.J.: Prentice-Hall, Inc., 1964), pp. 193–5. Cf. M. J. Wilks, *The Problem of Sovereignty in the Later Middle Ages* (Cambridge, 1963).

[3] Cf. *Hiob* (1497–8) 11.95.5–8; *Libellus* (1517) 22, 26, 33. In fact, Staupitz's doctrine of the Church is so subordinate to his doctrine of election that Kolde could say: "Eine Heilsvermittlung durch die Kirche lehrt Staupitz genau genommen gar nicht...." *Augustiner-Congregation*, p. 341. Against this one must point out that the same codex which Kolde uses to argue that there is no *Heilsvermittlung* through the Church (Hs: b II 11, St. Peter) also teaches that the priest actually looses the penitent from his sins (see No. 24, Kolde, *Augustiner-Congregation*, p. 455) and makes the intention to confess to a priest the precondition of forgiveness (Hs: b II 11, St. Peter (1523), Sermo 11, fol. 93ª).

[4] For a discussion of Biel's position see H. A. Oberman, *Harvest*, pp. 131–45. Cf. Staupitz, *Lieb Gottes* (1518), Kn. 103.

Like Biel, and unlike Thomas, Staupitz argued that the structures of justice rested on the will of God, and not vice-versa.[1] Like Biel, and unlike Giles, Staupitz defended the doctrine of the immaculate conception of the Virgin Mary.[2] When Staupitz emphasized the primacy of uncreated grace,[3] quoted Gerson on the acceptation of human works by God,[4] and stressed the covenantal relationship of God to the world,[5] he demonstrated the extent to which he was influenced by nominalist theology.[6]

---

[1] "Deus potest aliquid facere quod non est iustum fieri a deo; si tamen faceret iustum esset fieri. Unde sola voluntas divina est prima regula omnis iustitie." Biel, I *Sent.* d.43 q.1 art. 4 cor. Cf. Staupitz, *Hiob* (1497–8) 3.12.7–8: "Sola divina voluntas est regula sui actus, quia non ordinatur ad superiorem finem." *Ibid.* 3.16. 1–3: "Itaque non nisi dei voluntas causa est prima sanitatis, egritudinis, praemiorum atque penarum, graciarum et retribucionum." *Ibid.* 15.134.37–8: "Neque enim tibi placent hominum facta, quia bona sunt, sed pocius ideo sunt bona, quia tibi placent."

[2] "Beatissima genetrix dei Virgo Maria ab omni originalis peccati contagio fuit penitus preservata." Biel, III *Sent.* d.3 q.1 art. 2 concl. 1F. Cf. Staupitz, Hs: b II 11, St. Peter (1523) fol. 179ª: "Das ist dy aller heiligist mueter gots Maria gewesen, dy got auch aus seiner sünderleicher gewaltigen Kraft und gnad enthalten hat vor dem vall, das das liecht jn jr nye geswecht is warden."

[3] There are three ways in which he did this: (1) by emphasizing the infusion of the Holy Spirit or the inhabitation of Christ in justification rather than the created gift of love. *Lieb gottes* (1518), Kn. 98: "Derhalbenn ist die erste, die hochste und groste begnadung der ausserwelten seel, das got sein wonung yn yr macht." (2) By stressing the merciful acceptation of God which gives infinite rewards for finite works. Cf. *Libellus* (1517) 43. (3) By using the picture of marriage as a metaphor for justification. The *viator* possesses the merits of Christ only by being united to Christ. The dowry is not separable from the bridegroom. Cf. *Libellus* (1517) 77.

[4] *Hiob* (1497–8) 23.186–9 contains lengthy citations from Gerson, "De Vita Spirituali Animae, Lectio Prima," *Oeuvres Complètes*, Vol. III, *L'oeuvre Magistrale*, ed. Glorieux (Tournai, 1962), pp. 113–28. On acceptation compare Gerson, *op. cit.*, p. 124 with *Hiob* (1497–8) 23.186. 41–187.3. Cf. *Libellus* (1517) 43, 50; *Hiob* (1497–8) 5.32.13–24.

[5] All men owe God *laus*, though because of the fall they do not render it to God. God does not owe fallen man anything; He could in perfect justice abandon fallen man to his fate. *Hiob* (1497–8) 9.70.36–8. In his great mercy, however, He binds Himself to the elect. Through election—which is wholly gratuitous—He makes Christ the *debitor* of salvation to the elect. The elect, when they are justified, are enabled to render to God the *laus* which they owe Him. Cf. *Libellus* (1517) 22, 26, 33. Though the content of the covenant which Biel describes is very different from the covenant which Staupitz envisions, the differences should not blind us to the points of similarity. Cf. Biel, II *Sent.* d.27 q.u. art. 2 concl. 1G: "...nam licet Deus nullius debitor esse possit ex natura rei, potest tamen se facere debitorem nostrum ex sua libera voluntate nobis promittendo pro talibus actibus tantum praemium...."

[6] Ritschl noted that Staupitz taught a doctrine of acceptation, though he attributed its presence to the influence of Scotus rather than of the nominalists: "...the

Wolf did not note the agreement between Staupitz and Biel, because he was hampered by an incorrect understanding of the nominalist doctrine of God. The nominalists did not think of God as arbitrary or petulant.[1] His absolute power did not undercut the reliability of the created order, though it revealed its contingency. The nominalists wished to show that the reliability of the order established *de potentia ordinata* was grounded in a radical way in the free decision of God who kept covenant with creation, not because He was compelled to do so by any forces exterior to Himself, but because He had freely chosen to act in a certain way and had committed Himself accordingly.

This failure to understand Biel correctly has implications, not only for Wolf's understanding of Staupitz, but also for his explanation of the relationship between Staupitz and Luther. If Staupitz is not a committed representative of the *via antiqua* but rather shares many common presuppositions with Biel, then the old generalizations about Staupitz's influence on Luther must be re-examined. The question of *certitudo salutis* is a case in point. Wolf argued that Staupitz had presented Luther with a picture of a God who acted purposefully and reasonably in His dealings with man, in place of the arbitrary God of the nominalists. In point of fact, both Biel and Staupitz believed that God's relationship to the world should be covenantally understood. Staupitz did not ground the certitude of the elect in a norm which, in some sense at least, was independent of the will of God. Certitude was based, rather, on the *Bundestreue Gottes*, the unswerving faithfulness of God to His own purposes for the elect.[2] Biel and Staupitz differ on many issues, but the reliability of the will of God is not one of them. A study of the influence of Staupitz on the young Luther must take this agreement between Biel and Staupitz into consideration.

---

acceptance of the works wrought in grace is also a grace which makes them meritorious (this with Duns as against Thomas)..." *Justification and Reconciliation*, Vol. I, p. 110. Wolf also admits that Staupitz may have been influenced by Scotus. He explains this fact by pointing to the influence of Paul Scriptoris. *Staupitz und Luther*, p. 45. While Staupitz may have been influenced by Scotus, his rejection of supralapsarianism and his stress on the simplicity of God (Cf. *Hiob* 11.84.36–85.1) —to mention only two points—argue for the influence of nominalism.

[1] H. A. Oberman, *Harvest*, 30–56.

[2] "Mein zusag wil ich halten, sie halten jr pflicht oder haltens nicht." *Glauben* (1525) Kn. 127.

IV. The Shape of a New Study

There are, then, three problems which have served as foci for previous studies of the theology of Staupitz and which will recur, in some form or other, in any new study; namely, the relationship of Staupitz to scholastic theology, to mysticism, and to Luther. This book will concentrate on the first two of these problems, though it will touch on the third when it seems appropriate to do so.

Staupitz is not, in the customary sense of the term, a scholastic theologian. He does not attempt to comment upon all the doctrines of the Christian faith or to resolve profound metaphysical problems. His theology is expounded in the service of preaching. The range of issues which he discusses is limited by his immediate purpose as a preacher. That does not mean, however, that his understanding of issues is shallow. His touch, if light, is nevertheless sure.

Yet the fact remains that we have few writings from his hand which could be considered academic works.[1] The *corpus* of writings which we do possess consists for the most part of sermons and treatises written for the edification of a specific congregation and circulated among a wider audience only after they had proved their worth within a more limited circle. Evidence concerning Staupitz's attitude on a difficult and sensitive issue of theological controversy is often limited to occasional and scattered remarks embedded in a context directed, not toward the resolution of the issue itself, but toward another, more practical end. Theological speculation is always for Staupitz the servant of the Church, not its master.

One could say that Staupitz was a mystical theologian, not in the sense that he was a recluse devoted to exciting an immediate intuition into Being itself or that he elaborated a technique for acquiring such an intuition, but rather in the sense that his theological reflections were directed toward the cultivation and strengthening of the spiritual life. His theory of the religious life was not a decoration, resting lightly and precariously on top of his theological speculations and without any real relationship to them. On the contrary, the service of God is for him the crown and fruition of the knowledge of God.

Nevertheless, the scholastic foundations of his thought, however deeply hidden they at times may be, can still be uncovered and separated from the warm and compassionate piety which they serve. In the

---

[3] The sermons on Job were written for an academic audience, as was the *Decisio*. The *Libellus*, though it is systematic, was based on popular sermons.

chapters which follow we shall attempt to do precisely that—to abstract from the sermons and addresses of a warm-hearted and deeply
spiritual preacher of the cross the hard lines and structures of his
thought. We shall do this, not simply to show how deeply the mystical
piety of Staupitz was rooted in his scholastic theology—though that
would be a profitable exercise in and of itself, and would contribute
significantly to our understanding of the genius of late medieval mysticism. Our aim is somewhat different. We intend to show, more accurately than Wolf was able to do, the position of Staupitz within late
medieval thought, and thus to perform the necessary preliminary
work for any re-consideration of the influence of Staupitz on the theological development of the young Luther.

By re-examining the structures of Staupitz's theology we hope to
sustain two theses. First of all, we intend to show that Staupitz, even
though he disagreed with Biel and Gerson profoundly on many issues,
was nevertheless deeply influenced by them. We have already indicated in our discussion of Wolf's book some of the issues on which the
influence of nominalist thought can be discerned—the doctrine of the
divine will, the notion of a covenantal relationship to the world, the
doctrine of acceptation, to name only a few. Enough has already been
said on this subject to give an idea of the direction in which our argument will be developed.

Our second thesis, however, requires some further preliminary explanation. We contend that in his doctrine of grace and predestination
Staupitz is a representative of a late medieval Augustinian sentiment
in theology. The debate which underlines this thesis is not a new one.

The question has frequently been raised whether there was in the
later Middle Ages a school of theologians who represented a purer
form of Augustinian theology than that taught by Thomas and
Bonaventura, a form of theology inspired either by Augustine himself
or by the early scholastic tradition. In the first decades of the twentieth
century A. V. Müller published a series of articles and books which
defended the thesis that Luther was the heir of just such a tradition
within and outside the Augustinian Order.[1] Luther, according to
Müller, had learned many of his theological ideas—especially his
views of original sin and double righteousness—from a school of
theological inquiry to which Simon Fidati of Cassia (d. 1348), Hugo-

---

[1] For a complete list of the relevant articles cf. E. Stakemeier, *Der Kampf um
Augustin auf dem Tridentinum* (Paderborn, 1937), p. 241. The initial work in the
series was A. V. Müller, *Luthers Theologische Quellen* (Giessen, 1912).

lino of Orvieto (d. 1374), Augustinus Favaroni of Rome (d. 1443) and Jacobus Perez of Valencia (d. 1470) belonged.

In 1937 Eduard Stakemeier took up the thesis of A. V. Müller in his book, *Der Kampf um Augustin auf dem Tridentinum*. Stakemeier's interest centered not on Luther but on the General of the Augustinian Order, Girolamo Seripando; not on the genesis of Protestantism but on the proper interpretation of the Council of Trent. Stakemeier began with the indisputable fact that Seripando had defended a generally Augustinian position on a number of the theological questions discussed at the Council of Trent. By doing so, asked Stakemeier, had Seripando carried on the theological traditions of his order? The answer, he believed, was yes.[1] Seripando's doctrines of original sin and double righteousness were foreshadowed by a cloud of witnesses stretching from Simon of Cassia through Gregory of Rimini to Giles of Viterbo.

Stakemeier's contribution was sharply criticised by Hubert Jedin in an article for the *Theologische Revue*.[2] Stakemeier had only placed these theologians in parallel columns, argued Jedin. He had not shown their interconnection, nor could he, since the necessary materials for such a task were still largely unedited. Indeed, Jedin remarked, Stakemeier's footnotes and discussion showed that he was unfamiliar with the primary sources and that he relied for his citations on the earlier work of A. V. Müller.[3] It is thus impossible for historians to speak with any assurance of a late medieval Augustinian school or to deny its existence before some careful work with the primary sources has been completed. Generalizations must be grounded in evidence.

In the years since 1937 many of the figures cited by Stakemeier and Müller have been studied. The evidence which has been gathered so

---

[1] Stakemeier argued that Seripando "...nur im Zusammenhang mit jener Tradition seines Ordens verstanden werden kann, deren Sachwalter er in Trient gewesen ist." *Der Kampf um Augustin*, p. 53.

[2] *Theologische Revue* 36 (1937), 425–30. Twenty years later Jedin reaffirmed his position: "Not proven, and scarcely capable of proof, is the hypothesis that Seripando was the most prominent upholder of a school-tradition of his Order so that he and his fellow Augustinian Luther were as two branches on one and the same tree." Hubert Jedin, *A History of the Council of Trent*, Vol. II, *The First Sessions at Trent*, trans. by Dom Ernest Graf, O.S.B. (Edinburgh: Thomas Nelson and Sons, Ltd., 1961), p. 258. In conversation at Harvard University in May, 1966, Jedin indicated that he felt it was possible to speak of an Augustinian line, but not of an Augustinian school.

[3] Note the evidence for this provided by Wilfrid Werbeck, *Jacobus Perez von Valencia, Untersuchungen zu seinem Psalmenkommentar* (Tübingen, 1959), p. 212. footnote 6.

far makes it clear that the thesis of Müller and Stakemeier was hastily
drawn and ill substantiated. That there are theologians in the later
Middle Ages who represent (at least on certain questions) a more
genuinely Augustinian position than that, say, of Thomas Aquinas is
undeniable; that these theologians form a cohesive school and that
this school can be identified with the main theological tradition of the
Augustinian Order remains as yet unproven. The real situation, as we
are beginning to discover, is far more complicated that either Müller
or Stakemeier imagined.[1]

1. Müller and Stakemeier were correct to argue that there were
theologians in the late Middle Ages who belonged to the Order of the
Hermits of St. Augustine and who defended at the same time theological positions which were radically Augustinian. Gregory of
Rimini, for example, defined original sin in language which would
have dismayed Duns Scotus. Not only was he willing to say that the
essence of original sin was concupiscence, but he insisted as well that
the loss of man's original righteousness, so emphasized by Anselm and
Scotus, was nothing more than the effect of original sin.[2] Concupiscence was primary.

2. The advocacy of radically Augustinian positions was not limited
to the Augustinian Order. To be sure, Gregory of Rimini was the
most famous defender in the late Middle Ages of the Augustinian
doctrine of the absolute necessity of grace for the performance of
every morally good act.[3] In advocating this position, however, he was

---

[1] Lau typifies the cautious spirit with which this question is now approached:
"Whether in Luther's order, that of the Augustinian Hermits, which by a naive
distortion of history revered Augustine as its founder, there existed a special theological Augustinian tradition, is a difficult question that ought not to be hastily
affirmed. Certainly an Augustinian cult was promoted in Luther's order. Whether
a special theological Augustinianism existed in Luther's order, however, is another question." *Luther*, pp. 30-1. Though the hypothesis about an Augustinian
school in the Order of Augustinian Hermits remains unproven, it is possible,
to speak of late medieval Augustinianism as a sentiment in theology, which cuts
across the boundaries of the Augustinian Order and unites theologians of diverse
backgrounds.

[2] "Nec tamen nego quin etiam homo careat originali iustitia, cuius est debitor
ante baptismum. Sed huiusmodi carentiam non dico esse originale peccatum, sed
potius effectum originalis peccati...." Gregory of Rimini, II *Sent*. d.30–33 q.1 a.1
fol. 112 M. Gregory's doctrine of sin is discussed by Martin Schüler, *Prädestination, Sünde und Freiheit bei Gregor von Rimini* (Stuttgart, 1934) and Gordon Leff,
Gregory of Rimini, Tradition and Innovation in Fourteenth Century Thought (Manchester,
1961), pp. 171–7.

[3] "Homo non potest absque speciali Dei auxilio facere aliquem actum moralem
non culpabilem; igitur homo non potest absque speciali auxilio Dei facere aliquem

joined not only by Hugolino of Orvieto[1] and Dionysius of Montina[2] but also by such an important secular priest as Thomas Bradwardine.[3]

3. Finally, it must be admitted that all medieval theologians, even the most Pelagian, were indebted to the great father of Western theology for many of their ideas. All medieval theologians are, in some measure at least, Augustinian theologians. The question is not whether a theologian is indebted to Augustine but rather what is the degree and nature of his indebtedness. John Hus, for example, who clearly stands in the Augustinian tradition on the question of predestination and merit was, nevertheless, a semi-Donatist in his doctrine of the Church.[4]

In spite of all the qualifications which must be added to our thesis in order to make it as precise as possible, the thesis itself still stands. There was in the later Middle Ages a tradition of theology which stressed the centrality of grace for justification and which minimized, without eliminating, the significance of the human contribution. It was a tradition which attempted to preserve the Augustinian heritage against the corroding acids of contemporary semi-Pelagianism, represented by nominalist theologians such as Ockham, Biel and Holkot. Wherever the moral capacities of fallen man were overestimated, whenever the sovereignty of the prevenient grace of God was threatened, Augustinian theologians such as Bradwardine, Wyclif, Hus, Gregory of Rimini, Perez, Hugolino of Orvieto, Dionysius of

---

actum moraliter bonum." Gregory of Rimini, II *Sent.* d.26–29 q.1 a.1 fol. 93 I.

[1] Adolar Zumkeller, "Hugolin von Orvieto (gest. 1371) über Urstand und Erbsünde," *Augustiniana* 3 (1953), 43ff.

[2] Adolar Zumkeller, *Dionysius de Montina, ein neuentdeckter Augustinertheologe des Spätmittelalters* (Würzburg, 1948), p. 81.

[3] "Quod gratia quae est habitus gratis data a Deo una cum voluntate humana est causa efficiens proprie cuiuslibet boni et meritorii actus sui." Thomas Bradwardine, *De Causa Dei* I.40.364ff. For a comparison of Gregory and Bradwardine see H. A. Oberman, *Archbishop Thomas Bradwardine, a Fourteenth Century Augustinian* (Utrecht, 1957), pp. 211–23.

[4] Hus distinguishes between a *verus* priest (office) and a priest who is *vere* a priest (merit). Though Hus argues in several places that a moral life *(vere)* is a necessary constituent for being a true priest *(verus)*, he holds to a minimal anti-donatism, which makes the label semi-donatist a more accurate description of his thought. "Et non audivisti, quia sunt in libro meo, et hic in proximo lectae sunt? Quid refert dicere, episcopos, praelatos vel sacerdotes malos et praescitos non esse vere, nec digne secundum praesentem justitiam, episcopos, praelatos vel sacerdores, sed esse indignos ministros sacramentorum dei, nisi ipsos non vere nec digne quoad meritum esse tales, sed quoad officium, cum ut in libro meo ponitur, sunt indigni ministri sacramentorum, per quos deus baptisat vel consecrat; stat ipsos esse tales sacerdotes, praelatos vel episcopos etc." *Documntea Mag. Joannis Hus,* ed. Frantisek Palacky (Prague, 1869), p. 302.

Montina—and Johannes von Staupitz—raised their voices in protest.[1]

Thus we intend to show both that Staupitz was strongly influenced by nominalist thought and that he opposed its doctrine of grace. Both the agreement and disagreement are evident in the earliest writings of Staupitz. Indeed, most of the ideas which are developed later in individual treatises are found—at least *in nuce*—in the sermons on Job.[2] This fact makes it possible for an interpreter of Staupitz to place quotations from the earlier and later writings side by side, without stumbling over dramatic discontinuity and development. Staupitz's growth and development takes place, for the most part, within the same framework of thought. He explains in a later writing what he said in an earlier writing, or simply presupposes it. His development was unilinear rather than dialectical.

There are, of course, exceptions to this rule. His later writings redefine *prima gratia* and *gratia gratum faciens*, rejecting the habit of grace—a clear change of mind on his part.[3] Christology, which was treated as a locus in the sermons on Job, permeates his thought in the later writings, qualifying doctrines not traditionally associated with Christology. However, these exceptions tend to prove the rule. The changes take place within a larger framework of continuity. Since this proves to be the case, we will not separate the earlier and later writings in our treatment of Staupitz, except on those few points where it is evident that the development of his thought had led to a break with the past.

This thesis, then, will attempt to do what, as we have indicated, still remains to be done; namely, to place the theology of Staupitz once again in the context of the theological discussions of his own age. We shall begin by examining his doctrine of God.

---

[1] In speaking of Staupitz as a late medieval Augustinian, it should be noted that Gregory of Rimini theologians within the Augustinian Order from the time of onward had a more complete edition of Augustine with which to work than had Giles of Rome. Damasus Trapp. O.E.S.A., pointed this out in his article, "Augustinian Theology of the 14th Century; Notes on Editions, Marginalia, Opinions and Book-lore," *Augustiniana* 6 (1956), p. 186: "Aegidius remained the venerated figure of the Augustinian School before and after Gregory, but after Gregory especially more corrective reservations were made in regard to Aegidius. What is so new in Gregory is the fact that he is the best Augustine scholar of the Middle Ages from the milieu which created the Milleloquium." In the sermons on Job, Staupitz himself cited Augustine 163 times from 24 works. Cf. Wolf, *Staupitz und Luther*, p. 23.

[2] Even the theme of *laus Dei*, so prominent in the *Libellus*, is found in the sermons on *Hiob* (1497–8) 1.3.8–10; 2.11.17–24; 5.32.26–33; 7.44.36–7; 7.44.41–45.3; 30.229.2–4.

[3] Compare *Hiob* (1497–8) 30.232.17–19; 21–2; with the *Libellus* (1517) 36, 40, 86, 131, 152.

CHAPTER ONE

THE DOCTRINE OF GOD

I. God as the Summum Bonum

In his treatise *De doctrina christiana* Augustine introduced into Western theology a distinction which was repeated again and again by theologians of all schools and persuasions: the distinction between *uti* and *frui*.[1] According to Augustine *frui* is love directed toward an object for its own sake, while *uti* is love directed toward an object for the sake of something else.[2] Each kind of love is legitimate so long as it is linked to the proper object. But each kind of love is also capable of perversion, if misdirected.

There is only one object, Augustine maintained, which can be loved for its own sake as the absolute end of all human striving and aspiration, and that object is God Himself.[3] All other objects of human affection are temporal and subject to the same laws of change and decay to which man himself is subject. Neither in himself nor in his world can man find a permanent good to which he can affix himself and out of whose boundless resources he can live. Only in God can man find an enduring and unchanging Good which is the answer to his restless striving after rest.[4]

---

[1] Gerhard Ebeling attempts to show the importance of the distinction between *uti* and *frui* as a medieval hermeneutical principle. Gerhard Ebeling, "Der hermeneutische Ort der Gotteslehre bei Petrus Lombardus und Thomas von Aquin," *ZThK* 61 (1964), 283–326. See especially pages 294–301. For the use of *frui* in the thought of Augustine see R. Lorenz, "Fruitio dei bei Augustin," *ZKG* 63 (1950-51), 75–132; "Die Herkunft des augustinischen Frui Deo," *ZKG* 64 (1952-53), 54–60.

[2] "Frui enim est amore alicui rei inhaerere propter seipsam. Uti autem, quod in usum venerit ad id quod amas obtinendum referre, si tamen amandum est." Augustine, *De doctr. chr.* I.4.4., *PL* 34.20–21.

[3] "Res igitur quibus fruendum est, Pater et Filius et Spiritus sanctus, eademque Trinitas, una quaedam summa res, communisque omnibus fruentibus ea...." Augustine, *De doctr. chr.* I.5.5., *PL* 34.21.

[4] "In his igitur omnibus rebus illae tantum sunt quibus fruendum est, quas aeternas atque incommutabiles commemoravimus; caeteris autem utendum est, ut ad illarum perfruitionem pervenire possimus." Augustine, *De doctr. chr.* I.22.20., *PL* 34.26.

The world, on the other hand, while not a proper object for enjoyment, is nevertheless a proper object for use.[1] Creation cannot be loved in and of itself as that reality out of which man lives and in which he finds his final fulfillment. The world may be loved to some degree, however, as a creature of God and as a means for attaining a perfect love of God for Himself alone. It has an instrumental though not an independent value.[2]

Sin, however, inverts this relationship.[3] Instead of enjoying God and using the world, man the sinner enjoys the world and uses God. A creature is exchanged for the Creator, a temporal good for Goodness itself, a momentary respite for eternal Rest. Though sinful man never ceases to search for the eternal Good which he has lost, he is condemned to seek it in the wrong place. Only grace can redirect love back to its proper object.

Staupitz, acting in harmony with a broad medieval tradition, set his doctrine of God within the framework established by Augustine. God, argued Staupitz, is essential Love itself, that highest Good in which all other relative goods find their meaning and by which they are to be judged.[4] Everything which is good can be ascribed to this one eternal Source, who is the Author of all human righteousness.[5] He is, to use Anselm's phrase, that Being than which no better can be con-

---

[1] "...sic in huius mortalitatis vita peregrinantes a Domino, si redire in patriam volumus, uni beati esse possimus, utendum est hoc mundo, non fruendum; et invisibilia Dei, per ea quae facta sunt, intellecta conspiciantur, hoc est, ut de corporalibus temporalibusque rebus aeterna et spiritualia capiamus." Augustine, De doctr. chr. I.4.4., PL 34.21.

[2] "Illae quibus fruendum est, beatos nos faciunt. Istis quibus utendum est, tendentes ad beatitudinem adiuvamur, et quasi adminiculamur ut ad illas quae nos beatos faciunt, pervenire, atque his inhaerere possimus." Augustine, De doctr. chr. I.3.3., PL 34.20.

[3] "Charitatem voco motum animi ad fruendum Deo propter ipsum, et se atque proximo propter Deum: cupiditatem autem, motum animi ad fruendum se et proximo et quolibet corpore non propter Deum." Augustine, De doctr. chr. III. 10.16., PL 34.72.

[4] "Es begreyfft auch ein yetzlichs hertz, das diser lieb sonderlich nichts lieblichers ist, und nichts unlieblichs aus yre fliessen kun, Darumb das sye die selbst bestendige wesenliche lieb ist, die in ir selbst gut ist. Unsere lieb nymbt yrer guethe mass von des geliebten guete. Ist gut wann sy etwas guts liebt, Pesser, so sy einn bessers liebt, Allerbest wen sy das hochst guet liebt, und ist boss, wann sy liebt was nit gut ist." Lieb gottes (1518) Kn. 93–4.

[5] "Sed recurret homo in cor suum et inde recurrit ad deum et novit dicere: quicquid bonum dixi, quicquid verum dixi, dei dixi, de deo dixi. Quicquid forte aliud dixi, quod dicere non debui, homo dixi, sed sub deo dixi." Hiob (1497–8) 11.94.27–30. Cf. Nachfolgung (1515) Kn. 58.

ceived.[1] He is in Himself complete, perfect, and self-sufficient. There is nothing which He needs which he cannot find in Himself. As a result of this fact, beatitude is for God, as it is not for His creatures, something which is natural to Him, which is inherent in His own Being.[2] He is, to put the matter succinctly, His own supreme Good.

Beatitude, however, is not the natural state of man, but the ultimate object of his quest.[3] It is, of course, possible for man to seek his fulfillment in the created world around him, to attempt to substitute a temporal good for an eternal one.[4] But all such misdirected love yields bitter fruit.[4] The truly righteous man, like Job in the Old Testament, knows that God alone is to be enjoyed.[6] The created order, however attractive it may be, is only to be used. Either God is loved for Himself alone, Staupitz asserts, or He is robbed of His glory.[7]

Idolatry arises when something other than God is treated as God.[8] That is not to say that the temporal goods which man substitutes for God are in themselves evil. One's wife or children are certainly worthy of respect and love, but they are not worthy to be treated with that supreme love which belongs to God alone. Indeed, Staupitz main-

---

[1] "Cum autem melius deo cogitari non possit et infinite perfectioni, nihil addi, nihil demi; praeter laudem, honorem et gloriam non requirit aliquid." *Libellus* (1516) 3.

[2] "Soli enim deo beatitudo perfecta est naturalis, quia idem est sibi esse et beatum esse." *Hiob* (1497–8) 12.102.29–30.

[3] "Cuilibet autem naturae esse beatum non est natura, sed ultimus finis." *Hiob* (1497–8) 12.102–30-1.

[4] True peace is not to be found in the created order. "Non licet in creaturis, non in praesenti vita querere requiem, sed vitam eternam tamquam summum bonum totis postulare viribus fugereque mortem eternam." *Hiob* (1497–8) 6.33. 26–8.

[5] "...alle ungeorndte lieb is piter und all creatur soltu weniger lieb dan got das höchst guet und der lieb soltu nichtz fürsetzen." Hs: 23 E 16, Nonnberg, fol. 35a-b.

[6] "Sed quia homines victi pocius stulticia sua in bonis creatis ad praesentem vitam beatitudinem traxere, ideo exemplum tibi proponitur Sanctus Job, qui felicitate omni terrena spreta, quam tamen abundancius possedit, studuit omnibus sic uti, ut solo deo desideraret frui." *Hiob* (1497–8) 6.35.10–14.

[7] "Welcher aber goth liebt umb seins nutz willen, oder etwas zeytlichs, der setzt die creatur fur den schepffer, und beraubt got seiner glorien, seiner hochsten ere, unnd macht ym das zu got, das nit got ist." *Lieb gottes* (1518) Kn. 94–5.

[8] "Wer weiss nicht, das einn christen mensch der hewt sprech, seinn weib were sein got, ader seine kindt, ader guet etc. zum feur vorurteilt wurd, so er darinne verharret. wer sicht aber nicht in teglichen wercken, das got so gemeinlich dem guet, den wollusten, der zeytlichen eere nachgesetzt wirt, das es zuerbarmen ist. Abgotterey ist bey uns ym namen nicht, in der tat aber villeicht nichts weniger den gewesen." *Lieb gottes* (1518) Kn. 95.

tained, what one loves above all else, that is one's God.[1] It makes no
difference at all what one's religious professions may be. It is the deed
and not the profession which must be assessed.

As man's supreme Good, God expects to be both loved and feared—
though more loved than feared.[2] And by fear, Staupitz means not a
slavish terror or paralysing anguish at the thought of the Last Judgment, but rather the kind of fear which a son has in the presence of his
father—a fear grounded in the confidence that, whatever the ap-
pearances may be, the son is one who is always dear to his father.
Even though the father judges and punishes him, he does so out of
love and with the good of the son as his ultimate objective.[3] Un-
worthy or servile fear has no place whatever in this relationship. God
is never for Staupitz the Stranger, but always the End in which man
finds the fulfillment for which he was created.

---

[1] "Den was das hertz am hochsten liebt, das eretz als got, es rede der mund
sonst oder so von got." *Lieb gottes* (1518) Kn. 95. For Luther it is *Glaube* rather
than *Liebe* which makes God or an idol. Cf. WA 30.1.132.32–133.8 (1529); WA
40.1.360.2–361.1 (1531). Commenting on the second of these passages, the section
from the *Commentary on Galatians* of 1531, Ebeling remarks: "Die Schöpferkraft
des Glaubens—Luther sagt unüberbietbar gewagt: creatrix divinitatis—meint
eben gar nichts anderes, als dass der Glaube nicht Werk des Menschen, sondern
Werk Gottes ist, oder wie Luther im Wortspiel sagt, nicht ein facere deo (ein Tun
für Gott), sondern facere deum (ein Gott machen), aber das heisst doch allein:
Gott wirken lassen, Gott Gott sein lassen, Gott werden durch Glauben allein.
Wenn man ernst nimmt, kann man Gott nicht durch ein Tun, sondern allein durch
den Glauben, sagen wir jetzt: durch Freude an Gott, entsprechen. Allein der
Lobpreis Gottes ist sachgemässes Reden von Gott, nicht etwa im Sinne besonderer
literarischer Form, sondern als Grundbestimmung allen rechten Redens von
Gott." Gerhard Ebeling, *Luther, Einführung in sein Denken* (Tübingen, 1964), pp.
297–8.

[2] "Also wil auch got von unns seinen creaturen mer geliebt dann geforcht
werden, dorumb Ine der mensch mer lieben dann forchten soll." *In was gestalt der
mensch got lieben oder forchten soll* (1517) Kn. 25.

[3] "Dann ob wol ainer Vom nachrichter und dann von seinem Vater mit ruten
gezuchtigt wurd, fleust doch dieselb straff nit aus ainem gleichmessigen grundt,
wiewol der vater Und der nachrichter den Son mit gleicher hertigkait zuchtigen
mogen Sonder des zuchtigers straff entspringt aus ainer forcht die er dem Ver-
schulten Son damit verursachen wil und des vaters straff allein aus ainer lieb die
er als ein vater zum sone tregt. Dorumb sollen wir got lieben als den aller freunt-
lichsten parmherzigsten Vater und forchten als ein gerechten milten Richter nit
mit ainer knechtlichen Sonder ainer kindtlichen forcht." *In was gestalt der mensch
got lieben oder forchten soll* (1517) Kn. 25–6.

II. Distinction of Intellect and Will:
The Problem of Divine Simplicity

When we turn our attention to the problem of the distinction between God's intellect and will, we find, as we had been led to expect, that Staupitz is greatly indebted to Thomas Aquinas and Giles of Rome for insight into the intricate issues involved in this distinction. Thomas Aquinas argued that all Ideas pre-exist in God as the models or patterns of things to be created.[1] That is to say, the forms of all things, which in creation are united with matter, exist in the divine intellect before they exist actually. By the simple act of knowing His own essence, therefore, God takes knowledge of the whole of reality.[2] In no sense is divine knowledge abstractive or discursive.[3]

On the other hand, divine knowledge is not simply limited to the forms of things. Thomas suggests in the *Summa Theologiae* that divine knowledge extends as far as divine causality.[4] Since divine causality embraces matter as well as forms, divine knowledge does so, too. God knows singulars individuated by matter. But He knows them, not through abstraction nor by a process of discursive reasoning, but immediately through His own essence.

Every act of creation presupposes divine knowledge. In the broadest sense, therefore, one could say that God's knowledge is the cause of things. Acts of intellection, however, and acts of volition can be distinguished. Properly speaking, divine knowledge is causative only when the divine will cooperates with it to produce an effect.[5] To attribute causality to divine knowledge without immediately emphasizing the role of the will is to be guilty of theological imprecision.

In contrast to divine knowledge, human knowledge is derived by a process of abstraction from sense experience. Objects in the material world affect the human senses by means of their sensible qualities.[6] The senses, then, produce an image of this object which is made intelligible through the operation of the active intellect. This image, having been rendered intelligible, is impressed by the active intellect

---

[1] For a brief introduction to the epistemology of Thomas Aquinas see Frederick Copleston, S.J., *A History of Philosophy, Vol. II, Mediaeval Philosophy, Augustine to Scotus* (Westminster, Md.: The Newman Press, 1952), pp. 312–434.

[2] I *Summa contra Gentiles* 58.

[3] I *Summa contra Gentiles* 57.

[4] *Summa Theologiae* I q.14 a.11.

[5] *Summa Theologiae* I q.14 a.8 and I q.14 a.8 ad 1.

[6] *Summa Theologiae* I q.78 a.4 and ad 2.

on the mind or possible intellect of the knower. The final result or expression of this process is the concept. The act of knowing is thus in reality the act of isolating what is universal from particular things.[1]

Staupitz agrees with Thomas that the *species intelligibiles* are necessary for an act of human or angelic cognition.[2] In the case of human cognition, these *species* are abstracted from sensible things, while for angels the *species* are immediately present to their intellect. Fallen angels, or demons, are not able to read the thoughts of men *in se*, though they know what *species* are in the memory.[3] In any event, angels are denied the knowledge of future contingents, since the knowledge of future contingents is reserved for God alone.[4]

When Staupitz turns in particular to the question of divine knowledge, he deals with it by reproducing a lengthy quotation from Giles of Rome, the official doctor of the Augustinian Order.[5] The context

---

[1] *Summa Theologiae* IaIIae q.2 a.6; I q.79 a.4; q.84 a.6; q.85 a.1.

[2] "Intellectus vero humanus, qui cognoscit per species a rebus acceptas, habet scienciam per adequacionem, quia ipse adequatur rebus. In sciencia vero angelorum adequacionem salvamus, non quia res imitentur intellectum eorum, nec quia intellectus eorum imitetur res eo, quod non cognoscit per species acceptas a rebus, sed quia ambo imitantur tercium. Nam ab ideis in mente divina existentibus habent esse formae in propriis materiis et species in mentibus angelorum." *Hiob* (1497–8) 11.87.20–26. Cf. 11.86.32–87.36 with Giles of Rome, I *Sent.* d.38 q.1. Wolf is correct to argue that Staupitz's retention of the doctrine of *species intelligibiles* separates him from Biel and Ockham. It is not wholly accurate, however, to conclude from this that "...damit grenzt sich Staupitz deutlich gegen die Erkenntnistheorie der via moderna ab." Wolf, *Staupitz und Luther*, p. 29. Gregory of Rimini, who certainly has a claim to be considered a representative of the *via moderna*, also retains this doctrine. II *Sent.* d.7 q.3. Cf. Gordon Leff, *Gregory of Rimini, Tradition and Innovation in Fourteenth Century Thought* (Manchester: Manchester University Press, 1961), pp. 31–6. Leff relies on the more reliable J. Würsdörfer, *Erkennen und Wissen nach Gregor von Rimini* in BB, vol. XX, pt. 1 (Münster i. W., 1917).

[3] "...demones cogitaciones humani cordis in se non cognoscunt. Vident quidem intellectum nostrum et species intelligibiles, quas habemus apud nos, et vident eciam, qua vel quibus utimur." *Hiob* (1497–8) 17.144.38–40.

[4] "Ideo angeli ista cognicione non cognoscunt futura contingencia, quae non sunt determinata in esse." *Hiob* (1497–8) 26.204.40–1. "Intelligere namque dei modum naturae eius sequitur, quae non determinatur per aliquid esse. Ideo nec oportet scita a deo per esse actuale determinari, quoniam sine determinacione actualis esse scire poterit quodlibet scibile, ut scibile est, omnesque modos scibilitatis eius, ut scilicet uno atque simplici intuitu rem ipsam et eandem praesentem, praeteritam, et futuram cognoscat, quippe cognoscit influxibiliter rei fluxibilis totum esse, et future esse futura, absque eo, quod sit, in sciencia sua futuri racio intelligit." *Hiob* (1497–8) 11.85.15–22.

[5] The citation is from Giles of Rome, I *Sent.* d.38 q.1 and is reproduced in *Hiob* (1497–8) 11.86–32–87.36. See also 8.62.21–2. Our quotations are from the citation as it appears in *Hiob*. The teaching of the causality of divine knowledge is not limited to Giles' *Commentary on the Sentences*. See Giles of Rome, "Aegidii Romani

of this quotation is the thirty-eigth distinction of the first book of the *Sentences* of Peter Lombard, question one. In this distinction Lombard asked whether the knowledge or foreknowledge of God is caused by things or whether things are in fact caused by the knowledge or fore-knowledge of God. Lombard concluded that the knowledge of God is the cause of the things which it knows, though it is not, of course, the cause of evil.

Giles uses the distinction as an opportunity to discuss the three classes of knowledge: divine, human, and angelic.[1] Divine knowledge can be likened to the knowledge an artist has of the created product of his own hands. His knowledge is not caused by things but rather, as Lombard had already pointed out, causes them.[2] Human knowledge, on the other hand, does not cause things but is caused by them. It is, in other words, derived from sense experience.[3] Angelic knowledge falls into a third category. It neither causes things nor is caused by them. The *species*, which the human mind must abstract from the sensible world, are already present to angelic intellect.[4]

Human knowledge is thus made possible by an adequation of a sensible object to the intellect. The human mind abstracts the *species intelligibiles* and by means of them retains an impression of what the sensible object itself was really like. The mind, in other words, imitates or copies reality. The real world, however, antedates the mind which perceives it.

Impugnatio Doctrinae Petri Ioannis Olivi An. 1311–12," ed. P. Leo Amorós, O.F.M., *Archivum Franciscanum Historicum* 27 (1934), p. 443: "Secunda via ad hoc sumitur ex scientia Dei que est causa rerum, quia, ut Commentator vult, super XII, [Averroes, *Comm. in Metaph.* XII.18.44.51.] differentia est inter scientiam Dei et scientiam nostram, quia scientia Dei causat res, scientia nostra causatur a rebus." Cf. Thomas, *Summa Theologiae* I q.14 a.8.

[1] "Secundum autem hoc tres modos adequaciones est triplex sciencia: divina, humana et angelica." *Hiob* (1497–8) 11.87.14–15.

[2] "Nam intellectum divinum omnia imitantur. Comparantur enim omnia ad eum sicut arificialia ad artificem, quia omnium est artifex, omnem habens virtutem, unde et Commen. xii. metaphysicae vult, quod omnia, quae sunt in istis inferiori-bus, proveniunt ad una arte intellectuali ipsius dei... Cum igitur omnia comparen-tur ad deum sicut artificialia ad artificem et res sciantur a deo, in quantum divinam scienciam imitantur, vere dicimus divinam scienciam causam omnium rerum esse." *Hiob* (1497–8) 11.87.15–20 and 26–9. Cf. also: "Dei autem noticia res causat, cum nostra a rebus causatur, ut vult commen. xii. meta." *Hiob* (1497–8) 8.62.21–2.

[3] "Advertendum tamen, quod licet respectu aliquorum aliquomodo sciencia nostra se habeat ut causa, tamen quia inicium cognicionis nostrae a sensu incipit et nihil scimus nisi prout res aliquam cognicionem in nobis efficiunt, simpliciter concedere possumus scienciam nostram causari a rebus." *Hiob* (1497–8) 11.87.5–9.

[4] See p. 40, footnote 2.

Moreover, the real world, to carry the argument one step further, is a copy of an Idea in the divine intellect. God does not abstract knowledge from sense data. On the contrary, by a single act of simple intuition God knows past, present and future alike. The world is not the presupposition or precondition of divine knowledge, but its result. Everything which has being is fashioned after an Idea which existed first of all in the divine intellect. Or, as Giles himself says, "Sciencia enim dei causa entis. Ens autem est causa scienciae nostrae."[1] Divine knowledge is thus not passive, but active. It does not imitate or reflect reality, but rather shapes and forms it.

Staupitz, however, diverges from both Thomas and Giles, who maintained that the distinctions which the mind draws between the attributes of God correspond to real distinctions in the nature of God Himself.[2] Giles defended the doctrine of a *distinctio realis* against Henry of Ghent by arguing that the *esse* and *essentia* of God are not only distinct, but in some sense separable.[3] For late medieval Thomism the *distinctio realis* signified that "...die Fülle von Namen, die wir dem Göttlichen beilegen, nicht nur in dem unvollkommenen Menschenverstand ihren Ursprung findet, sondern zugleich in der göttlichen Natur selbst."[4]

Scotus maintained that the divine attributes, though inseparable from one another, are nonetheless objectively distinct.[5] Mercy and justice, for example, are not merely mental concepts which correspond to no objective distinction in the divine nature itself. Though each is really identical with the divine essence, they can and should be formally distinguished.

Ockham and the nominalists pushed beyond Scotus and Thomas by denying both the *distinctio realis* and the *distinctio formalis*.[6] Their

---

[1] *Hiob* (1497–8) 11.87.35–6. Staupitz nowhere acknowledges in this passage that he is reproducing a citation from Giles of Rome. It is the careful editorial work of Ernst Wolf which has uncovered this fact. See the addenda to *Hiob*, p. 267.

[2] Thomas Aquinas, *Summa Theologiae* I q.13 a.1–6.

[3] For a brief discussion of Giles see F. Copleston, *History of Philosophy*, II, pp. 460–5.

[4] This is the position of the late medieval Thomist Heinrich von Gorkum as described by A. G. Weiler, *Heinrich von Gorkum (ob. 1431), Seine Stellung in der Philosophie und der Theologie des Spätmittelalters* (Hilversum, 1962), p. 144.

[5] Duns Scotus, *Ox.* II d.16 q.unica n.17.

[6] For a brief discussion of Ockham's position see Paul Vignaux, *Philosophy in the Middle Ages: An Introduction* (New York: Meridian Books, 1959), pp. 165–79. Leif Grane summarizes the doctrine of divine simplicity in this way: "Spricht man von Gottes Wissen, Intellekt, Willen, Allmacht oder Prädestination, sind keine selbständigen Eigenschaften gemeint. Allein die *Objekte* für Gottes Wirken machen

tenacious hold on the doctrine of the simplicity of God led them to argue that God's will and intellect are one with His essence. This meant, in point of fact, that the nominalists believed the attributes of God to be mental concepts, created by the mind in its attempt to understand the simple essence of God, but corresponding to no objective distinctions in the nature of God Himself.

Staupitz touches briefly on this issue in the eleventh sermon on Job, when he attempts to explain the relationship between God's *sciencia*, *providencia* and *praedestinacio*.[1] According to Staupitz, divine knowledge (which, as we have already seen, does not imitate or reflect reality, but rather shapes and forms it), divine providence (which refers to God's governing or care of the world) and divine predestination are words used to describe the same activity. Staupitz does not attempt to base the terminological distinction between them on a distinction in the divine essence itself, whether real or merely formal. That knowledge, providence, and predestination are distinguished at all is due to the imperfection of the human intellect, which can comprehend the divine essence only by drawing such multiple distinctions. Staupitz does not go on to say that the distinction between divine intellect and volition

diese Begriffe zu Nicht-Synonymen. Sie repräsentieren in sich selber nichts anderes als Gottes Wesen, mit dem sie in jeder Weise identisch sind." Leif Grane, *Contra Gabrielem, Luthers Auseinandersetzung mit Gabriel Biel in der Disputatio Contra Scholasticam Theologiam* 1517 (Gyldendal, 1962), p. 69. See also Leif Grane, "Gabriel Biel's Lehre von der Allmacht Gottes," *ZThK* 53 (1956), 53–75. We disagree, however, with Grane when he finds the guarantee for the reliability of the divine will in the simplicity of God: "Die übliche Behauptung, dass das bedeute, dass Gott in seinem Verhältnis zur Welt 'willkürlich' sei, beruht auf einem Missverständnis, denn Gottes Willen ist mit seinem Wesen identisch. Der berühmte Satz: *bonum est, quia Deus vult*, gibt keinen Anlass dazu zu überlegen, ob Gott nun auch gerecht sei, denn Gottes Willen und Gottes Gerechtigkeit sind nicht zwei selbständige Grössen, die in ihrem Verhältnis zu einander abgewogen werden können, sondern real identisch, weil alle Begriffe von Gott das gleiche unteilbare, göttliche Wesen bezeichnen, nur in verschiedenen Relationen zum Geschöpf." Leif Grane, *Contra Gabrielem*, p. 11. Cf. infra, footnote 81.

[1] "Quia igitur non repente, sed causarum verborumque incrementis quasi quibusdam ad eternitatem passibus ducimur, igitur diem divinum in his, in quibus nostro modo intelligendi quandam intellectualem luminositatem speculamur, ut sunt divina sciencia, divinia providencia, divina insuper praedestinacio, non quod sint tres dies, sed est una tantum, divina scilicet essencia a nobis tamen ob nostri intellectus imperfeccionem sub quadam multiplicitate comprehensa." *Hiob* (1497–8) 11.84.36–85. We do not wish to place undue emphasis on a single quotation from the writings of Staupitz. Nevertheless, the clear disagreement with Thomas on the relation of intellect and will and the preference of Staupitz for a covenantal view of God's dealings with man gives a significance to Staupitz's view of divine simplicity which it might not have in isolation. This quotation is significant as one piece in a larger pattern of evidence.

is only a nominal one, but the drift of his argument is clear. The nominalist position on the simplicity of God is preferable to the Thomistic —Aegidian—alternative.

III. Relation of Intellect and Will: Problem of Divine Bonitas

The problem of the relation of divine intellect and will shows even more clearly than their distinction the way in which the influence of Thomas on Staupitz was qualified by the influence of Scotus and the nominalists. When Staupitz discusses the question of the omnipotence of God, he begins by placing it in the setting provided for that doctrine by Thomas Aquinas. Being is for Staupitz primary and acting a consequence or expression of being. Or, to put the matter in Staupitz's own language, the *modus agendi* follows the *modus essendi*. A person who acts does not by that action create, but rather expresses the being which he has, or perhaps more accurately, which he is. The possibility of action does not exist where being is not presupposed.

The doctrine of the omnipotence of God does not mean, therefore, that God can do anything at all, or as Staupitz himself says, anything which can be enumerated. God can actualize only those potentialities which have the possibility of being. However, since every being or possibility of being is contained, at least in potency, in the Being of God, God can bring these possibilities to expression in His activity.[1]

To be sure, God does not act of necessity when He chooses to actualize one possibility and to leave some other possibility in mere potency. Staupitz cites the *Summa Contra Gentiles*, Book II, to demonstrate that God is limited by no necessity of nature, knowledge or of intellect.[2] However, having said this, he feels obliged to add immediately in agreement with Thomas that God is guided in His activity by His

---

[1] "Deus enim est omnipotens, non, quia possit, quicquid enumerari potest, sed quia potencia activa et modus agendi sequitur modum essendi, et cum esse dei sit esse, in quo omne esse reservatur, posse suum est illud posse, in quo omne posse continetur; unde potest, quicquid habet racionem entis." *Hiob* (1497–8) 24.195. 15–19.

[2] "S. Tho. 2 contra gentiles multis ostendit racionibus, quod sicut deus non agit de necessitate naturae, sic quod eius potencia ad determinatos effectus limitetur, ita nec agit de necessitate sciencie vel intellectus, ut eius sciendia vel intellectus ad determinatos effectus solummodo possent extendi." *Hiob* (1497–8) 11. 88.34–8. Cf. Thomas, II *Summa contra Gentiles* 23.

wisdom. Freedom from necessity does not mean for Staupitz freedom to act arbitrarily.[1]

In order to explain the relationship of the divine will of the Creator to the creation which that will brought into being and which it continuously governs, Staupitz appeals to the causal scheme used by St. Thomas.[2] God is the First Cause apart from whom no secondary cause can act. All created being has its power of motion from God and in cooperation with Him is enabled to move toward its end. Even Satan relies on this power in order to move in opposition to God.[3] There is nothing redeeming about this influence of the First Cause. Indeed, what Staupitz seems to be defending, although he does not label it as such, is the Thomistic doctrine of *praemotio physica*.[4]

According to Thomas, every action is a form of being, a movement —to use his vocabulary—from potency to act. No action can take place, therefore, apart from God, who as First Cause enables all secondary causes to act in accordance with their natures.[5] In dealing with rational beings, however, God is not merely the First, but also the Final and Efficient Cause. As a Final Cause God works from without the human personality, drawing it by a kind of moral attraction toward its end. As an Efficient Cause God penetrates the human personality and by cooperation with the human will enables it to actualize a selected number of the possibilities which are presented to it.[6] The human will is not obliterated by God's activity, but rather

---

[1] "Tamen subdit: quamvis divinus intellectus ad certos effectus non coarctetur, ipse tamen sibi statuit determinatos effectus, quos per suam sapienciam determinate producat et ad terminos determinatos producat." *Hiob* (1497–8) 11.88.38–41. Cf. Thomas, II *Summa contra Gentiles* 23, 26, 27.

[2] "Nam agens secundum non agit, nisi simul influat primum agens, nec agere potest, nisi motum fuerit...." *Hiob* (1497–8) 29.222.39–40. Cf. Thomas Aquinas, *De Potentia* q.3 a.7.

[3] "Ideo Sathan post ea, quae superius licentiatus exercuit, non poterat ad alia progredi, nisi divina manus cooperaretur sibi." *Hiob* (1497–8) 29.223.2–3.

[4] For an exposition of *praemotio physica* cf. R. Garrigou-Lagrange, O.P., art. "Prémotion," in *DThC* XIII (1936), col. 31ff.; G. M. Manser, *Das Wesen des Thomismus*, 3 ed., *Thomistische Studien* (Fribourg, 1949), pp. 603–25; Reinhold Seeberg, *DG* III³ (Basel, 1953), pp. 400–4.

[5] "Deus est causa omnis actionis prout quodlibet agens est instrumentum divinae virtutis operantis." Thomas Aquinas, *De Potentia* q.3 a.7; "Dicendum, quod tam Deus quam natura immediate operantur, licet ordinentur secundum prius et posterius." *De Potentia* q.3 a.7 ad 4; "Voluntas Dei, quae est origo omnis naturalis motus praecedit operationem naturae; unde et eius operatio in omni operatione naturae requiritur." *De Potentia* q.3 a.7 ad 9.

[6] "Deus igitur est causa nobis non solum voluntatis, sed etiam volendi." Thomas Aquinas, III *Summa contra Gentiles* 88. Cf. *De Malo* 3.3 and *Summa Theologiae* I q.105 a.5 ad 3.

is freed to act as an instrumental cause in accordance with its nature.

We do not mean to infer that Thomas is in any way (if we may be permitted to use an anachronistic term) inclined toward deism. God acts upon the created will, not merely externally, but internally and immediately as well. That does not mean that Thomas by-passes the distinction between creature and Creator. The cooperation of the divine and the human will presupposes not merely an intimate causal relationship, but also a metaphysical distinction which makes the term "cooperation" meaningful. If there were no such distinction of essence between the divine and the human will, then one could not properly speak of divine-human cooperation, but only of divine action. The human will, far from dissolving indistinguishably into the will of God, preserves its own integrity as an instrumental cause.[1]

This doctrine of the causal priority of God in every human action *(praemotio physica)* appears to lie behind Staupitz's own scattered and occasional comments on divine volition. God is for Staupitz the First Cause from whom all secondary causes receive their power of motion, and He is the final End toward which all things move. He is the universal, principal and, Staupitz can even say, the most immediate Cause of every event.[2] Staupitz does not, of course, deny freedom to the human will. Indeed, as we shall later see, he even argues that man in sin has some freedom of the will remaining to him, though not the freedom to reconstruct his broken relationship to God. Grace is needed for meritorious actions and even—and here Staupitz is undoubtedly more radically Augustinian than Thomas or Giles—for morally good actions. But it is not needed for action as such. The general causality of God, what Thomas would call the *praemotio physica* and the nominalists would term the *concursus Dei*,[3] is enough to make the action of secondary causes possible.

The universe, then, is ordered by the will of God, which acts as a First (but by no means remote) Cause and which wisely directs all things to their proper end.[4] The activity of God is qualified by His

---

[1] "Sic igitur intelligendum est Deum operari in rebus, quod tamen ipsae res propriam habent operationem." Thomas Aquinas, *Summa Theologiae* I q.105 a.5.

[2] "Sed sciendum est quod deus est universalis, principalis et immediatissima cuiuslibet rei causa, et omnium actionum operator." *Libellus* (1517) 39. Cf. *Hiob* (1497-8) 3.15.32–16.3; 5.29.21–24.

[3] Biel also taught that a cooperation between the First Cause and all second causes makes the action of second causes possible. See Biel II *Sent.* d.28 q.1 a.1 nota 2.

[4] "Verum quia sapienter ordinantur secundum disposicionem finis omnes operaciones et passiones, et tamen creaturae huiusmodi sapiencia non plene innotuit,

goodness.[1] According to His distributive justice He apportions to each what is due Him.[2] Nothing falls outside of this will nor has it—and here Staupitz calls on the authority of St. Augustine—ever been known to fail.[3] Even sin can be said, in some sense, to fall inside the divine will.[4] After all, Satan is powerless to work except within the boundaries set for him by God and by means of the power which God as the First and Final Cause provides. God does not will sin, however, in the sense that He is its Efficient Cause.[5] Sin does not have an efficient cause, but only a deficient one. In saying this, Staupitz appeals to the authority of Giles of Rome, though it is clear that Giles himself was only repeating a well known teaching of Augustine, refined in the controversy with the Manicheans.

Evil is fundamentally a privation of the good—a definition which Staupitz takes from Augustine and supports by a reference to Pseudo-Dionysius and John Damascene.[6] It has, therefore, no existence of its own independent of the existence of the good. Indeed, Staupitz wishes to maintain that a particular evil can best be known through the study of its opposite.[7] In order to know pride, one must first come to know humility; in order to recognize greed, one must first have learned to

---

sequitur, quod nemo aliquid paciatur seu operetur, quod divina sapiencia, eciam quantum ad omnem circumstancium actus, non ordinaverit prout aptum natum est in finem ordinare." *Hiob* (1497–8) 29.223.6–11.

[1] "Dicet profecto: o domine deus meus, qui solus es, qui es, cuius bonitate sunt nec est, quod sine te esse vel operari posset, conserva, optime deus, miserrimam creaturam tuam, quas te non manutenente in nihilum versa est." *Hiob* (1497–8) 13.118.8–11.

[2] Hiob (1497–8) 8.55.36–56.9. Cf. Thomas Aquinas, *Summa Theologiae* I q.21 a.1 and Dionysius, *De divinis nominibus* c.8 lect. 4.

[3] "Neque enim extra providenciam dei esse potest, cui omnia subsunt." Hiob (1497–8) 11.90.9–10. "Illa enim voluntas, ut ait S. Augus. in enche. semper impletur aut de nobis aut a nobis," Hiob (1497–8) 3.16.26–8. Cf. Augustine, *Enchiridion* 100 (*PL* 40.279). This is not a quotation, but a rather free summary of Augustine's teaching.

[4] "Haec dicendo non excludimus eciam peccata humana, quoniam nec ista ordinaccionem dei fugere possunt, quapropter Sathan respiciens, quia deus est omnium finis, non potest prius temptare quam deus suam temptacionen in se ipsam ordinare." *Hiob* (1497–8) 29.223.11–14.

[5] "Declarabo autem, quomodo non habeat [malum] causam efficientem, sed deficientem." *Hiob* (1497–8) 5.26.33–4. Cf. 11.88.3–7.

[6] "Scire te oportebit, quod malum non est nisi boni privacio..." *Hiob* (1497–8) 5.29.32–3.

[7] "Vis cognoscere hoc vel illud malum studeas virtuti contrarie, ut scilicet per temperanciam intemperancie habeas cognicionem, per humilitatem superbiam cognoscas, per liberalitatem avariciam etc." *Hiob* (1497–8) 5.29.34–37.

recognize generosity. Evil is at best only a parasite which draws its life from an already existing good.

Wolf argued that Staupitz's undertanding of the *bonitas Dei* "...geht nicht über das der thomistischen geläufige Mass hinaus..."[1] To grasp what Wolf meant when he asserted this, one must remember that Thomas Aquinas was not satisfied to confess that the created order rests on the free decision of God and would have no being apart from that free decision—though he certainly wished to affirm at least that! Thomas believed it necessary to assert as well that the divine will acts in partnership with the divine intellect to create and maintain an order guided by right reason.[2] The will of God moves creation toward ends, which it in wisdom has chosen, but it does so under norms which, from the perspective of Duns Scotus, are independent of the divine volition. The attempt to ground justice in the will of God alone is, within the framework of Thomistic thought, at the very least superfluous and quite possibly dangerous.[3] Good is good, not simply because God wills it, but because it conforms to the order of right reason. The will of God is good, not so much because it is the will of God,

---

[1] Wolf, *Staupitz und Luther*, p. 121. Cf. *ibid.*, p. 80: "Der Gedanke der bonitas Gottes ist eng verbunden mit der Vorstellung von der Vollkommenheit eines Gesamtorganismus, in dem kein Glied verkürzt werden soll und, damit Gottes Zweck erreicht werde, auch nicht darf...." The principal difficulty with this thesis is, as we attempt to show in what follows, Staupitz's attitude toward *bonitas* is Scotistic rather than Thomistic. Goodness is not the standard for the will of God; the will of God is the standard for goodness. One should also note the following: (1) Staupitz often speaks of *sapiencia* rather than *bonitas* as the ordering principle of the universe. *Hiob* (1497–8) 6.35.27–9; 30.235.9–12; *Libellus* (1517) 1. Once it is *sapiencia per bonitatem*. *Hiob* (1497–8) 30.229.32–36. (2) While *sapiencia* is linked with *providencia*, *bonitas* is linked with *restauratio* and is used as a synonym for *misericordia*. *Hiob* (1497–8) 6.35.27–29; 12.104.18–20. Compare 12.108.4–12 with 12.107.32–36. Man is recalled to penance in the first passage by *divina bonitas*, in the second by *misericordia*. (3) Staupitz's interest in the doctrine of creation is religio-ethical rather than cosmological. The important thing about creation is that (a) it is gratuitous. *Hiob* (1497–8) 23.188.35–189.2. (b) and it reveals man's absolute dependence upon God. *Hiob* (1497–8) 13.118.8–11; *Libellus* (1517) 1, 18. (4) Prominence in the later writings is given to a covenantal view of salvation, which, while it does not wholly replace the causal scheme prominent in *Hiob*, tends to deemphasize it.

[2] For a discussion of Thomistic intellectualism cf. Odon Lottin, O.S.B., *L'ordre morale et l'ordre logique d'apres St. Thomas* (Louvain, 1924); "L'intellectualisme de la morale thomiste," *Xenia Thomistica*, I (1925), 411–27. G. M. Manser, *Das Wesen des Thomismus*, pp. 200–4.

[3] "Dicere autem quod ex simplici voluntate dependeat iustitia est dicere quod divina voluntas non procedat secundum ordinem sapientiae quod est blasphemum." Thomas Aquinas, *De Veritate* 23.6.

but because it chooses those ends which right reason dictates.[1] Justice is grounded in divine wisdom, not in the divine will.

The sovereignty of God is safeguarded, not by an attempt to maintain the independence of God vis-à-vis creation, but rather by stressing His all-pervading causal activity within the created order which He in wisdom has established. God is the First Cause who moves all secondary causes in accordance with their nature toward the ends which He ordained when He created them. God is Pure Act in whom there is no potency whatever and yet who enables created beings to actualize their own potentialities. That God could have ordered things differently is self-evident. That there is no purpose to be served by contemplating this fact is equally clear. The designs of infinite wisdom however cloudy they may appear, can scarcely be improved upon.

The Thomistic subordination of will to intellect seemed to Scotus to endanger the radical freedom of God and to give contingent being, however tentatively, a ground outside of the divine will. No being exists necessarily except the Being of God, asserted Scotus, and therefore no essence is the necessary object of the divine will except, of course, the divine Essence itself. Every finite essence exists contingently and depends for its existence upon a free decision of God. God wills what He wills because He wills it. There is no norm independent of that will to which He must conform.[2] In rejecting the Thomist position on the *bonitas Dei*, Scotus was joined by Ockham and the nominalists.

The question, then, is whether Staupitz follows Thomas or Scotus in interpreting the *bonitas Dei*. The evidence supports the latter alternative. The good, Staupitz maintains, is what is directly willed by God or whatever conforms exactly to His intention.[3] The standard for both distributive and retributive justice is the divine will. That is to say, there is no standard outside of this will or independent of it by which it can be judged. Although the divine will is essentially good, its goodness rests on the character of God and not on the abstract norm of right reason.[4] Indeed, Staupitz can affirm—in agreement with

---

[1] Thomas Aquinas, *Summa Theologiae* Ia IIae q.93 a.1.

[2] Duns Scotus, *Par.* I d.48 q. unica. Cf. Werner Dettloff, O.F.M., *Die Lehre von der Acceptatio Divina bei Johannes Duns Scotus: mit besonderer Berücksichtigung der Rechtfertigungslehre* (Werl-Westf., 1954), pp. 173–83.

[3] "Sola divina voluntas est regula sui actus, quia non ordinatur ad superiorem finem. Sed homo non est deus, ergo sicut causatum dependet a deo quo fit, ut sibi ipsi derelictus non est rectus..." *Hiob* (1497–8) 3.12.7–10. Cf. 3.15.1–2.

[4] Cf. the following statements concerning the relation of justice to the divine

Scotus and in disagreement with Thomas—that good deeds do not please God because they are good, but rather that they derive their goodness from the fact that they please God.[1]

While God directly wills the good, He permits evil, not for the sake of the evil itself, but in order to gain a greater good.[2] He permits unbelief, therefore, which is evil, in order (in the words of St. Paul) to have mercy upon all. He permitted Satan, whom He created good, to fall into evil, in order that the saints might have an occasion to profit from the testing to which Satan would subject them.[3] The same kind of statement can be made about the suffering of Jesus Christ on Golgatha. God is the One who makes the evil deeds of men praise Him. There is no tragedy which is not, so to say, anticipated and directed by divine goodness.

Temptation clearly has a place within the will of God.[4] God, of course, does not tempt men to sin; that would be unthinkable. But He—in a manner of speaking—domesticates it and uses it to His own advantage. Through temptation men learn to abandon their self-confidence and to flee to God, who can give them strength to overcome the wiles of Satan. And it is through temptation as well that men learn that conformity to the divine will in which their blessedness is to be found. Even evil is taken up into the divine plan and turned to good effect.

---

will and the relation of the divine will to the divine character: "Conclude: Solus itaque honorare deum plena iusticia cernitur, qui praeter eum nihil rectum esse sentire cognoscitur." *Hiob* (1497–8) 3.13.22–3; "Deus enim, quia iustus est, non punit iniuste nec quod iuste corrigit, repente affigit, sed expectat." *Hiob* 22.177. 25–7; "Itaque non nisi dei voluntas causa est prima sanitatis, egritudinis, praemiorum atque penarum, graciarum et retribucionum." *Hiob* 3.16.1–3.

[1] "Neque enim tibi placeant hominum facta, quia bona sunt, sed pocius ideo sunt bona, quia tibi placent." *Hiob* 15.134.37–8.

[2] "Incredulitas enim peccatum est, quae non fit agente, sed permittente deo. Verum, quia non permitteret, nisi inde melius bonum eliceret, addit S. Paulus: 'ut omnium misereatur.' [Rom. 11:32]" *Hiob* (1497–8) 16.139.9–12. Cf. Giles of Rome, *Errores Philosophorum*, ed. Josef Koch, trans. by John O. Riedl (Milwaukee: Marquette University Press, 1944), p. 40: "Potest enim Deus impedire mala conservando res in esse suo, non tamen permittet mala fieri nisi ut ex eis eliciat maiora bona."

[3] "Figmentum ergo dei dicitur, quia cum sciret eum deus voluntate malum futurum, ut bonis noceret, creavit tamen illius, ut de illo bonis prodesset. Hoc autem fecit, ut illudatur ei. Illuditur enim ei, cum sanctis proficit temptacio eius." *Hiob* (1497–8) 12.101.38–102.1.

[4] *Hiob* (1497–8) 11.86.18–24; 11.88.21–32; 24.194.30–195.7.

IV. The Covenanting God

Staupitz's most important deviation from the Thomistic pattern of thought is what we may call his covenantal view of the relationship of God to the world. This deviation can, perhaps, best be clarified by considering briefly the late medieval discussion of the *potentia Dei absoluta* and the *potentia Dei ordinata*.[1] According to Thomas Aquinas, the *potentia absoluta* is the power of God considered abstractly and in isolation.[2] Can God, asked Thomas, in view of His absolute power actualize possibilities which He has chosen rather to leave in potency— that is to say, unactualized? The answer, of course, is yes, although Thomas was quick to point out that even the absolute power of God cannot do the inherently impossible or whatever implies contradiction.[3] Yet, leaving to one side what is by definition impossible, there is no question that God could have ordered the created world far differently than He has.

The term *potentia ordinata*, on the other hand, refers not to what God could have done, but rather to what He has done or is in fact about to do.[4] It refers, in other words, to all those possibilities which God in His infinite wisdom has decided to actualize. While God could have chosen other possibilities to actualize, His wisdom led Him to create a universe which, all things considered, can scarcely be improved

---

[1] One should keep in mind the fact that the distinction between *potentia absoluta* and *potentia ordinata* served an epistemological function in late medieval theology. H. A. Oberman asserts that Gabriel Biel does not intend "...to ascribe to God an arbitrary and lawless code of behavior but rather to formulate that God, in all his *opera ad extra*, does not act in accordance with *our* but in accordance with *his* own justice, which transcends our preconceived ideas as to the nature of justice." H. A. Oberman, "'Iustitia Christi' and 'Iustitia Dei', Luther and the Scholastic Doctrines of Justification," *HTR* 59 (1966), p. 3. Wolf, by attempting to show that Staupitz is in the Thomistic tradition, believes that for Staupitz the harmony and order of the universe, which are prehensible to man's reason, reflect the *bonitas Dei*. See above, p. 48, footnote 1. One can argue *per analogiam* from one's idea of justice gained from observation of the functioning of the universe to a conception of divine justice. Actually, Staupitz shows no interest in this kind of analogical argument. His Scotistic-nominalistic idea of the *bonitas dei* and use of *potentia absoluta* and *ordinata* provide the background for his disinclination to pursue the arguments of natural theology. Staupitz's reflection about God begin at that point where the *Barmherzigkeit Gottes* was revealed in its greatest intensity: in the ministry of the incarnate Lord—more specifically in His passion. See *Hiob* (1497–8) 11.91.32–3; 19.158.29–31; *Libellus* (1517) 8, 9, 13, 14.

[2] Thomas Aquinas, *Summa Theologiae* I q.25 a.5 ad 1.

[3] Thomas Aquinas, *Summa Theologiae* I q.25 a.3.

[4] Thomas Aquinas, *Summa Theologiae* I q.25 a.5 ad 1.

upon.[1] Indeed, it would be fair to say that so far as Thomas is concerned the wisdom of God displayed in the *potentia ordinata* has very nearly rendered the question of the *potentia absoluta* superfluous. That God could have chosen otherwise is granted; that He could have chosen more wisely is denied.[2]

For Duns Scotus the distinction between the *potentia absoluta* and the *potentia ordinata* took on an importance which it had not previously possessed.[3] It became in his hands an indispensable tool for the defense of the freedom of God as an acting Subject, particularly in relation to the question of the justification of the sinner. Scotus asked whether in fact a habit of grace is necessary in order for a sinner to be made acceptable to God or for him to act meritoriously. If one examines this question from the viewpoint of the *potentia absoluta*, then, of course, the answer is no. The structures of grace have been created by God. They have not been imposed upon Him from without; they have no necessary or independent existence apart from His will.[4] God could, if He so wished, accept the person or work of anyone who lacks the normally requisite habit of grace.

On the other hand, while the law that a sinner needs a habit of grace in order to be acceptable to God is not absolutely valid in itself, it is, nevertheless, a law laid down by the *potentia ordinata* of God and derives its validity from the faithfulness of God to that course of action to which He has publicly committed Himself. In no sense is God thought of by Scotus as arbitrary or petulant. The reliability of the created order is not undercut or even, indeed, weakened. But its reliability is grounded in a radical way in the free decision of God who keeps covenant with creation, not because He is compelled to do so by any forces exterior to Himself, but because He has freely chosen to act in a certain way and has committed Himself accordingly.[5]

---

[1] Thomas Aquinas, *Summa Theologiae* I q.25 a.6 ad 3.

[2] Thomas Aquinas, *Summa Theologiae* I q.25 a.6 ad 1.

[3] "Fere omnes doctrinas theologicas Scotus considerat non solum respectu Dei potentiae ordinatae, sed etiam respectu potentiae absolutae." Parthenius Minges, *Ioannis Duns Scoti doctrina philosophica et theologica*, Vol. I (Quaracchi, 1930), p. 578f. See Duns Scotus, *Ox.* I d.44 q. unica n.1. Cf. Paul Vignaux, *Justification et prédestination au XIVe siecle, Duns Scot, Pierre d'Auriole, Guillaume d'Occam, Grégoire de Rimini* (Paris, 1934), pp. 9–38. Wolfhart Pannenberg, *Die Prädestinationslehre des Duns Skotus* (Göttingen, 1954), pp. 133–9.

[4] To speak of God as *exlex* does not mean that He is arbitrary. It means, rather, as Oberman argues, that God "...is not dependent upon any heteronomous law, extra deum, *except for* the law of his own being, the compound of his will, his goodness and mercy." H. A. Oberman, "Iustitia Christi," p. 4.

[5] When we describe this relationship as covenantal, we are following the help-

The theologians of the nominalistic tradition, although they were by no means in full accord with Scotus in their understanding of the doctrine of God, took over, nevertheless, his distinction between the *potentia absoluta* and *potentia ordinata* and adapted it to their own systems.[1] The nominalists wished to know, as had Scotus before them, whether a created habit of grace could in any sense be said to be necessary to salvation.[2] Faced with this question, the nominalists admitted freely that God could have established *de potentia absoluta* a quite different order of justification. There is no inherent worth in the good works of man, even in the good works of a man in a state of grace, which compels God to acknowledge them or to reward the man who is doing the very best that he can with justifying grace. The laws and principles governing justification have been established by God *de potentia ordinata* and have no other ground than the divine will which brought them into being.

This does not mean that the prescribed steps in the process of justification are unreliable or that God acts arbitrarily in granting grace to one man and withholding it from another. It means rather that the reliability of the order of grace is grounded in the covenant which the Creator has made with His creation. God promises to act in accordance with the structures which He has established *de potentia ordinata*, though He could have established, had He chosen to do so, an altogether different order of things. The *potentia absoluta* does not undercut the created order, but rather reveals its contingency.

Staupitz introduces the distinction between the *potentia absoluta* and the *potentia ordinata* in the sermons on Job, when he discusses the distinction between mortal and venial sins. To be sure, he does not use the terms *potentia absoluta* and *potentia ordinata* themselves, but rather the equivalent terms *de possibili* and *de lege statuta*.[3] Furthermore, the passage is itself a citation from *De Vita Spirituali Animae* of Gerson.[4]

---

ful suggestion of H. A. Oberman, "Iustitia Christi," p. 4; *Harvest*, pp. 166ff. In part, too, we are dependent upon Paul Vignaux, who describes divine justice as a "fidélité aux promesses." Paul Vignaux, *Luther, commentateur des Sentences* (Paris, 1935), p. 48.

[1] For a discussion of *potentia absoluta* and *ordinata* in the theology of Gabriel Biel see H. A. Oberman, *Harvest*, pp. 30–56.

[2] Gabriel Biel, I *Sent.* d.17 q.1 a.3 [H].

[3] For evidence that these are synonyms see H. A. Oberman, *Harvest*, p. 100.

[4] Compare Jean Gerson, "De Vita Spirituali Animae, Lectio Prima," *Oeuvres Complètes*, Vol. III, *L'oeuvre Magistrale*, ed. Glorieux (Tournai, 1962), pp. 120–1 and 123 with *Hiob* (1497–8) 23.186.27–33; 23.187.12–20.

However, a comparison of the text of Sermo 23 by Staupitz with the
original *Lectio Prima* of Gerson indicates that Staupitz has been very
careful to cite only those passages from Gerson which he wishes to use.[1]

The distinction between mortal and venial sins, argues Staupitz,
rests on a free decision of God. Properly speaking—i.e. *de possibili*—
every sin is worthy of infinite punishment, even those sins which are
commonly termed venial.[2] It cannot be said that God punishes every
sin *ad condignum* in the sense that He punishes every sin with a boundless and eternal penalty. As a gracious Father, God has introduced
finite limits to His wrath. He has, so to say, redefined the meaning of
ad condignum. To punish *ad condignum* no longer means to punish infi-
nitely (which God could do *de possibili*), but rather to punish to the
limits established by His justice (which He has determined *de lege statuta*). That does not mean that the category of mortal sin no longer
exists. On the contrary, there are still mortal sins which will bring
their perpetrator into eternal damnation unless they are remitted by a
divine act in justification. It does mean, however, that *de lege statuta*
not all sins are mortal. Divine mercy has made discriminating judgments in a sphere in which, when viewed absolutely, no such distinctions exist. The structures of justice are themselves contingent
creatures of God. Their reliability is dependent upon the faithfulness
of God to His own decision.

Staupitz's view of the covenantal relationship of God to the world
depends less on the distinction between the *potentia Dei absoluta* and
the *potentia Dei ordinata* than on his use of the terms *debitum nature*,
debitum gratie, *debitor salutis*, *ius ad celum* and the verbs *decrevit* and
debetur. A detailed discussion of these terms should be reserved for the
contexts in which they occur. We can, however, outline this covenantal
relationship briefly.[3]

---

[1] Staupitz omits, for example, a passage such as this: "Nolo tamen negare quin
anima possit ex sua vita naturali bene moraliter agere et faciendo quod in se est,
se ad vitam gratiae disponere." Gerson, "De Vita," p. 117. Staupitz rejects this
idea: "Et sic ante mundi constitutionem conclusum fuit neminem sine Christi
gratia bene facere posse." *Libellus* (1517) 19.

[2] "Obligamur ergo deo ad gratificacionem et graciarum accionem ex hoc, quod
peccata nostra venialia non imputat ad mortem, sicut tenemur ex remissione mor-
talium, quoniam utrobique concurrit misericordia dei non imputans peccata nisi
ad penam temporalem, quae de sua indignitate imputabilia sunt ad mortem, unum
de possibili; aliud de lege statuta." Hiob (1497–8) 23.186.27–32. Cf. Gerson, "De
Vita," p. 120.

[3] We will only give the references here. Full citations will be given in the
appropriate places in later chapters.

God created men to praise Him; i.e. to love Him as their highest good and to conform their wills perfectly to His.[1] All men by virtue of their creation owe God *laus*, though because of the fall they do not render it to Him. God is not compelled by His justice to demand *aut poena aut satisfactio* of man. In point of fact, God does not owe fallen man anything. He could in perfect justice abandon fallen man to his fate, allow him to fall back into the non-being out of which he was called.[2]

In His great and unexplainable mercy, however, God binds Himself to the elect. Through election—which is wholly gratuitous—He makes Christ the *debitor* of salvation to the elect.[3] The mediatorial work of Christ does not make men dear to God—as Anselm argued. They are already dear to God through election.[4] Although Staupitz can speak in Anselmian terms of satisfaction, his emphasis falls elsewhere. The principal work of the mediator is to make God dear to the elect.[5]

The elect, when they are justified, are enabled to render to God the *laus* which they owe Him.[6] And it is certain that the elect will be justified, not because they deserve it *(ex debito nature)*, but because God is faithful to His decree of election *(ex debito gratie)*.[7] Thus validity of the *ius ad celum* which God gives to the elect rests on the faithfulness of God to His own free decision.[8] Although, as we shall see later, the content of the covenant which God establishes *de potentia ordinata* is radically different from the covenant which Biel describes, the structure of the covenant itself is not dissimilar.

V. ASSESSMENT

Our examination of Staupitz's doctrine of God indicates that Wolf's thesis regarding the influence of Thomism on Staupitz, while partly true, requires modification. Staupitz is clearly indebted to Thomas and to Giles of Rome for insight into problems of epistemology and for the doctrine of the *praemotio physica*. However, his views on the sim-

---

[1] *Hiob* (1497–8) 5.32.26–33; 7.44.36–7; 7.44.41–45; 30.229.2–4; 18.153.19–21; *Libellus* (1517) 3; *Lieb Gottes* (1518) Kn. 94; Hs: 23 E 16, Nonnberg, fol. 56ᵃ.
[2] *Hiob* (1497–8) 9.70.36–8. Cf. *Libellus* (1517) 18.
[3] *Libellus* (1517) 22, 27. Cf. 22, 26, 33. See *Lieb Gottes* (1518) Kn. 111.
[4] *Libellus* (1517) 36, 40, 86, 131, 152.
[5] *Lieb Gottes* (1518) Kn. 105.
[6] *Hiob* (1497–8) 1.3.8–10. *Libellus* (1517) 8, 9, 13, 14. 33.
[7] *Libellus* (1517) 26.
[8] *Libellus* (1517) 62; *Glauben* (1525) Kn. 126–7.

plicity of God, on the goodness of God, and on the covenant of God
with the world have been influenced by Scotus or the nominalists.
The goodness of God at work in the world does not bind or determine
all present and future activity of God, but is itself a product of a free
determination of the divine will. One cannot argue *per analogiam* from
a human conception of justice to a description of the character of the
divine will. The human understanding of divine mercy and justice is
dependent upon the revelation of those attributes in the person and
work of Jesus Christ. There is no proper knowledge of God *extra
Christum*, if one understands by proper knowledge the knowledge
which springs from faith, is motivated by love, and issues in praise.
Staupitz's serene piety—to use Henri Strohl's phrase[1]—is not the
product of his devotion to the *via antiqua*, but rather rests on the conviction that the God who has bound Himself to the elect is a merciful
Father—a knowledge gained from a contemplation of the wounds of
Christ.[2]

---

[1] Henri Strohl, *Luther jusqu'en* 1520, 2 ed. revised (Paris, 1962), p. 71.
[2] Hs: b V 8, St. Peter (1512), Sermo 6, fol. 28a-*b*; *Libellus* (1517) 8, 13; *Salzburger Predigten* (1523), No. 5, Aumüller, p. 125.

CHAPTER TWO

CREATION AND FALL

I. Man as Created

God created the world, according to the Christian tradition, out of nothing.[1] The world is not, so to say, an overflow of the divine essence, existing co-eternally with God, spontaneous, uncaused and inde-structible. That there is a world at all is due to a free decision of God, who, acting entirely without coercion, chose to create something other than Himself. What He made is good, though not divine; metaphysically distinct, though not causally independent. Indeed, if the world were not every moment preserved by the continuous ac-tivity of the God who made it, it would fall back into the nothingness out of which it has been called.[2]

The relationship of God to the world may be partly described as the relationship of a First Cause to secondary causes. Nothing happens in the world without the prior causal activity of God, though God is not—except in the very loosest sense—the Author of sin. By His wisdom He makes what He created desirable and sweetly disposes all things to their proper end. Independence is a word which can only

---

[1] "...potentiam dei, qua cuncta ex nihilo in esse produxit et secundum gradus suos in ordine rerum sapientissime collocavit." *Libellus* (1517) 137. The term *nihil* has two meanings for Staupitz, which, though related, should not be confused. (1) It may be used ontologically to designate non-being, as in the quotation above. With Augustine, Staupitz affirms that matter is *prope nihil* and that evil is the privation of being or *nihil*. See *Hiob* (1497–8) 5.27.16–21; 23.184.4–7. Man is absolutely dependent upon God every moment for the preservation of his being. *Libellus* (1517) 1. (2) The fact of this dependence is the basis of the second; namely, the religio-ethical use. To stress the nothingness of the creature and the *annihilatio sui* is to confess man's absolute dependence upon God. *Nihil* becomes in this context an expression of *humilitas*. See *Libellus* (1517) 4, 5, 257. These two meet in *Libellus* 252, when a man is so resigned to the will of God, that he is willing to be consigned to non-being if it would redound to the glory of God. But though they meet they are still distinguishable. The confession of the *nihileitas creature* is the obverse side of the *laus dei*.

[2] "Nec ergo sorte sed ex proposito condidit universa, sapientiaque sua deco-ravit et desiderabilia fecit, bona singula, valde bona cuncta, non tamen optima. Neque enim creature convenit optimam esse, quae hoc ipso quod creatura est, ad nihilum tendit, in nihilum vadit, nisi is conservet eam qui creavit." *Libellus* (1517) 1.

properly be ascribed to God. He alone is metaphysically and causally prior. He alone is original. All else is derivate and dependent. Thus there is laid in the doctrine of creation a foundation for the *humilitas* of the creature.

Staupitz is willing to speculate at times why God created the world. There are three reasons which he puts forward. The first reason is simply to say that God created the world for His own sake *(propter semetipsum)*—not that He needs the world for His own fulfillment![1] God is, as we have already seen, the Source of His own blessedness. But He was pleased to create something which He could love and with which He could share what He is and has. Creation rests on the free decision of God. The phrase, *propter semetipsum*, underlines that fact.

The second reason, which Staupitz occasionally suggests, is that God created the world out of sheer goodness.[2] Creation is, to borrow a term from later theology, a benefit.[3] God was not compelled to create the world, just as He is not compelled to justify a sinner. Neither did the world cooperate with God in its creation. Everything which man has received as a creature of God, he received, not on the basis of his own merit, but freely as a gift. Man's natural existence, no less than his fellowship with God, is a grace. Creation and redemption are in some sense analogous. Both depend on the unheard of goodness of God.

The third reason is the most characteristic of all. God created the world, Staupitz asserted, in order that it might praise Him and find in Him its supreme fulfillment and its final end.[4] This is true both of rational and of irrational creation, though it is not true of each in

---

[1] "Quemadmodum enim creat universa, ut sint propter semetipsum, sic et lapsa reparat, ut bona sint, ut iusta sint propter semetipsum." *Libellus* (1517). 1.

[2] "Got hat aus seiner aigen ungemessen güet peschaffen alle ding…" Hs: 23 E 16, Nonnberg, fol. 56ᵃ. Cf. *Hiob* (1497–8) 12.117.23–8.

[3] "Esse naturale hominis vel animae tamquam principales partes a deo sine nostris meritis accepimus… Magnum itaque tum ad hoc, ut nihil nobis asscribimus, tum ad hoc, ut de misericordia dei confidamus, ex eo suscipimus, quod, cum non essemus, sine nostra cooperacione creati sumus." *Hiob* (1497–8) 23.188.35–189.2.

[4] "Finis itaque creationis et reparationis est laus creatoris redemptorisque." *Libellus* (1517) 3. Cf. *Hiob* (1497–8) 30.229.2–4, where Peter Lombard is cited as the authority for the view that man is ordained to praise God [II *Sent.* d.1]. Staupitz stresses the point that man as created owes praise and honor to God. Though he does not speak of man as a *debitor laudis*, he does use the phrase *laudes debitas* and insists that God alone is to be glorified by man *ex debito*. See *Hiob* (1497–8) 5.32.26–33; 8.56.14–22.

quite the same way.[1] The difference is to be found in the element of free will.

Irrational nature praises God by moving in accordance with its nature toward the ends for which God created it. It is therefore by no means out of the way to suggest that God is praised by a summer shower or by a winter migration of wild geese. The world praises God by fulfilling His creative purposes, even though it has not consciously chosen to do so and is, in the nature of the case, unable to choose. God is praised where His will is followed.

Man, however, as a rational creature has the freedom to apostasize from the purpose for which God has created him.[2] Man has the freedom, which he may abuse, to seek his fulfillment in something which is not God—though he will not, of course, find it. God is praised by man when man does the will of God. But this doing of the will of God always implies conscious choice, affirming one course of action over against its opposite. To do the will of God, it should be emphasized, does not benefit God—though God is delighted when men love and serve Him. The benefits are all one-sided.[3] It is man who profits by praising God—that is, by loving (frui) and serving Him. In this service and in no other way man finds the fulfillment for which he desperately yearns. A life which does not praise God is a life which is unfulfilled.

Yet the emphasis in Staupitz's theology falls not on the *esse* but on the *bene esse* of the created order, not on the divine act of creation but on the still mightier act of redemption. Though creation is a gracious

---

[1] "Nunc sic omne, quod in eodem ordine invenitur, in quo deus invenire constituit, bonum est et deum ipso ordine laudat." *Hiob* (1497–8) 7.44.41–45.2. "...in allen übung der creatur wirt got gelobt, in menschen, in tiern und in kreütern, ein yegleichs in seiner art. Und so ein yegleichs zw seinen volkömen endt kümbt. So hats sein Säligkait erraicht." Hs: 23 E 16, Nonnberg, fol. 56ᵃ.

[2] Creation and fall are not synonymous for Staupitz. Man's problem is not his creatureliness but rather his inordinate self-love. His doctrine of salvation is not, as it was for Eckhart, that "...the creature, which of itself is nothing, has no essence, being, or value, may come to 'being' and essence..." Rudolph Otto, *Mysticism East and West* (New York: Collier Books, 1962), p. 105. The problem of man is in the will. Thus "...das Ziel der Religion nicht die Verschmelzung der Seele mit Gott in der grossen grauen Einheit ist, in der es weder Subjekt noch Objekt gibt, sondern—ethisch gedacht—die Verbindung des menschlichen mit dem göttlichen Willen." Erich Seeberg, *Luthers Theologie in ihren Grundzügen*, 2 ed. (Stuttgart, 1950), p. 17.

[3] "Et si quaeritur, ad quid creata sit racionalis creatura, respondetur ad laudandum deum, ad serviendum ei, ad fruendum eo, in quibus proficit ipsa, non deus." *Hiob* (1497–8) 18.153.19–21.

benefit and should be received as such it is still a lesser benefit than redemption. In creation God gives man his natural faculties and all the goods which belong to nature. But in redemption God gives Himself.[1] Though the divine *misericordia* is in some sense the presupposition of both, it is only in the latter instance that the full meaning of divine mercy becomes clear. The God of the Christian faith is not merely the God who gives gifts; He is the God who shares Himself. Creation is thus only a grace of a lower order.

When God created man He endowed him with the threefold gifts of nature, grace and glory.[2] The gift of glory, to be sure, was not man's in the sense that he already possessed it. Glory is another name for the goal which lies at the end of the road for man the *viator*; namely, the fruition of the relationship between man and God in which man finds his final fulfillment. In order to reach this goal, man needs not only the gifts of nature, but also the gifts of grace. Staupitz does not explain what these gifts of grace may be, except to identify one as

---

[1] "Magna certe gracia est, quod dedit nobis bona naturalia, sed maior, quando dat, quae per naturam adipisci non possunt, illa autem maxima est quando dat seipsum et quando nobis graciam gratum facientem, quam habendo sumus deo digni bono increato..." *Hiob* (1497–8) 30.232.19–22. In the earliest writing we have from his hand, Staupitz distinguishes created and uncreated grace and gives priority to the latter. Biel also—although he has a very different theology of grace—gives priority to uncreated grace. I *Sent.* d.17 a.2 concl. 3 E. See Paul Vignaux, *Luther, commentateur des Sentences* (Paris, 1935) p. 89: "Gabriel Biel distingue la grâce qui sauve de tout don créé: ex gratia sua, non ex quacumque forma vel dono creato. La grâce première, essentielle, c'est l'action divine, une avec Dieu."

[2] "Dominus dedit (ut intelligimus) triplicia bona hominibus: naturae, graciae et gloriae. Inter quae bona gloriae sunt finaliter intenta, ut scilicet sint ipsa bona naturae et graciae maxime gratis datae quasi media pertingendi ad finem gloriae. Vulgata vero regula habet media debere ordinari iuxta disposicionem finis pro et non contra finem. Vitam autem gloriae non vidimus, sed speramus et cognovimus per fidem. Movemur autem ad eam per caritatem. Ipsa namque caritas pondus est, quo celum attingimus. Caritas autem non consentit malo. Ideo simul cum peccato mortali non stat." *Hiob* (1497–8) 24.194.16–24. In the sermons on Job Staupitz argues that justifying grace can be lost. Cf. *Hiob* (1497–8) 26.208.8–14; 12.107.12–14, 107.14ff., 115.3–9. In his later *Libellus* with its greater stress on election, which cannot be lost, and with its emphasis on the intimate bond between election and justification, the doctrine of the amissibility of justifying grace disappears. In view of his early statements on the subject of perseverance, it seems to us less likely that he has repudiated this doctrine entirely than that he has narrowed the focus of his discussion in such a way as to make the treatment of this subject unnecessary. The theology of the sermons on Job is a *theologia viatoris*. It describes the pilgrimage of all men, just and unjust alike, toward their eternal destiny. The theology of the *Libellus de executione eterne predestinationis* is a *theologia electi*. It describes the journey of a select band of those pilgrims, the *electi*, as God's eternal decree is brought to fruition in their experience.

caritas, the unhindered love of God and neighbor.[1] It is not mere nature, but nature aided by grace, which enables man to attain his appointed end.

Man was created in the image of God. This means, on the one hand, that the faculties of the soul—will, understanding, and memory—are a reflection of the triune nature of God the Creator.[2] And it means, on the other hand, that man was placed in a relationship of immediate subjection to God.[3] Man was not made in the image of the image of God. There is not a mediating image, "whether of a good angel or of Satan himself," which is interposed between man and God. The doctrine of the *imago dei* serves as the guarantee that man was placed in an immediate relationship to the God he images forth and not in a relationship of obedience to some creature.

Staupitz preserved, however, if not the term *imago imaginis dei*, at least its substance when he asserted—using one of his most characteristic phrases—that man was created *ad conformitatem Christi*.[4] Christ alone is the revelation of the nature of the invisible God, the *figura* of His substance. Man is not made in the image of the image of God, if one means by this that he is made in the image of a creature. He is, however, created in the image of the image of God, if one means by this that he is made in the image of Christ.

Staupitz is not willing, in other words, to interpret the doctrine of creation without reference to Jesus Christ. His standpoint as an interpreter of Scripture is not in the Old Testament, but in the New.[5] The *imago dei* is not simply a way of saying that man was created to live in subjection and obedience to God. The nature of this obedience and subjection is Christologically defined. The obedience for which man was created is the obedience evidenced in the life, sufferings and

---

[1] "In ym [Adam] war unvorhinderte liebe tzu got, warhafte trew und geselschafft tzum nechsten..." *Nachfolgung* (1515) Kn. 52.

[2] "Dy drey kreft der sel, willen, verstäntnus und gedächtnus, das ist dy pildnüs gotz, ist zuegeaigent dem geist." Hs: 23 E 16, Nonnberg, fol. 3ª.

[3] "Homo siquidem habet in se imaginem dei; ad imaginem enim ipsius dei creatus est, secundum quam ita deo subicitur, ut nihil mediat inter deum et ipsum. Si enim alia imago media vel angeli boni vel ipsius Sathanae inter deum et hominem reperta fuerit praeter illam, quae ipsa deus est, homo iam non ad imaginem dei, sed melius ad imaginem imaginis dei creatus diceretur." *Hiob* (1497–8) 30.234. 35–41.

[4] "Ab initio creavit deus hominem rectum, iustum ad ymaginem et similitudinem ac conformitatem Christi, qui est 'splendor glorie et figura substantie dei.' [Heb. 1:3]" *Libellus* (1517) 29.

[5] For Staupitz's attitude toward the Old Testament, see chapter six, section five, "The Inner and the Outer Word."

death of Jesus Christ. It is this kind of obedience and not obedience
in general to which man is summoned. The *imago dei* is given concrete
form in Jesus Christ.

Adam had as a hope or promise the gift of glory (what Staupitz
following Thomas Aquinas sometimes refers to as the *visio dei* and
sometimes calls *fruitio*—the unhindered enjoyment and love of God
as the *Summum Bonum*).[1] Unlike nature and grace, which are immediate
unmerited gifts of God, glory must be earned by Adam. Man gains
his own glory *(beatitudo)* only by rendering glory *(laus)* to God. God
is to be loved *(frui)* and the world to be used *(uti)*. Man's will is to
be perfectly conformed to the will of God, just as the will of Jesus
Christ is perfectly conformed. He is created to praise God with word
and work.[2] All of which, of course, Adam was perfectly equipped to
do, having at his disposal not simply his natural faculties—which by
themselves would be insufficient to attain a supernatural goal—but,
more importantly, a gracious endowment of *caritas*.[3] Adam had then,
as he would soon cease to have, the freedom to do the will of God, to
be conformed to Christ. The beatitude which he desired would, if he
had persevered in the good, lie within his grasp. He was not tantalized
by the unattainable; he was lured to a goal which he could achieve.

The life to which Adam was invited was a life characterized by the
praise of God *(laus dei)* and by the denial, or as Staupitz can even say,
by the annihilation of self.[4] Nothing can be allowed to compete with

---

[1] "In speciali consistit enim beatitudo hominis in visione et fruicione... Visio
autem divinae essenciae replet animam omnibus bonis, cum coniungit fonti tocius
bonitatis." *Hiob* (1497–8) 12.103.18–29. This is a quotation from Thomas Aquinas,
Summa Theologiae Ia IIae q.5 a.4.

[2] "All menschen sein endtlich darzu beschaffen das sy got loben und eren, und
yn in sich selbst grossmachen und glorificiern sollen mit hertzen, wortten und
wercken. Nw ist kein wey, darin das hertz und der will gote sein eygne, sonder-
liche, hochste ere geb, den in dem, das es in seiner lieb rue, unnd yn umb nicht
anders den sein selbst willen lieb, aus gantzem hertzen, seelen, unnd gemuete, yn
seiner gotlichen volkommenheit gantz und gar gesettiget, und von aller anderer
lieb erlediget." *Lieb gottes* (1518) Kn. 94.

[3] See p. 60, footnote 2.

[4] "Nihil ergo creature felitius, quam redire cum laude in suum principium, recedere a se, accedere ad deum. Neque enim potest digne laudari deus a quoquam
sine sui annihilatione. Hinc tanto felitior quisquam est quo fuerit a seipso abso-
lutior, et in eternum felix est qui a laude dei non recedit." *Libellus* (1517) 5. As
already noted (see above, p. 57, footnote 1), *annihilatio sui* is confessional, rather than
ontological language. It refers to utter *humilitas* in the presence of God. Much the
same idea is conveyed in the German writings by the word *Gelassenheit*. Self-will
is abandoned in order to do the will of God. *Nachfolgung* (1515) Kn. 80ff. The
exitus-regressus theme which appears here in the *Libellus* (1517) 5, 40, 50, 138–40,

the love of God above all else, certainly not feelings of self-concern. The temple in which God is rightly praised is swept bare of all idols.[1] No creature will be allowed to take the place of the Creator as the object of the soul's affections. The praise of God presupposes a singleness of heart.

Praise is impossible, than, apart from love. But love itself in turn is impossible apart from knowledge.[2] One cannot love something with which one is not acquainted. For fallen man, as we shall see, this knowledge with which love is bound and on which it depends is mediated to him through Jesus Christ. For man before the fall, apparently, it forms part of his original endowment. Man knows God in the sense that he stands in a personal relationship of love and obedience to him.

But knowledge is never merely personal acquaintance, never merely a matter of relationship. Man not only knows God, he knows something about Him—something about the characteristics of God which define the relationship in which man stands. For Staupitz there are four characteristics which it is essential for man to know: that God is powerful, that He is wise, that He is just, and—above all—that He is merciful.[3] The man who knows this about God, Staupitz maintains, is the man who can praise God and who has something to praise him for.

---

257 should not be interpreted to mean that there is a divine spark in man which, though separated from God in creation, is reunited with Him in redemption. Older scholarship was correct to insist that Staupitz strictly preserved the distinction between creature and Creator. Staupitz merely wishes to assert that God is man's *principium* and *finis*, that human existence—to use Ebeling's phrase—is an "Unterwegssein...zwischen Gott und Gott." Cf. Gerhard Ebeling, "Der hermeneutische Ort der Gotteslehre bei Petrus Lombardus und Thomas von Aquin," *ZThK* 61 (1964), p. 319.

[1] "Laudi dei nunquam potuit deesse fructus salutaris, eius qui rite laudavit. Siquidem laudando deum in se immensum, in nobis magnificamus, comparatione illius et universam creaturam nihili facientes paramus dignum deo habitaculum et efficimur templum Spiritus Sancti, deo plenum et omni creatura vacuum." *Libellus* (1517) 4.

[2] "Quemadmodum incognita non diligimus et minus cognita non satis diligimus, ita nec laudare possumus simpliciter ignotum et nulla ratione dilectum. Nec digne laudare obscure visum et tepide dilectum." *Libellus* (1517) 8.

[3] "Tertium ceteris plus necessarium est novisse sublimitatem infinite misericordie dei et quod miserationes eius supra omnia opera eius." *Libellus* (1517) 12.

II. Man as Fallen

There are in the later middle ages three schools of interpretation concerning the doctrine of original sin.[1] The first school is the strictly Augustinian school, of which Peter Lombard and Gregory of Rimini are representative. These theologians agreed with Augustine that the essence of original sin is concupiscence.[2] The second school, of which Anselm, Scotus and Ockham are typical, redefined original sin in terms of the Augustinian doctrine of evil. Evil is nothing other than the absence of good. It has no positive nature of its own. Therefore original sin is nothing other than the absence of original righteousness.[3] Like evil, it has no positive nature of its own. The third school, to which Alexander, Bonaventura and Thomas belong, attempted to steer a middle course between both extremes. Alexander, for example, defined original sin as both *culpa* and *pena*, as both guilt and penalty. The guilt of original sin consists, as Anselm taught, in its lack of original righteousness, while its penalty consists, as Lombard maintained, in concupiscence.[4] Or, to use the formula of Thomas Aquinas, the absence of original righteousness is the form of original sin, while its matter is concupiscence.[5]

The results of original sin, according to Thomas, are twofold. On the one hand, man has lost the supernatural gift of grace which he was obliged to have and has therefore become liable to punishment. On the other hand, man's nature, which was harmonious and integrated has been disrupted and disordered by his fall into sin *(natura inordi,*

---

[1] These three schools follow roughly the divisions made by Gabriel Biel, II *Sent.* d.30 q.2 a.1. H. A. Oberman argues that Biel is a good historian of Christian thought and that these divisions are appropriate. H. A. Oberman, *Harvest*, pp. 121–26.

[2] "Ex his datur intelligi, quid sit originale peccatum, scilicet vitium concupiscentiae, quod in omnes concupiscentialiter natos, per Adam intravit, eosque vitiavit." Lombard, II *Sent.* d.30 c.10.

[3] "Nam de facto est sola carentia iustitie originalis cum debito habendi eam..." Ockham, II *Sent.* q.26 U.

[4] "Ad quod dicendum quod originale habet utrumque in se: et culpam et poenam. Culpa est carentia debitae iustitiae sive deformitas quaedam, qua ipsa anima deformatur; concupiscentia vero est ipsa poena, quae in parvulis dicitur concupiscibilitas, in adultis vero dicitur concupiscentia actu." Alexander of Hales, *Summa Theologica* Inq. 2 tract. 3 q.2, 221, pp. 236–7.

[5] "Sic ergo privatio originalis iustitiae, per quam voluntas subdebatur Deo, est formale in peccato originali; omnis autem alia inordinatio virium animae se habet in peccato originali sicut quiddam materiale." Thomas Aquinas, *Summa Theologiae* Ia IIae q.82 a.3.

nata).[1] Giles of Rome described the corruption of original sin when he maintained that man is not only *spoliatus a gratuitis* but also *vulneratus in naturalibus.*[2] Fallen man needs not only to be forgiven, but also to be healed.

Scotus rejected the mediating position of Thomas.[3] The material of original sin is not concupiscence, but rather the unfulfilled obligation to have original righteousness.[4] Indeed, Scotus so limited the significance of concupiscence for the doctrine of original sin that he defended the notion that concupiscence belongs to the nature of man as such. Concupiscence is, therefore, not in itself sinful, though it can lead the will into sin once the restraining influence of the superadded gift of grace is removed. With this view of concupiscence, Scotus could even appear to teach that the nature of man was not disordered when the *donum superadditum* was lost.[5]

Gabriel Biel did not agree with Scotus that the nature of man was left intact at the fall. The nature of man is corrupted by sin.However, this corruption is primarily psychological and not, if one may be permitted to put it this way, metaphysical.[6] The will no longer delights in doing the good and is hampered by fear and anxiety. Nevertheless, the will has not lost the freedom to do good, however intense the psychological struggle surrounding such an act may be. Indeed, not only can the will perform virtuous deeds, but it can even bring forth by the exercise of its fallen powers an act of love for God *super omnia.* On this point, Biel and Staupitz differed sharply.

According to Staupitz, Adam had a twofold freedom. On the one

---

[1] Thomas Aquinas, *Summa Theologiae* Ia IIae q.87; q.109 a.7.

[2] "Ostensum est ergo ex parte Dei quod sine infusione gratie non fit deletio culpe.—Potest autem hoc idem ostendi si ipsum peccatum vel ipsam culpam comparemus ad nos, quibus tria mala facit: quia spoliat nos gratuitis, vulnerat nos in naturalibus et obligat ad eternam penam, et maxime si sit culpa mortalis, pro cuius deletione semper requiritur infusio nove gratie." Giles of Rome, "Aegidii Romani Impugnatio Doctrinae Petri Ioannis Olivi An. 1311–12," ed. P. Leo Amorós, O.F.M., *Archivum Franciscanum Historicum* 27 (1934), p. 445. Cf. Gabriel Biel, *Sermones dominicales de tempore* (Hagenau, 1510), 19 B.

[3] For the position of Scotus see Reinhold Seeberg, *Die Theologie des Johannes Duns Scotus* (Leipzig, 1900), pp. 218ff. and P. Minges, *Ioannes Duns Scoti doctrina philosophica et theologica,* Vol. II (Quaracchi, 1930), pp. 318ff.

[4] "...ad istud peccatum concurrunt duo, carentia iustitiae, ut formale, et debitum habendi eam, ut materiale, sicut in aliis privationibus concurrit privatio et aptitudo ad habitum." Duns Scotus, *Ox.* II d.32 q.1 nota 5.

[5] Note the opinion of P. Minges, *Ioannes Duns Scoti,* p. 332: "Per contractionem peccati originalis non videtur esse vulnerata ipsa natura."

[6] H. A. Oberman, *Harvest,* pp. 128–31.

hand, he had the freedom to do the will of God, to praise his Creator
with every daily word and action. On the other hand, he had the
opportunity and ability to turn aside from the purpose for which he
was created and to seek in himself or in the world around him the
satisfaction of his desires. Ideally, Adam should have exercised his
first freedom and voluntarily abnegated the second. In point of fact,
however, he chose instead the second and tragically forfeited the first.

Staupitz suggests two reasons to explain why man fell. The first is
the traditional answer. Man fell out of pride.[1] Though he could have
obeyed God and loved and honored his Creator above all else, he
elected rather to honor himself with the love which belongs to God
alone and to exchange what is creaturely for the Creator Himself. He
who was merely *imago dei* attempted to become *sicut deus* by turning to
himself *(ad se conversus)*, and in this desperate gamble forfeited the
heritage which he despised. *Superbia* is the source of Adam's sin.

The second reason, which is found only in the late sermons preached
in Salzburg (1523), is one which Staupitz may have learned from
Luther.[2] In these sermons it is not pride but unbelief *(ungelauben)*
which is singled out as the source of every other sin.[3] He who does
not trust God cannot love Him properly. The nature of sin as misdirected love is, it should be noted, a basic conception to which Staupitz
still clings. He has not abandoned the Augustinian doctrine of sin as
amor sui. But this perverted love expresses itself fundamentally as unbelief rather than as pride.

The characteristic position of Staupitz, apart from these later
sermons, is the undiluted Augustinian view that the beginning of sin
is self-love.[4] Adam turned aside from his highest good, namely God,

---

[1] "Non enim malum est aurum, quod deus condidit, sed malus est homo relin-
quens creatorem ad se conversus, quod sine superbia non est." *Hiob* (1497–8) 7.
51.12–14.

[2] Ebeling explains Luther's view of unbelief as the fundamental sin in this way:
"Nicht die abstrakte Leugnung der Existenz Gottes, sondern die Leugnung des
eigenen Angewiesenseins auf Gott, also die Leugnung der eigenen Existenz als
Gottes Kreatur ist die eigentliche Gottlosigkeit. Der Unglaube ist darum die
Grundsünde des Menschen." Gerhard Ebeling, *Luther, Einführung in sein Denken*
(Tübingen, 1964), p. 153. Cf. Erich Seeberg, *Luthers Theologie in ihren Grundzügen*,
p. 106; Reinhard Schwarz, *Fides, Spes und Caritas beim jungen Luther, AKG* 34
(Berlin, 1962), pp. 268–9. See *WA* 57 III.151.13ff.

[3] "dan all sünt komen aus dem ungelauben; wan ains nit fest gelaubt & vertraut jn God, wie kan er jn dan recht lieb habn; wan ainer dan got nit liebt, so kan
er auch sein nagstn nit lieb habn, darauss komen alle sünt." *Salzburger Predigten*,
No. 6, Aumüller, p. 128.

[4] "Sunt, qui ex nobilitate et formositate naturae inducuntur ad se amandum,

and sought to find his *Summum Bonum* in himself. In this way, sin began
and out of this false posture of the soul all other evils flow. The sinner
loves as God what is not God and which can never take His place.
Adam made a fateful exchange but found no substitute.

Sin is, in the nature of the case, voluntary.[1] At no time was Adam
compelled to fall into sin, either by the pleas of his wife or through the
temptations of the evil. Quite spontaneously *(sua sponte)* he chose to
disobey God, to launch out on his own course,[2] to attempt to become
like God.[3] He turned from what was spiritual and eternal to what was
material and temporal. But he did so freely. He chose the destiny under
which he ever after labored. It was not fruit, as Staupitz once remarked,
but disobedience which brought man into his sorry condition.[4]

The nature of man's sin is generally described as *amor sui*. But it can
also be described—following St. Augustine—by another word, *nihil*,
nothingness.[5] Staupitz does not mean to suggest by this that sin is not
a reality with which man must reckon and to which he frequently
succumbs. Sin is, on the contrary, all too frighteningly real. But its
reality is not primary or independent. It depends for its existence on
the existence of the good. It is a parasite which perverts what is good.

This means, of course, that God, who created everything, cannot
have created evil. *Nihil* has no Creator. Sin is not being, but rather the
absence or privation of being. Thus the man who has chosen to sin
has been drawn into the sphere where being is not affirmed but rather

---

quod est peccati principium. Quanto enim nosipsos amare dulcius incipimus,
tanto nobis amaricatur deus, quo fit, ut ab ipso avertamus, ad nos convertamur,
et hoc est peccatum, quo perpetrato alieni sumus ab isto optimo bono, quod
finaliter nobis dare intendit deus. Ideo praenovit sua misericordia et auffert hoc,
quod impeditivum est salutis." *Hiob* (1497–8) 24.194.24–30.

[1] "Pro primo scire debemus secundum S. Augustinum [De diversis quaestioni-
bus 24, *PL* 40.17], quod peccatum adeo est voluntarium, quod si non est voluntarium, non est peccatum nec est in aliis viribus secundum se peccatum, nam si
actus virium sunt peccata, hoc est, quia voluntarii." *Hiob* (1497–8) 25.199.16–19.

[2] "Ipse autem sua sponte se infinitis immiscuit questionibus atque misere lapsus
est et labitur continue proh dolor." *Libellus* (1517) 29.

[3] "Cumque audisset quod esse lignum scientie boni et mali, voluit non subesse
sed similis esse deo et conversa in seipsam transgressa est preceptum; amisit obedientiam." *Libellus* (1517) 31.

[4] "Do sichstu ein klein verbot, under tausenten eins holtzes, einer frucht, nicht
das sie, sunder der ungehorsam gifftig were und den todt wirckete..." *Nachfolgung*
(1515) Kn. 53.

[5] "Sola autem peccati servitus praeter erubescenciam et obligacionem ad penam
nihil conferre dignoscitur. Bene profecto, quia peccatum nihil est." *Hiob* (1497–8)
23.184.4–6.

denied. The servant of sin is the servant of *nihil* and receives *nihil* as his just reward.

Although Staupitz describes sin as *nihil* and admits that the fall involves a loss of the original gift of *caritas*, he does not think of original sin primarily in Anselmian but rather in Augustinian terms, not as a privation but as the debilitating power of a perverted affection. The essence of original sin is concupiscence, understood not as an illicit sexual impulse, but as *amor sui*.[1] The notion defended by Scotus that concupiscence is natural to man[2] and that the fall, while it destroyed the supernatural gifts, left the nature of man intact is wholly foreign to Staupitz.[3] The problem with fallen man is that the basic posture of his will is misdirected. Sinful man is by nature an idolator. A radical act of God is needed to rescue man from his idolatry and to redirect his perverted will back to the true object of its affections. Man in sin is not merely incomplete; he is thoroughly corrupted.

The first effect of Adam's sin is that he becomes liable to mortality.[4] There are, Staupitz maintains, three kinds of death: of the soul, of the body, and of the soul and body together.[5] And Adam, by sinning, became liable to all three.[6] First comes the death of the soul; that is to say, the loss of its right-being *(recht sein)*. Then follows in its train the death of the body or the loss of being *(sein)*.[7] And lastly falls the final judgment of all, eternal death, when the body which is separated from the soul and the soul which is abandoned by God are reunited and given over to unending pain and sorrow.[8]

---

[1] "Ex Adam adgeneratur nobis amor in nos..." *Libellus* (1517) 46.

[2] Duns Scotus, *Ox.* II d.29 q.1 nota 4.

[3] Duns Scotus, *Par.* II d.33 q.2 nota 3. See above, footnote 33.

[4] At one place Staupitz lists seven effects of Adam's sin: "...nemlich, angeborne sunde, des fleischs widerspenickeit, mussen sterben, todes bitterkeit, schwacheit wol tzu thuen, unvorstandt des waren, begirlickeit tzum bosen." *Nachfolgung* (1515) Kn. 55.

[5] "Also das ungehorsam der selen todt, des leibs tzeitlichen und leibs und selen ewigen todt vorschuldet hat." *Nachfolgung* (1515) Kn. 54.

[6] "Oben ist geschrieben, das der leib sein todt, die sele yren todt hab, leibs und selen todt tzu gleich, auch sunder sey, dem nachfolget ein ewig sterben, Weiter das alle tode auss der selen eignem tode erwachsen sein, der in dem stehet, das got die sele vorlest, das dann geschicht, wan sich der mensch in ungehorsam von Got wendet." *Nachfolgung* (1515) Kn. 58.

[7] "Des leibs todt ist augenscheinlich und is vorlyrung des seyns, Der selen todt ist vorstentlich und ist vorlyrung des recht seins, in dem ersten vorlest die sele den lieb, von der er sein wesen hat. Im andern vorlesset got die sele, von dem sie yr recht sein hat." *Nachfolgung* (1515) Kn. 53.

[8] "Dem gantzen ersten tode folget nach und henget ann der ewig todt ader besser das ewige sterben, das dan recht anfecht, Wan die verdampten verlassenen

The second result of sin is that man falls under the bondage of concupiscence. This means, first of all, that his intellect, which had formerly some knowledge of God, is plunged into ignorance of Him.[1] Indeed, not only is Adam deprived of the knowledge of God, but he is prevented by concupiscence from ever regaining it.[2] Self-love acts like a magnet to draw his intellect back to earth. It is only faith in Christ, as we shall see, which can release the intellect from this earthward attraction and enable it to grasp afresh what God is like.

Not only, however, does concupiscence result in the loss of the knowledge of God. It means as well that man loses the knowledge of the truth about himself. He remains blissfully ignorant of the corrupting influence of sin or of the disorder which has been introduced into his soul as a result of his disobedience. He has lost all perspective on himself. Not only has he not correctly diagnosed the nature of his illness, he is not even aware that he is sick. He believes, in fact, that he perfectly well.[3]

Man's basic problem as a sinner, nevertheless, is not intellectual but volitional, not a matter of knowledge but a matter of will. If man's problem were merely cognitive, then a revelation of the truth or a disclosure of certain essential information could quickly and easily resolve it. But the fundamental problem is conative rather than cognitive. Man does not know the truth because he does not want to know it. And he does not want to know it because his will is misdirected. The human will is in bondage to concupiscence as well as the human intellect.

That is not to say that the will has lost its spontaneity or that man serves sin under a kind of compulsion. On the contrary, fallen man

---

selen mit verlassenen leiben wider durch gots gestrengs urteil tzu ewigem sterben vereint werden, do wird wolentpfindung aber alle tzeit mit pein und schmertzen." *Nachfolgung* (1515) Kn. 53–4.

[1] "Ideoque captivum ducitur ingenium, ligata est voluntas ut iam omnis sapientia mundi, omnis intellectus, scientia quoque, prudentia et ars ita concupiscentie serviunt, quasi ad eam solam et propter eam sint." *Libellus* (1517) 48.

[2] "Hinc rectissime sapientia, que ceteris merito prefertur, mundi stulticia est apud deum, quippe que concupiscentie servit, in notitiam dei sublevari nequit. Quod enim ab amore sui cepit, ultra quam ad se non tendit; quapropter in operibus humanis extra fidem Christi non potest deo serviri sed mammone." *Libellus* (1517) 49.

[3] "Es ist alles menschlichs geschlächt kranck und tod kranck gewesen und habent jr kranckait nit erkennt. Ja sy haben auch nit hilf noch ertzney gesuecht. Ja sy haben sy halt geflochen und haben jn selber wellen helfen, und haben jn jrem verstandt alle ding wellen erkennen und wissen und haben gedacht es sey nyemant gesünter dan sye." Hs: b II 11, St. Peter (1523), Sermo 11, fol. 98ᵃ⁻ᵇ.

serves sin with great joy *(gaudenter)* and abandon.[1] To be sure, he has lost the freedom to serve God (though he is totally unaware of this fact), but he has not forfeited the freedom to disobey. He sins, therefore, necessarily, but not as a result of coercion. Though his will is, so to say, metaphysically bound, it is nevertheless psychologically free. The bondage of the will does not hamper its spontaneity or diminish its delight in its misdeeds.

Sin has, however, a progressively debilitating effect on the will, so that indulgence in one sin leads to another.[2] This means in effect that the man who has been abandoned by God contributes nothing to his salvation but rather the opposite.[3] He uses the gifts which God has given him to increase his damnation.[4] Without *caritas* man finds it impossible to love God above all other things.[5] Indeed, without the grace of God man finds it impossible to do anything which is morally good.[6]

---

[1] "O flendam miseriam et hoc miserius quod leti ferimus hanc maledictam damnationem, et peccato servimus gaudenter." *Libellus* (1517) 32.

[2] "Facile vincitur ab uno vicio, qui in alio peccare non desistit, quoniam peccatum, quod penitencia non abluitur, mox suo pondere ad aliud trahit." *Hiob* (1497–8) 25.199.6–8.

[3] "Dan es mag der selen von got verlassen nichts tzum leben vereiniget werden, nichts tzu gutem dienen, nichts tzu heil wircken, dem dybe wirckt reichtumb tzu ewiger durstckeit, dem unkeuschen wollust tzu ewigem unlust, dem hoffertigen ere tzu lautteren schanden, dem gewaltingen hoher standt tzu ewiger unterdruckung, und in einem beschlus, was im der sunder tzum besten gedacht, kumpt in alles tzum bosesten." *Nachfolgung* (1515) Kn. 54.

[4] "...ia mer wo die lieb nit ist, da kombt einem menschen zuschaden, das ehr ein mensch ist, und die hochsten gaben gottes bringen yn zu mererm verdamnuss." *Lieb gottes* (1518) Kn. 113.

[5] "Unsere hertzen werden durch gossenn (spricht Paulus) mit der lieb von dem heiligen geist, der uns geben ist, der geist des hymelischen vaters, der geist Christi, wer der nit hat, der ist nit Christi, yme ist auch unmuglich got uber alle ding zeliebenn." *Lieb gottes* (1518) Kn. 98.

[6] "Et sic ante mundi constitutionem conclusum fuit neminem sine Christi gratia bene facere posse." *Libellus* (1517) 19; "Siquidem natura destituta nec nosse habet, nec velle, nec facere bonum, cui et deus ipse formidini est." *Ibid.* 33. Cf. 42. One of the criteria of the Augustinian sentiment in the late middle ages is the denial of the capacity of the free will of fallen man to act either meritoriously or morally before the infusion of justifying grace. Gregory of Rimini asserts that "...nemo potest habere ante primum gratiam actum aliquem liberi arbitrii non culpabilem." II *Sent.* d.26–8 q.1 a.1 fol. 93Q. Thomas Bradwardine, though he differs with Gregory in several respects, agrees with him in affirming that grace is necessary for good as well as for meritorious deeds: "Quod gratia quae est habitus gratis data a Deo una cum voluntate humana est causa efficiens proprie cuiuslibet boni et meritorii actus sui." *De Causa Dei* I. 40.364ff. Gregory's position was adopted by Dionysius de Montina. See Adolar Zumkeller, O.E.S.A., *Dionysius de Montina ein neuentdeckter Augustinertheologe des Spätmittelalters.* (Würzburg, 1948), p. 81. They were joined by Hugolino of Orvieto, Augustinus Favaroni of Rome, and Jacobus

He is the servant and not the master of his own disobedient members.[1]

The essence of man consists not merely in *sein* but in *recht sein*, not merely in *esse* but in *bene esse*.[2] No son of Adam, however, has the integrity of being he was meant to have. He is, in fact, wounded and impotent (or to use the language of the parable of the Good Samaritan, *semimortuum*), unable to act either virtuously or meritoriously.[3] If it were not for the providential care of God which preserves man's being and for redemptive grace which restores his right-being, man would instantly plunge into *nihilum*.[4] It is impossible, once the hand of God is withdrawn, for man not to fall.[5] Man's *sein* no less than his *recht sein*

Perez of Valencia. Except for Thomas Bradwardine, who was a secular, all these men were members of the Augustinian Order. See Adolar Zumkeller, O.E.S.A., "Hugolin von Orvieto (gest. 1373) über Urstand und Erbsünde," *Augustiniana* 3 (1953) 35–62, 165–93; 4 (1954) 25–46; Nicolaus Toner, O.E.S.A., "The doctrine of original sin according to Augustine of Rome (Favaroni)," *Augustiniana* 7 (1957) 100–17, 349–66, 515–30; Wilfrid Werbeck, *Jacobus Perez von Valencia, Untersuchungen zu seinem Psalmenkommentar*, BHTh 28 (Tübingen, 1959), pp. 228–239.

[1] "Ach edler gott, nymandt ist sein selb gewaltick, seiner eignen glid herre, ungehorsam gebierdt ungehorsam." *Nachfolgung* (1515) Kn. 56.

[2] "Ach got, nuh sehen wir, wie gar kleiner trost es ist, das die sele, von got gescheiden, bey dem leibe bleibet, und der mensch mensch bleibet, wann er nicht eyn recht wesen beheldt, dann nicht sein, sunder recht sein ist des menschen wares wesen." *Nachfolgung* (1515) Kn. 57.

[3] "Si autem illud naturae concedis et non aliud quam ab Adam accepisti, fidem, spem et caritatem non habes, sed semimortuum tantum hominem debilem, vulneratum et impotentem etiam ad opera nature possibilia, minus ad ea quae supra nos sunt, quae omnem facultatem nostram transcendunt; nosse scilicet deum trinum et unum, et filium dei, deum de deo, lumen de lumine, incarnatum, passum, crucifixum, mortuum." *Libellus* (1517) 16.

[4] "Ne frusta crearentur universa, decreta est pro natura divine potentie conservatio, pro libero arbitrio divine incarnationis gratia. Et sic per conservationem esse, per gratiam persistat bene esse, utrumque per ipsummet deum." *Libellus* (1517) 19. Wolf, commenting on this passage, says: "Hier unterscheidet sich Staupitz wiederum vom Gabrielismus; Biel III, d.20, q.un. a.1 u.B diese Anselmsche Begründung der Notwendigkeit der Reparatio ab..." *Staupitz und Luther*, p. 73, footnote 2. While it is true that Biel omits the *necessitas* motif in view of the *potentia absoluta* of God, nevertheless Biel "structurally...preserves the argument of Anselm's *Cur deus homo*." H. A. Oberman, *Harvest*, p. 266. Cf. Biel, III *Sent.* d.16 q.1 a.2 concls. 1–4; d.20 q.1 a.2 concl. 1. Furthermore, one should not stress too emphatically Staupitz's dependence on Anselm: (1) because Staupitz like Biel rejects the notion that the divine will is subject to any necessity imposed upon it from without (see chapter 1) and (2) because Staupitz like Biel stresses the man-directed Abelardian understanding of the work of Christ. *Lieb gottes* (1518) Kn. 103, 105. The elect are already dear to God through election. *Libellus* (1517) 36, 40, 86, 131, 152.

[5] "Cum igitur divinitus disponeretur hominem creandum fore eique corporalia cuncta submittenda pro dei laude et gloria, mox in lucem prodiit creature nihileitas et quod esset impossibile eam sibi derelicta non labi, non cadere, non reverti ad

is a gift of God. He is not and cannot be autonomous vis-à-vis God.[1]

All men have fallen under the power of original sin—with, however, two exceptions: Jesus Christ and the Virgin Mary.[2] Nevertheless, aside from these two who (for reasons which will later be explained) were preserved from the taint of sin, the entire world lies in bondage to cuncupiscence.[3] Exactly how this has come about is not fully elucidated by Staupitz. He does indicate, however, that he accepts Augustine's interpretation of Romans 5:12.[4] Man has inherited *amor sui* from Adam.[5] The process by which original sin is transmitted from generation to generation is not explained, although Staupitz is careful to point out that sexual intercourse is a gift of God which antedates the fall.[6] If man's sexual being plays a role in the transmission of original sin, it is not because man's body is as such inherently corrupt. The locus of sin is the will, not matter.

Every sin receives its just punishment from God. Even though one

---

et in nihilum, tam in esse quam in posse, et agere in naturalibus et minus possibile non deficere in moribus." *Libellus* (1517) 18.

[1] The fall, however, does not quench man's desire for the *Summum Bonum*: "Naturalis appetitus fertur in summum bonum volendum et in summum verum intelligendum naturaliter, non libere, ita scilicet, quod, velit, nolit, si tamen ita dici potest, non poterit non velle ista. Semper vult et dulciter vult, quia naturalia suavia." *Hiob* (1497–8) 4.24.25–28. Nevertheless, man cannot know God in this present life by means of natural knowledge. He needs the theological virtues of faith, hope, and love: "...et quia deus unus et solus eternus a nobis in praesenti vita cognosci non potest cognicione naturali nec amari per consequens, voluntas enim in bonum cognitum fertur, similiter impossibile est in illo sperare, quam nec intellectus cognovit nec appetiit voluntas. Ideo mittunt et vocant sorores, quas mistice fidem, spem et caritatem intelligimus, ut simul edant et bibant." *Hiob* (1497–8) 9.70.16–21. In the *Libellus* (1517) 14, Staupitz argues that the knowledge of God has a Christological center: "Ex ante dictis satis, ut estimo, apparuit deum absque notitia et delectione sui laudari non posse, nec digne laudari absque certissima notitia, quam, sine Christi fide, nemo consequit."

[2] See the chapter on Christology and Mariology.

[3] "...de primis parentibus nos habemus intellectum obtenebratum, voluntatem flexibilem atque ita totam naturam infirmam, quam infirmitatem nos patimur maxime propter peccatum originale, quod fuit actuale Adam." *Hiob* (1497–8) 12. 104.15–8. Cf. *Hiob* (1497–8) 1.5.6; *Nachfolgung* (1515) Kn. 55.

[4] "Cum ergo primus homo per Sathan a domino motus est, tunc est dominus contra humanam naturam commotus. Omnes fuimus in illo uno, quando omnes ille unus corrupit..." *Hiob* (1497–8) 27.212.40–213.1.

[5] "Ex Adam adgeneratur nobis amor in nos, amor commodi, curvitas in electione, obscuritas in iudicio et inde malicia in opere." *Libellus* (1517) 46.

[6] "Et nunc probari satis potest ex Augustine, quod fuisset generacio filiorum in paradiso primis parentibus non peccantibus: primo ex benediccione divina, secundo ex multiplicacione electorum, tercio ex bonis, quae oriunter ex institucione reipublicae." *Hiob* (1497–8) 6.36.21–5. Cf. Augustine, *De Civitate Dei* 14.22, *PL* 41.429.

must assert that divine justice is tempered by mercy, it is not abolished by it. God matches a fitting penalty to each transgression.[1] This means in effect that everyone who has not been elected by God to salvation is punished by Him, not because he was not predestined but rather on the basis of his own sin. The non-elect is, in other words, punished for real guilt.[2]

What about those people, such as babies or very young children, who die before committing actual sins of their own? Staupitz does not shrink back from supplying the same answer to this question which Augustine had provided. Those who are innocent of actual sin are punished on the basis of the original sin which they inherit from Adam.[3] No sinner, however extenuating the circumstances, is exempted from punishment. All the children of Adam share by nature Adam's fate.

III. EVALUATION

Staupitz's teaching on the creation and fall of man is characterized by its strongly Augustinian flavor. The essence of original sin is *amor sui*, concupiscence. This misdirected love has worked such havoc in the soul of man that there is no corner of his being, no inner undefiled citadel, no divine spark which has escaped its corrupting influence. Fallen man is impotent, not merely to act meritoriously but to act virtuously as well. There is no natural basis on which the good life can be built. Not only does Staupitz reject the nominalistic faith in the natural powers of man and its optimistic anthropology, but he also rejects the moderate, mediating position of Thomas Aquinas. His theo-

---

[1] "Si autem dicamus: punior ad condignum, quia punit, quantum recta racio et iusticia de facto taxant talo peccatum esse puniendum, tunc omne peccatum punitur aut punietur ad condignum, quia scilicet tantum punitur, quantum puniri deus vult et ordinat rectissima iuris racione." *Hiob* (1497–8) 23.187.16-20. This is, with only slight variations, a citation from Gerson, *De Vita*, p. 123. The limits of condignity have been established by God *de lege statuta*. See chapter one above, section four.

[2] "Culpam igitur deus odit et eum qui culpam in se habet semper punit; ut qui semper peccator est, semper puniatur; qui ad tempus est peccator, ad tempus puniatur." *Libellus* (1517) 89.

[3] "Hoc idem S. Pau. ad ro. v.c. [Rom. 5:12] dicit: 'Sicut per unum hominem in hunc mundum intravit peccatum et per peccatum mors et ita in omnes homines mors pertransiit, in quo omnes peccaverunt,' non quidem, actuali, sed originali peccato. Quamobrem dominus commotus est contra naturam humanam ita, ut eciam innocens a proprio peccato actuali nihilominus punitur." *Hiob* (1497–8) 27. 213.9-15.

logical affinities on this question are with the school of Peter Lombard
and the more conservative interpreters of St. Augustine. Man is absolutely dependent upon God for both his *sein* and *recht sein*. The stage
has thus been set for a discussion of the gracious intervention of God's
in the *miseria* of man. What has God done to set right man's miserable
predicament? That is the question which must now be answered.

CHAPTER THREE

PREDESTINATION AND PRESCIENCE

I. The Mystery of Election

A theologian in the late middle ages inherited not merely the Augustinian tradition, which stressed predestination and reprobation as acts of the divine will, but also the manifold modifications of this tradition, which emphasized to a lesser or greater degree the role of divine foreknowledge in predestination. A stress on prescience and the impartiality of God allowed a theologian to underscore the significance of human activity and to preserve the notion of divine justice. At the same time, a theologian who stressed prescience was forced by the logic of his position to dilute the doctrine of the sovereignty of God and to leave the door open for synergistic theories of grace, whether Pelagian or merely semi-Pelagian. If, on the other hand, a theologian wholeheartedly embraced the Augustinian doctrine of predestination, he was forced to confess that the universal offer of grace was in fact not universal at all and to explain, as best he could, in what sense human activity was significant in the redemptive process. Most theologians wished to preserve, insofar as that was possible, the advantages of both positions with the disadvantages of neither. They wished to assert both that God is just and that He is sovereign, both that grace is prevenient and that good works are essential to faith. In order to balance these elements, the late medieval theologian was forced to consider in what sense predestination can be said to be an act of the will and in what sense it can be said to be an act of the intellect.

Alexander of Hales asserted that the will follows the lead of the intellect.[1] The divine will acts to elect or reject men only after it has been supplied certain information by the intellect; namely, whether

---

[1] "...praedestinatio enim secundum rationem intelligentiae praecedit voluntatem et sequitur scientiam et attenditur in dispositione consequente scientiam." Alexander of Hales, *Summa Theologica* I (Quaracchi, 1924), p. 317. For the position of Alexander see Wolfhart Pannenberg, *Die Prädestinationslehre des Duns Skotus* (Göttingen, 1954), pp. 30–33, 77–9. Klaus Reinhardt, *Pedro Luis SJ (1538–1602) und sein Verständnis der Kontingenz, Praescienz und Praedestination* (Münster Westf., 1965), pp. 178–82.

the free will of man will make good use of the grace which is granted to it.[1] The locus of decision is shifted from heaven to earth, from the divine will to the human.

According to Alexander, predestination is not so much an action on the part of a sovereign God as His reaction to the free decision of His creatures. God is, so to say, an impartial Judge who views the human scene without bias and without predisposition *(se aequaliter habet ad omnes)*.[2] No distinction is drawn between men which does not find some basis in the men themselves. Election to life is not an expression of the unheard of goodness of God, of the boundless and mysterious mercy which can be gratefully received but never rationally explained. It is, rather, a demonstration of the fairness of God, who wills all men to be saved and who condemns no one without adequate ground.

Thomas Aquinas reinterpreted the Augustinian doctrine of predestination within the causal schema adapted from Aristotle. Predestination is, when rightly understood, a subdivision of divine providence.[3] God is the First Cause who moves all second causes toward the ends which He has chosen; He is the supreme Governor of the world, who sovereignly chooses the elect and provides them with the necessary means to arrive at the supernatural goal of eternal glory. His choice is in no sense qualified by His prescience, not even—and here Thomas broke sharply with Alexander—by His prescience of the good use of grace.[4] Thomas agreed with Augustine that election is an act of divine sovereignty.

The key to Thomas' theory of predestination is his clear and rigid distinction between *electio* and *praedestinatio*.[5] Of the two terms *electio*

---

[1] "...voluntate antecedente vult Deus omnes homines salvos fieri: haec enim est voluntas quae respicit creaturam rationalem salvabilem. Voluntas consequens cum praescientia quod bene usurus est dono Dei: sic non vult omnes homines salvos fieri, sed electos solum, et sic dicitur voluntas Dei rationabilis; si enim vellet alicui finaliter salutem qui male usurus est per liberum arbitrium, non esset iustus." Alexander of Hales, *Summa Theologica* I (Quaracchi, 1924), p. 320; "Electio vero connotat usum gratiae...unde etiam respicit usum liberi arbitrii." *Ibid.*, p. 316. Cf. John of Damascus, *De fide orthodoxa* II.29, *PG* 94.979.

[2] "Praescientia se habet aequaliter ad omnes, voluntas similiter uno modo se habet ad omnes; sed voluntas cum praescientia non se habet aequaliter ad omnes. Non tamen hoc est propter diversitatem quae sit in praescientia, sed quia nos non habemus nos aequaliter ad ipsam; unde praedestinatio non solum dicit voluntatem Dei, sed voluntatem cum praescientia quod bene sunt usuri dono suo." Alexander of Hales, *Summa Theologica* I (Quaracchi, 1924), p. 320.

[3] Thomas Aquinas, *De Veritate* VI a.1.

[4] Thomas Aquinas, *Summa Theologiae* I q.23 a.5.

[5] The following schematization is indebted to the suggestive essay by G. W. Locher, "Die Prädestinationslehre Huldrych Zwinglis," *ThZ* 12 (1956) 533–4.

is primary.[1] Moved only by His mysterious and groundless love *(dilectio)*, God chooses *(electio)* certain men to be redeemed and to share in the divine benefits. In the same way He passes over others. Both election and non-election are acts of divine sovereignty. In neither case is God moved to act because of His foreknowledge or by any consideration of merit or demerit in the elect and non-elect.[2] His decision is free and uncoerced.

But here the parallelism cases. Those who are elected are first predestined to grace and then to glory. They are granted the means to attain the supernatural goal and then to glory. They are granted the means to attain the supernatural goal and then predestined, by the use of these means, to attain the goal itself. All three decisions—election, predestination to grace, and predestination to glory—are acts of divine sovereignty. In no sense is the redemptive activity of God a response to the prior activity of His creatures. Election and predestination are gratuitous. But non-election and reprobation are not—or at least not wholly.

Of course, the decision to pass over some men is an act of divine sovereignty in the sense that God is moved to do so by no consideration of their demerits. Non-election is, so to say, the dark side of election. God cannot choose some men without leaving other men unchosen. Nevertheless, the non-elect are not condemned on the basis of their non-election. They are permitted to fall into sin and then reprobated on the basis of that sin.[3] An act of divine sovereignty (non-election) is followed by an act of divine permission and finally by an act of divine justice. The Thomistic doctrine of election is thus asymmetrical. Men are redeemed by divine grace but condemned by divine justice. Predestination is an act of divine sovereignty; reprobation— at least in part—a reluctant act of divine permission.[4]

The Franciscan theologian, Duns Scotus, immediately set himself in opposition to the older Franciscan tradition of Alexander of Hales by

---

[1] Note that Aquinas maintains that predestination presupposes dilection and election, *De Veritate* VI a.1; *Summa Theologiae* I q.23 a.4.

[2] "Praeexigitur etiam et electio per quam ille qui in finem infallibiliter dirigitur ab aliis separatur qui non hoc modo in finem diriguntur. Haec autem separatio non est propter diversitatem aliquam inventam in his qui separantur, quae possit ad amorem incitare, quia antequam nati essent aut aliquid boni aut mali fecissent, dictum est: Jacob dilexi, Esau odio habui." Thomas Aquinas, *De Veritate* VI a.1.

[3] Thomas Aquinas, *Summa Theologiae* I q.23 a.4 ad 2.

[4] Note that Aquinas makes use in this connection of the distinction between *voluntas antecedens* and *voluntas consequens*. *Summa Theologiae* I q.19 a.6 ad 1.

denying the role of prescience in predestination.[1] Predestination is an act of will, not an act of intellect. The decision of God to redeem some men out of the mass of fallen humanity is not a response to certain information made ascessible to the will by the intellect. On the contrary, the central theme of Scotus' doctrine of divine election is the conviction that this eternal decision is arrived at independently of all consideration of human merit *(ante praevisa merita)*. In the strongest possible terms Scotus indicated that predestination is an act of divine sovereignty. Nevertheless, he did not abandon the view that reprobation is by permission.[2]

Scotus clarified his position by an appeal to the example of Peter and Judas *(Ox.* I d.41 q.un. n.12). According to Scotus, Peter was first chosen by God *ante praevisa merita* to be added to the company of the redeemed in heaven. Having made this selection, God then prepared the means of grace which would enable Peter to arrive at the heavenly goal. Both Peter and Judas were then allowed by God to fall into sin. While Peter was helped out of his predicament by means of the grace provided for that purpose, Judas, for whom no such assistance was provided, was punished by God for his sin. Thus, while for Thomas God first predestines man to grace and then to glory, for Scotus the order is reversed—first glory, then grace.

Gabriel Biel differed with Scotus.[3] Although Biel recognized that certain persons—notably St. Paul and the Virgin Mary—had been granted grace apart from any consideration of their merits, they were clearly regarded by Biel as exceptional cases.[4] Ordinarily grace is given only to those who merit it.[5] Both election and reprobation are based on the foreknowledge of human behavior.[6]

Biel did not forsake the Augustinian doctrine of grace altogether. It would be fairer to say that he reinterpreted it. The mercy of God is understood by Biel, not so much as the redeeming activity of God within the order established by His *potentia ordinata* as His decision to

---

[1] For the position of Scotus see W. Pannenberg, *Prädestinationslehre*, 54–68, 90–119, 125–39.

[2] Duns Scotus, *Ox.* I d.41 q.un. n.11 and n.12.

[3] For a discussion of Biel's doctrine of election and reprobation see H. A. Oberman, *Harvest*, pp. 185–248.

[4] Gabriel Biel, I *Sent.* d.41 q.1 a.2 concl.3.

[5] "Statuit deus nullum damnare pena sensus nisi pro culpa personali. Nec adultum salvare regulariter sine merito personali..." Gabriel Biel, I *Sent.* d.41 q.1 a.3 dub.3.

[6] Gabriel Biel, I *Sent.* d.41 q.1 a.2 concl.2.

create an order in which men can perform meritorious works and be rewarded with the gift of salvation.[1] Fallen man has not immediately been hailed before the divine bar of justice. He has been given a way of salvation. That is certainly an act of mercy, even if the way itself is governed by the strictest justice. *Sola gratia* describes the freedom of the divine will in establishing an order within which redemption can be merited; it does not describe the nature of the activity of God within the order so established.

The Augustinian tradition of double predestination was reaffirmed by Gregory of Rimini. According to Gregory, the prescience of God plays absolutely no role in either election or in reprobation. God is not moved to predestine someone because He foreknows that that person will respond favorably to the proffered gift of grace. Neither does He condemn anyone—and here Gregory is clearly more Augustinian than either Thomas or Scotus—on the basis of foreseen demerit *(non propter demerita futura)*.[2] Both election and reprobation are acts of the sovereign will of God. Human good works are thus not the presupposition but rather the effect of divine predestination.

Staupitz sided with Thomas, Scotus and Gregory against Alexander and Biel. Election is the merciful decision of God to redeem certain men out of the mass of fallen humanity. In making this selection, God is moved by no consideration of the merits of the elect. Good works, according to Staupitz, are not the presupposition of election, but its fruit.[3] Or to put the matter differently, predestination is not an act of the divine intellect, but an act of the divine will. God does not respond to the prior activity of His creatures in apportioning out the gifts of grace. On the contrary, God seizes the initiative and by a sovereign act of the will makes the meritorious activity of His creatures possible. Nature, especially fallen nature, cannot merit grace. It can only receive it as a gift.[4]

---

[1] H. A. Oberman, *Harvest*, pp. 30–56.

[2] "Concludo...sicut deus quos voluit ab eterno predestinavit et non propter merita aliqua futura, ita quos voluit ab eterne reprobavit, non propter demerita futura." Gregory of Rimini, I *Sent.* d.40–41 q.1 a.2 fol. 160B.

[3] "Siquidem operis christiani principium est praedestinatio, medium iustificatio, finis glorificatio seu magnificatio, que gratie sunt effectus non nature." *Libellus* (1517) 52; "Nequaquam igitur sine bonis moribus et operibus sanctis vitam suam agit qui predestinatus est." *Libellus* (1517) 45.

[4] For a complete discussion of the relation of grace and works see chapter four on justification. It has already been shown in chapters one and two that fallen man is unable to act virtuously apart from the assistance of divine grace, i.e., *charitas*, and that left to himself he can only sin and merit damnation. *Libellus* (1517) 19,

The division introduced into the family of man between the elect
and the non-elect is a division resting on the sovereign will of God.
Apart from the intervention of God in predestination, the entire
human race would lie in bondage to concupiscence and death.[1] The
free will of man, so highly praised by the nominalists, is impotent, not
merely to act meritoriously, but even to act virtuously. Unless God
acts to redeem some, all will perish together in implacable disobedience.
Fallen man has retained the freedom to disobey God, but he has
forfeited the freedom not to sin. If predestination were based on foreseen merits, then all alike would be condemned to unending punishment. The nominalist doctrine of predestination taught by Biel is, so
far as Staupitz is concerned, tantamount to a universal sentence of
condemnation.

Nevertheless, while Staupitz insisted on the Augustinian teaching
of a gratuitous predestination to life apart from all consideration of the
merit of the elect, he shrank back from affirming with Gregory of
Rimini an Augustinian doctrine of predestination to death. The reprobate are condemned, not on the basis of their non-election, but on the
basis of the sins in which they impenitently die.[2] Reprobation is thus
not so much an act of divine sovereignty as it is an act of divine justice.
Man the sinner is punished for the sins which he has freely and spontaneously chosen—or, in the case of infants, for the sin which he has
inherited from Adam.

Moreover, to pursue the matter further, not even man's fall into sin
is a result of a decision of the sovereign will of God.[3] To be sure, no

33, 42; *Lieb gottes* (1518) Kn. 113. It remains to be shown that this *charitas* is primarily *Christus inhabitans* and only secondarily a created gift.

[1] "Ideoque captivum ducitur ingenium, ligata est voluntas ut iam omnis sapientia mundi, omnis intellectus, scientia quoque, prudentia et ars ita concupiscentie
serviunt, quasi ad eam solam et propter eam sint." *Libellus* (1517) 48. Cf. *Hiob*
(1497–8) 27.213.9–15. "Qui non est praedestinatus, non salvabitur." *Hiob* (1497–8)
11.92.9.

[2] "Ubicunque ergo legis deum irasci peccatoribus, cum reduplicatione intelligas
scilicet inquantum peccatores et ut peccatores. Ubi autem furit, indurationem
quandum insinuat et sic illos odisse dicitur, quos perpetuo cruciare decrevit propter peccata eorum in quibus moriuntur peccatores impenitentes." *Libellus* (1517)
88. One should not overlook the important verb *decrevit*. Staupitz has already made
it clear in the sermons on *Hiob* (1497–8) 23.186.27–32 that punishment for sin has
been set by the will of God *de lege statuta*.

[3] By using a quotation from Gregory the Great, Staupitz denies the supra-
lapsarian position of Duns Scotus: "'Sathan itaque ad affliccionem iusti tunc dominus commovit, quando in paradiso primum hominem a iusticiae culmine in-
obedienciae culpa prostravit.' Tunc eciam commotus est (sc. Deus), ut Christum
unigenitum dei filium cruci traderet. 'Nisi enim Adam primum per voluntarium

one can sin or disobey God apart from the *praemotio physica*, the power which God as the First and Final Cause supplies. God does not will sin, however, in the sense that He is its Efficient Cause. Sin does not have an efficient cause—as we have elsewhere noted—but only a deficient one. God thus does not directly will sin, but only permits it, in order thereby to gain some greater good. That man falls into sin is due to an act of divine permission; that he is punished for this sin is due to an act of divine justice. Neither act is an expression of divine sovereignty. Staupitz cannot bring himself in this instance to embrace the full Augustinian tradition of double predestination.[1] Instead he embraces what appears to be a Scotistic alternative—first election to glory, then to grace.[2]

Indeed, Staupitz with his view of the relation of the will of God to His justice and with his covenantal understanding of the activity of God in the world has already shown his inclination to differ with Thomas. The mystery of election is the mystery of the condescenscion of God, who binds Himself by His promises to the elect.[3] There is no

---

vicium in animae mortem traxisset, Adam secundus sine vicio in carnis mortem voluntariam non veniret,' ut ait S. Gre. [*Moralia super Iob* III.14, *PL* 75.613]..."
Hiob (1497–8) 27.212.35–40. Wolf is also inclined to doubt that Staupitz teaches supralapsarianism. See *Staupitz und Luther*, p. 75. The passage "Cum ergo primus homo per Sathan a domino motus est..." [*Hiob* (1497–8) 27.212.40–1] should be interpreted in the light of the doctrine of *praemotio physica*. Cf. *Hiob* (1497–8) 5.26. 33–4; 11.88.3–7; 29.223.11–14.

[1] Ernst Wolf is in agreement with this position: "Dass Staupitz die gemina praedestinatio vertreten habe, ist allerdings von vornherein nicht wahrscheinlich." *Staupitz und Luther*, p. 70.

[2] While Staupitz rejects the supralapsarianism of Scotus, he seems to hold to the order, first glory, then grace. The elect are immutably dear to God; they have a *ius ad celum;* by one eternal decree Christ is made to them a *debitor salutis*—which Scheurl translates to mean that: "...Christus is im schuldig worden die seligkeit. *Libellus* (1517) 22, Kn. 142. See *Libellus* (1517) 86 and 90 on the faithfulness of God to His electing decree; *Libellus* (1517) 62 on *ius ad celum; Libellus* (1517) 22, 26, 27, 33; *Lieb Gottes* (1518) Kn. 111 on Christ as *debitor salutis*. Justification is subordinate to the electing decree and is the means by which God brings the elect to the end He has chosen. Furthermore, like Scotus and unlike Thomas, Staupitz does not sharply distinguish between *electio* and *praedestinatio*. Compare *Libellus* (1517) 40 with 131.

[3] *Glauben* (1525) Kn. 126–7. Cf. "Cui data est illa gratia prima cetere sequentur singule necessitate consequentie, et Christus factus est ei debitor salutis." *Libellus* (1517) 22. *Necessitas consequentie* is not an absolute, but rather a conditional necessity. See H. A. Oberman, *Harvest*, p. 472: "The dialectics of the *potentia dei absoluta* and *potentia dei ordinata* are concerned with this second kind of necessity. *De potentia absoluta*, the necessity like the *necessitas absoluta* is declared inapplicable to God. The conditional necessity indicates that God, de potentia ordinata, has committed himself to his own decrees." Cf. Biel, IV *Sent.* d.1 q.2 a.1 n.1A.

necessity in the justice or goodness of God which compels Him to act.[1] One cannot argue from human conceptions of justice to an explanation of the unheard of mercy of God. If God places Himself under obligation to the elect, if He reveals Himself in Christ as man's debtor, He has done so freely and without constraint[2]. Man cannot anticipate the mercy of God nor bind God to a covenant which man in his fallenness initiates. There is no analogy in nature or in human relations which foreshadows the divine decree of election nor, indeed, fully explains it when it is revealed. God's indebtedness to man, the restriction of His freedom to act in His self-commitment to the elect, is only meaningful against the background of God's sovereign power, His freedom from all natural obligation to man. God who owes nothing to man *ex debito iusticie* freely assumes His covenant obligations *ex debito gracie*.[3] If He fulfils these obligations—as He assuredly will—there is no other explanation for His action than His fidelity to His own decree.

Not all fallen men are included in the decree of election. If Adam had not fallen, the number of the elect would have been assembled without the exclusion of anyone. All the sons of Adam would have ended their lives in unbroken fellowship with God and would have received from Him the gift of eternal life.[4] Neither sin nor death would have had any dominion over the family of man. But that is not

---

[1] God could have abandoned man in his predicament: "…'cum essemus inimici,' sola Cristi misericordia amici iam facti spem habemus vitae eternae. Poterat enim iuste nos deserere, cum essemus inimici, sed expectavit pacienter nostram emendacionem." *Hiob* (1497–8) 9.70.36–38. Cf. *Libellus* (1517) 18.

[2] It is important to note that Staupitz attributes the decree of predestination to the "sola…liberrima dei voluntas." *Libellus* (1517) 21. Staupitz's doctrine of the *libertas Dei* should be understood against the background of nominalist thought. For Biel the "*misericordia dei* has now become a synonym for the liberty and contingence with which God chose in eternity to make himself debtor and to reward acts which, in themselves, that is, *de potentia absoluta*, have only *bonitas* but not *dignitas*. Outside the established order, that is, before that moment in eternity when God set the present order, his *misericordia* is unconditioned. Inside that order, however, there is the double condition of justice." H. A. Oberman, *Harvest*, p. 44. For Staupitz *misericordia* describes both the freedom of God in making Himself a debtor to the elect and the character of the covenant so established.

[3] "Sicut enim consequens est omnes predestinatos debito vocari, ita vocati debent iustificari, non quidem ex nature sed gratie debito." *Libellus* (1517) 26.

[4] "…do die menschen seliklich yre tzeit hie geendet, die tzal der ausserwelten erfullet, als in von got aufgelegt, gewachsen und gemanchfeltiget, ane vormittelung des todes des vorsprochenen bessers ewigen lebens teyl und habhaftig worden weren, In welchem gewisse sicherheit ist, das in ym nymant sundet, nymandt stirbet…" *Nachfolgung* (1515) Kn. 53.

in fact what happened. Adam freely chose *(sua sponte)* to disobey his Creator and brought down upon himself and his descendents the just condemnation of God.

The reprobate are called to salvation in many ways—through the law, the prophets, the apostles and preachers of faith, and even through tribulations.[1] Yet these forms of the call are in vain unless God speaks directly to the heart of the listener.[2] Only this latter form of the call is genuinely efficacious. There is, in other words, a distinction to be drawn between effectual and ineffectual calling, between the call which is only the voice of Moses and the call which is truly the voice of God.[3] The reprobate may hear the one, but only the elect hear the other. Being called is not synonymous with being chosen.

Predestination is the source from which all other graces flow.[4] Indeed, Staupitz can even say, justification is owed by Christ to the elect—not, of course, in the sense that the elect have merited it, but

---

[1] "Multi namque sunt vocati per lumen quod super nos signatum est, per legem, per prophetas, per dona, per tribulationes, per apostolos et predicatores fidei, sed non fuerunt omnes electi." *Libellus* (1517) 24.

[2] "Verum hi, quos predestinavit libere, sunt necessaria consequentia in tempore ad fidem efficaci voluntate vocati, et quidem non per Moysen, prophetas aut apostolos sed per ipsummet deum, qui loquitur ad cor." *Libellus* (1517) 24.

[3] The question is how these two calls are related. Paul Zeller argues that Staupitz "...hält aber doch die Objectivität des Wortes, wie es in der Schrift gegeben und geoffenbart ist, fest, er theilt nicht die mystische Betonung und Bevorzugung des innerlichen Wortes—der subjectiven Erleuchtung durch den Geist—von dem äusseren..." Paul Zeller, "Staupitz, Seine religiös-dogmatischen Anschauungen und dogmengeschichtliche Stellung," *ThStKr* 52 (1879), p. 28. There is evidence to support this view. The importance of Scripture for Staupitz can scarcely be exaggerated. He himself says that the "facies, inquam, domini i.e. aspectus divinitatis in praesenti ambulantibus in spe et fide in sola scriptura sacra ostenditur." *Hiob* (1497–8) 31.239.13–15. Because the objective word of Scripture can be read without inward spiritual illumination, Staupitz discusses in some detail the problem of letter and spirit. Nevertheless, Staupitz seems to teach that the Spirit speaks to the heart apart from, as well as through, the letter of Scripture. Note that in footnote 31 Staupitz says "non per Moysen...sed per...deum." In the treatise on *Nachfolgung* (1515) Staupitz writes: "Der sechste gradt ist begirde geruets hertzen, innerer stille, des heimlichen gottes gespreche. In der hohe bittet man, O suesser einwoner der selen, du allerheimlichster freundt, gib mir die stille, dorinnen nichts dann du gehoredt wirst, unnd sprich ein wordt...Ein solch wort kan nymant reden, dan du allein, und redest es nicht, dan in geheim..." *Nachfolgung* (1515) Kn. 83. Cf. *Lieb gottes* (1518) Kn. 106, 108–9; *Salzburger Predigten* (1523) No. 1, Aumüller, 52–3; No. 7, 132. For a striking parallel see Thomas à Kempis, *De imitatione Christi* III.2.

[4] "Sicut enim ex notitia primi principii fluunt omnes notitie naturales, ita ex gratia predestinationis universe et singule gratie in qua et per quam, ut ante tetigi, Christus factus est minister salutis nostre." *Libellus* (1517) 27.

in the sense that all the steps in the process of justification—vocation, regeneration, glorification—must be included for the divine purpose in predestination to reach its goal.[1] No one is saved by a *fiat* of God apart from the infusion of *charitas*. There is no way around these steps but only a way through. Predestination is not the bare decision of God to snatch sinners from the jaws of hell. It is rather the decision to bring man to glory *(beatitudo)* by first bringing him into conformity with Christ.[2] Fallen man is thus not merely to be pardoned, but also to be healed. Justification is accordingly owed to the elect in order that the full purpose of God in their election might be fulfilled.

In order to stress the centrality of predestination Staupitz redefined *gratia gratum faciens*, the sanctifying grace infused in the sinner at the moment of justification.[3] According to the main scholastic tradition, from which Staupitz here deviates, *gratia gratum faciens* is the grace which renders the sinner, who was previously unacceptable, pleasing

---

[1] "Certe si exterior vocatio efficax esset, vocatos diceres universos et omnino iustificandos. Sicut enim consequens est omnes predestinatos debito vocari, ita vocati debent iustificari, non quidem ex nature sed gratie debito." *Libellus* (1517) 26; "Quapropter electis non modo vocatio, verum et iustificatio debetur." *Libellus* (1517) 33.

[2] Therefore Wolf is quite correct when he says: "Die Behandlung der Prädestinationslehre in geschlossener Weise zeigt jedoch deutlicher, dass es sich dabei für Staupitz nicht bloss um einen Gegenstand theologischen Denkens, sondern vor allem um eine Frage des frommen Lebens handelt..." *Staupitz und Luther*, p. 85.

[3] It is clear that Staupitz deviates from the main scholastic tradition by defining *gratia gratum faciens* in this new way. It is difficult to know whether he had a precedent for this redefinition in the writings of lesser known scholastic figures since so many texts have yet to be edited and studied. There is, however, at least a partial parallel in the anonymous treatise *De Praedestinatione et Praescientia* (attributed to Thomas Bradwardine), dating from the fourteenth century. It has been edited and published by H. A. Oberman (to whom I am indebted for this reference) in the NAK 43 (1960) 195–200. "9. Sumatur quomodo Deus Karitas est et qui manet in Karitate in Deo manet et Deus in eo...prout est habitus a prima vel secunda Karitate, scilicet divine voluntate, gratis anime infusu, qui habitus nedum gratis datur a Deo, verum etiam cui datur hunc efficit gratum Deo car[um] amicum et filium in presenti et consortem glorie in futuro. Vel forte, ut verius loquar eis quibus datur efficit gratum et car[um] ipsum Deum et non econtra, nisi secundum presentem iusticiam, cum predestinatio Dei huiusmodi habitus est et non econtra causa originalis existat..." The redefinition of *gratia gratum faciens* is not a central point of this treatise nor does the writer develop this new theme with any degree of care or thoroughness. Furthermore, he speaks of grace as a *habitus*, as Staupitz does not do. Nevertheless, the fact that he has redefined sanctifying grace in this way makes it necessary to use caution in speaking of Staupitz's originality on this point.

to God.[1] It is a transforming power which, when released, heals the wounds in the fallen nature of man and restores him to a state of moral integrity.

For Staupitz, however, *gratia gratum faciens* does not render the sinner pleasing to God.[2] On the contrary, it is election which makes

---

[1] The meaning of *caritas* was a subject under discussion in the late middle ages. The nominalists weakened the idea of *caritas* as a *habitus* (1) by indicating that the law that a *viator* must have a habit of grace is only valid *de potentia ordinata*; (2) by stressing the uncreated gift of the Holy Spirit and the divine acceptation of human works. Cf. Paul Vignaux, *Luther, commentateur des Sentences* (Paris, 1935), pp. 87–94; H. A. Oberman, *Harvest*, pp. 160–84. Reinhard Schwarz argues that Luther in his lectures on the Sentences of 1509–10 goes beyond the nominalist critique of the *habitus* doctrine to reject it completely: "Mit der vom Lombarden abgelehnten Ansicht übt Luther Kritik an dem Gedanken eines Gnadenhabitus. Die Gnade wirkt nicht durch die Schaffung eines habitus, sondern unmittelbar durch die Befreiung des Willens zu guten inneren Willensbewegungen. Es bleibt dabei, dass der heilige Geist nur im uneigentlichen Sinne ein habitus ist, da er auch nicht in der Gestalt der gratia zu einer inharierenden Qualität wird." *Fides, Spes und Caritas*, p. 39. Staupitz joins with Luther in the critique of the *habitus* doctrine: (1) by stressing the primacy of uncreated grace, i.e. the Holy Spirit, in justification. *Hiob* (1497–8) 18.154.11–14; 23.189.3–6; 30.232.19–34; 30.232.36–41; *Lieb gottes* (1518) Kn. 98–9; (2) by teaching that *dignitas* is bestowed through the acceptation of works. (Gerson is his authority). *Hiob* (1497–8) 23.186.39–187.3. Cf. Gerson, "De Vita", p. 124. *Libellus* (1517) 43. (3) by maintaining that the indwelling Spirit immediately moves man to good works: "Nymandt kann ainigen guten gedancken, Wort oder Werck haben, Got sey dann vor mit seiner parmherzigkait und seinen leiden in Ime gewest, damit er Ine Zu solchem hab bewegt." *Von der nachvolg cristi* (1517) Kn. 28. "...wir muessen den heiligen geist haben, das ist dy lieb gots an den wir nichtz tain mügen, dan got wil nichtz haben es geschach dan aus seiner lieb. Das ist das wass das allain jn das ewig leben springt." Hs: b II 11, St. Peter (1523) No. 15, fol. 137*b*-138ª. "...yn ym [a Christian man indwelt by the Spirit] wachsen fur und fur gotliche frucht, er wiss es oder wiss es nit, den der heilig geist feyret nit...Vil vil fruchte unsers hails wirckt er in uns, der wir gantz kein wissen tragen..." *Lieb gottes* (1518) Kn. 99. "Also sichstu tzu dem beschlus, das kein gut werck in uns kompt, der heilig geist sey den vor darin, wie oben gemelt. Wen er aber in uns ist, so ist er das lebendig wasser, das do in uns ein springender brun wirdt in das ewig leben, durch glaub, lieb und hoffnung." *Lieb gottes* (1518) Kn. 102. Staupitz can also speak of Christ inwelling the Christian. *Libellus* (1517) 179. This does not seem to represent a change from the emphasis on the Spirit in *Hiob*, since in *Von der nachfolg cristi* also dating from 1517 and in *Von der lieb gottes* from 1518 Staupitz speaks once more of the indwelling Spirit. See the references above. In *Lieb gottes* (1518) Kn. 98 he refers to the Spirit as the "geist Christi." There is a kind of Pauline imprecision in his language which does not yield to a rigid schematization. Cf. Wolf, *Staupitz und Luther*, pp. 36–42. Wolf does not see, however, how sharply Staupitz breaks with the ontological objectivity of the Thomistic theory of grace.

[2] Staupitz did teach, of course, in the sermons on Job that grace makes the Christian dear to God: "...gracia omnine specialiter, qua sumus digni deo et per quam sumus grati deo." *Hiob* (1497–8) 30.232.18–19. This position he later abandoned.

man pleasing to God. The proper function of *gratia gratum faciens* is
to make God pleasing to man.[1] Justifying grace restores to man the
ability, which Adam forfeited through his sin, to love God the
Creator and to deny himself. It frees him from the terrible bondage
of *amor sui* and leads him into the freedom which is the heritage of
the sons of God. The justified man is liberated from the fear of hell
and the desire for heaven and given the power to serve God in true
obedience. His *electio melioris partis*—namely, his choice to serve God
—is his response to the *electio* of God.[2]

With this view of predestination and justification Staupitz had no
difficulty in answering the allegation that predestination should not be
preached to common people.[3] Augustine had recommended that this
doctrine be discussed only by the learned. Apparently there were some
people in Staupitz's day who argued that the preaching of predestination takes away the freedom of the will, encourages moral lassitude,
and forms the basis for a presumptuous and spurious confidence in
God. Staupitz challenged this view. The preaching of predestination
cannot take away man's freedom, because he has none—or, rather, he
has no true freedom. He only has the liberty to sin and merit damnation. The preaching of predestination restores to man the freedom
to serve God which he has tragically forfeited in Adam. It demands
that he respond to the *electio* of God with his own free *electio*. It
motivates him to praise God with words and deeds. It destroys all
vain and foolish confidence and gives man true hope.[4]

The question was frequently raised in scholastic theology whether
a person who had been predestined by God could nevertheless be

---

[1] "Iterum cernis quod gratia gratum faciens non est illa qua deo placemus, sed
qua deus nobis placet et gratus est. Quapropter divine electioni eterne tribue
gratum facere te deo; justificationi gratum facere deum tibi." *Libellus* (1517) 131.
Cf. *Libellus* (1517) 36, 40, 86, 152.

[2] "Consequens est neminem invitum salvari sed per electionem melioris partis,
sincere scilicet obedientie dei; et quod liberior est predestinatus, qui infernum non
timet, celum non petit, sed optimo bono sui tantum gratia servit, quocunque alio;
liber inquam a creatura, liberrimus a peccato." *Libellus* (1517) 172.

[3] On the problem of *predestinatio predicata* see Klaus Reinhardt, *Pedro Luis*, pp.
215–17.

[4] "Dicunt aliqui quod predestinatio predicata tollat arbitrium, damnet electionem, permittat ocia et fit occasio stulte confidentie in deum. Revera imprudenter
enuntiant. Praedicatio predestinationis veram libertatem, qua nos Christus liberos
fecit, erigit. Electionem salutarem requirit, sine qua nulli adulto salutem concedit.
Ocia cuncta extinguit. Et non stultam confidentiam sed veram spem permittit et
efficit." *Libellus* (1517) 170.

finally rejected.[1] The question is not so strange as it may first appear.
Once it is granted that the works of God *ad extra* are contingent, on
the one hand, and that the will of man remains free vis-à-vis the will
of God, on the other, it is possible to wonder—at least—if anything
can be definitively settled in advance.[2]

Staupitz defended the thesis that the saving intention of God toward
the elect is absolutely immutable.[3] Those who have been chosen by
God will without fail be brought to the final goal of eternal glory.
However, by asserting this Staupitz did not mean to infer that the
elect lose their freedom of will through divine election or that they
can no longer sin and apostasize from a state of grace. On the contrary,
as long as the elect are *viatores*, they have the freedom to disobey their
Creator. Nevertheless, they do not—and here Staupitz is quite ada-
mant—have the freedom to luxuriate in their sins. God troubles the
elect in their disobedience and afflicts them, until they grow repentant
and cry for restoration. In other words (to put the matter in terms of
a medieval distinction), even though according to present justice the
elect are in a state of mortal sin, this is not in itself the decisive factor.
God is not disheartened by the apostasy of the elect. He chose certain
men to praise and enjoy Him and remains true to His own intention.
None of the elect, therefore, will die in mortal sin, not because he
lacks the capability to do so, but because God is faithful to His own
decree of election.[4] God pursues the elect and brings them back. Indeed, said Staupitz confidently, "Was er [Gott] ein mal versprochen
hat, muess ewig ja sein."[5] The very sins of the elect are pressed into

---

[1] Cf. Wolfhart Pannenberg, *Prädestinationslehre*, pp. 44–68.

[2] Cf. Klaus Reinhardt, *Pedro Luis*, pp. 148–62.

[3] "Semper amat qui amicus est, et immutabiliter qui immutabilis est. Non ergo
fit ingrata anima deo, que dei electione eterna stabili et immutabili est semel
gratificata. Deus enim dat cuncta moveri, immobilis ipse manens." *Libellus* (1517)
86.

[4] "Modo stante predestinatione, consequens est peccatum predestinati esse
temporale et non perpetuum. Et ideo pena temporali dumtaxat mulctandum. Ut
autem in anima electa nec macula, nec ruga, nec aliquid huiusmodi inveniri possit,
deus gravius in tempore hoc electiones punit, immo sepe ultra commissa peccata
infert piissimus pater penas, quatinus merita paciente obedientieque crescant et
accedat natus servus ad similitudinem filii per innocentem passionem." *Libellus*
(1517) 90.

[5] "...das ym [i.e. die ausserwelte seel] also sein eygne sund zu der seligkeit
helffen muess, dan was got einn mal beschlossen hat, muess mit nichte hindersich
geen, was er ein mal versprochen hat, muess ewig ja sein, und dem ehr wol wil,
dem muessen hymel und hell, boss und guts, zu seinem besten dienen." *Lieb
gottes* (1518) Kn. 111.

divine service and used by God to help them on to final salvation.[1] The reliability of the decree of election depends upon the faithfulness of God to His own decision. The faithlessness of man does not undermine or weaken the faithfulness of God.

II. ELECTION IN CHRIST

A. *Rejection of supralapsarianism.* Duns Scotus believed that it was a serious theological mistake to make the incarnation dependent upon the fall of Adam.[2] Jesus Christ had been chosen by God to acquire glory by becoming a man and living a life of obedience to the Father, wholly apart from all consideration of the fall of Adam. The incarnation would have taken place, therefore, even if Adam had not sinned. Both the election of Jesus Christ and of all his brethren occurred independently of and prior to all foreknowledge of the disobedience of Adam.

Biel rejected this position out of hand. To say that the incarnation would have occurred even if Adam had not fallen is tantamount to saying that the redemption of the elect can be separated from the work of Christ.[3] Redemption is not by a *fiat* of God, by, so to say, a general proclamation of pardon. On the contrary, the salvation of the elect is inextricably bound up with the incarnation and passion of Jesus Christ —if not as the total cause of their redemption (the *viatores* have their own part to play in meriting salvation), at least as an indispensable partial cause. Election does not issue in salvation apart from the redemptive work of Christ.

Staupitz sides with Biel against Scotus. The secret decision of God

---

[1] "Facit insuper deus hanc cum electo misericordiam, quod post lapsum fortier resurgit, preceptum domini cautius custodit...Scimus etenim quoniam diligentibus deum, his scilicet qui secundum propositum vocati sunt sancti, cooperantur omnia. ita omnia, ut etiam peccata, in bonum serviant ad salutem." *Libellus* (1517) 93. Staupitz seems to echo a teaching of Giles of Rome, *De Ecclesiastica Potestate*, ed. Richard Scholz (Leipzig, 1929), p. 124: "Dictum est supra de principatu angelorum, quod ordinatus est propter electorum salutem: dicendum est ergo de principatu demonum, qui eciam ordinatus est propter salutem electorum; non quod ipsi demones salutem electorum intendant, sed quia diligentibus Deum omnia cooperantur in bonum, ut dicitur ad Romanos VIII [Rom. 8:28]. Ideo ipse insidie demonum, quas demones ordinant in malum hominum, cooperantur in bonum electorum, quia electi per demonum insidias exercitati proficiunt et merentur. Nam non solum insidie demonum, sed tribulaciones quas paciuntur a malis hominibus, diligentibus Deum, et hiis qui secundum propositum vocati sunt sancti, idest electis, cooperantur in bonum; immo et peccata propria cooperantur eis in bonum, prout resurgentes a peccatis humiliores et devociores fiunt."

[2] Duns Scotus, *Ox.* III d.1 q.3 n.3.

[3] Gabriel Biel, III *Sent.* d.19 q.1 a.2 concl.4.

in eternity to redeem some men is not divorced from the redemptive work of Christ in history. Salvation is not by *fiat*, not by a proclamation of general amnesty. Rather it rests upon and is mediated through the suffering and death of Jesus Christ. Indeed, Staupitz affirms that the elect, although they have been destined by God for salvation from all eternity, are not in fact redeemed until the work of atonement is effected.[1] Predestination does not dispense with the cross, but rather issues in it. God makes Christ the *debitor* of salvation to the elect.[2]

B. *Election to conformity.* Election not only rests upon a Christological basis; it is directed toward a Christological goal. Election is the decision of God which selected certain men *ante praevisa merita* to recover their ability to praise God by regaining that conformity to Christ which Adam through his disobedience had forfeited.[3] Or to put it somewhat differently, election is the gratuitous choice of a part of fallen humanity in whom the *imago dei* will be restored. Man was created, as we have already had occasion to observe, to live in subjection and obedience to God—an obedience which, as we have also noted, was Christologically defined. The obedience which redounds to the praise of God is the kind of obedience which is evidenced in the life of the incarnate Savior.

Election is not merely the decision of God to glorify the elect and reward their good works, though it is clear that the elect, sustained by the covenantal fidelity of God, will unfailingly arrive at their eternal and heavenly goal. Neither is election simply the decision of God to equip the elect with grace and thus enable them to merit

---

[1] "Wie wol wir von ewigkeit erwelt sein, so sein wir doch nit von ewigkait erlost." *Salzburger Predigten* (1523) No. 1, Aumüller, p. 52. "...mein praut, ich [Jesus] muess als bezalen was dw verschult hast..." Hs: b V 8, St. Peter (1512), Sermo 5, fol. 20[b].

[2] One should keep in mind that the necessity which compels Christ to come as mediator is a *necessitas consequentie*, the necessity based on the faithfulness of God to His own decrees. *Libellus* (1517) 22. See above, footnote 25. Anselm attempts to show in the incarnation and death of Jesus Christ a necessity "...self-evident to, or accepted after proof as true by, believers and unbelievers." John McIntyre, *St. Anselm and His Critics* (Edinburgh: Oliver and Boyd, 1954), p. 59. Staupitz and the nominalists wish to maintain that "...God's justice transcends human calculations..." H. A. Oberman, "Iustitia Christi," p. 4. One cannot argue from the attributes of God or the nature of sin to the action of God in the atonement.

[3] "Et quia cunctipotentis laudi misericordia pariter et iusticia conservunt, decreta est electio et predestinatio certorum ad conformitatem imaginis filii Dei, ad fidem domini nostri Jesu Christi. Nam qui non credunt iam iudicati sunt." *Libellus* (1517) 20.

glory, though all the elect are in due course justified by grace and reborn through the sacrament of baptism. The purpose of God in creation was to enable men to praise Him by living in conformity to the image of His Son. This purpose was frustrated by man's disobedience. But God did not abandon His intention. Through grace fallen men are restored to the image of Jesus Christ—a grace faithfully imparted to the elect.

C. *Election to union.* The merits of Christ through which the elect are redeemed are only possessed by the elect in union with Jesus Christ. Staupitz uses the image of a marriage in order to explain how Christ, his merits and benefits, are communicated to the elect.[1] They are not bestowed on him like the natural gifts of sight, health, long life—gifts which are not bound up with the self-giving of God.[2] In justification Christ gives Himself to the Christian, just as the husband gives himself to the bride in marriage.[3] This is not an ecstatic experience reserved for a select few, though there may be estatic experiences of love connected with it as a foretaste of the joys of heaven.[4] God gives Himself to every Christian. Through the sacrament of baptism the Christian is united with Christ in the fellowship of the Church.[5]

With Christ come His merits.[6] They are not separable from His

---

[1] Staupitz asserts that "...matrimonium inter virum et mulierum apertissima veritate sit figura matrimonii Christi et ecclesie." *Libellus* (1517) 112. Cf. *Hiob* (1497–8) 2.8.7–9; 1.3.29–31; *Libellus* (1517) 353.

[2] *Hiob* (1497–8) 30.232.14–24.

[3] "Contractus Christi et ecclesia consumatus est et talis: Ego accipio te in meam, accipio te mihi, accipio te in me. Et econverso Ecclesia sive anima dicit Christo: Ego accipio te in meum, accipio te mihi, accipio te in me. Ut sic Christus dicat: Christianus est meus, Christianus est mihi, Christianus est ego. Et sponsa: Christus est meus, Christus est mihi, Christus est ego." *Libellus* (1517) 56. The two contracting partners do not lose their identity in this union. Union with God for Staupitz is always "...per voluntatis conformacionem, non substancie ydemptitate." *Hiob* (1497–8) 3.16.16–18. "Im hymnischen Lob der copula spiritualis, der geistlichen Liebeseinigung, liegt auch das Wesen dieser Art von Mystik, die mit Pantheismus nichts zu schaffen hat, ausgesprochen: Innerster Verband von Ich und Du—, 'Liebestausch,' 'Hochzeit,' 'Umarmung'—aber konsentibles Füreinander, Beieinander, nicht konsubstantiales Verrinnen ineinander." Joseph Bernhart, "Einleitung," *Der Frankfurter: Eine Deutsche Theologie* (München, n.d.), p. 66.

[4] God may give mystical ecstasy, but it is not necessary for salvation. Christ is in this respect "...non...debitorem, sed liberalissimum datorem." *Libellus* (1517) 160–1. He is not obligated to give it.

[5] On baptism see *Hiob* (1497–8) 11.94.15–19; 23.189.23–8. On the Church as mother see *Hiob* (1497–8) 23.189.42; 23.190.2–7. On union with the Church see *Hiob* (1497–8) 30.232.28–33; *Glauben* (1525) Kn. 129–30.

[6] "Insuper sublimiora sunt propria merita Christi, actiones scilicet passiones et

Person.[1] They are His *proprietates*.[2] Negatively, He bears the sin and folly of the Christian. Positively, He reconciles the Christian to God and enables him to praise God with his words and works. The Christian receives the gifts of Christ because dwells in him by His Spirit.[3] The merits of Christ do not belong to the Christian in the sense that they are his property. By right they still belong to Christ. But he has the use of them. They are his *possessio*.[4] He derives benefit from them only so long as he is thus united to Christ. Staupitz knows of no predestination which does not unite the elect to Christ in an intimate bond of love.

D. *Certitude in Christ.* The certitude that one is elect is also connected for Staupitz with Jesus Christ. The problem of the certitude of salvation will be dealt with in detail in the chapter on justification. However, we can at least note here that Staupitz agreed with the general medieval position concerning subjective certitude; namely, that no one could know whether he were elect or damned apart from a special revelation of God.[5] To be sure, there are external signs from which one can conjecture that one is elect. Conformity to Christ in undeserved suffering is such a sign;[6] temptation is another.[7]

---

mors eius, qui natura fuit et est filius dei, que et nobis ita donata sunt ut nostra sint." *Libellus* (1517) 51.

[1] "Tu es ille singularis sponsus qui es meus, es mihi, es ego. Ideo tu es meus et universa que habes mihi habes. Ego sum tuus et quicquid in me est tibi et quia sumus unum. Tua ita mea sunt quod maneant tua. Mea sic tua sunt quod etiam maneant mea." *Libellus* (1517) 76.

[2] For a discussion of *proprietas* and *possessio* and their significance for the theology of Martin Luther, see H. A. Oberman, "Iustitia Christi," pp. 22–6. Oberman conjectures that Staupitz may have been influenced by Luther on this point and cites the letter of Luther to George Spenlein dated April 8, 1516. *Ibid.*, p. 25, footnote 52.

[3] "Postremo si Christus est ego, ius ad celum habeo, spem habeo et glorior in spe filiorum dei." *Libellus* (1517) 62. "Sum igitur sic ego tua iusticia iustus. Tu es mea culpa peccator et tua iustitia iustus. Tua quoque virtute sum fortis, mea infirmitate infirmus. Et tu mea infirmitate infirmus, tua virtute fortis. Tua sapientia sum sapiens, mea stulticia stultus. Et tu mea stultitia stultus, tua sapientia sapiens." *Libellus* (1517) 77. Cf. *Libellus* (1517) 71. "wann seine [Jesus] gerechtigkait ist mein, so sint meine sünten sein." *Salzburger Predigten* (1523) No. 1, Aumüller, p. 54.

[4] Paul Vignaux uses the term *possessio* to describe the relationship between the justified soul and the Holy Spirit: "On recoit l'Esprit quand on est justifié...Une chose nous est donnée quand elle entre en notre propriété, ou plutôt en notre possession: il nous est désormais loisible d'en user. *Dominium, possessio, usus:* retenons ces termes juridiques." Paul Vignaux, *Luther commentateur des Sentences*, p. 58. Vignaux applies this term to the theology of Biel, in which uncreated grace is given to man as a *possessio*.

[5] *Libellus* (1517) 142–3.

[6] *Hiob* (1497–8) 11.92.6–22; *Libellus* (1517) 92.

[7] *Hiob* (1497–8) 11.93.2–6.

But these can at best form the basis for conjectural certitude.

In his posthumous tractate on faith Staupitz expressed his final opinion concerning the way of certitude. To speak of the elect, Staupitz noted, is to speak of those who believe in Christ. Since this is true, one should seek certitude by clinging to Christ and not torture oneself with endless speculations. It is indisputable that God will not condemn anyone who believes in His Son. Thus the troubled conscience can find peace at last it if will take its gaze off of itself and fix it on Christ. "If we believe in Christ," said Staupitz, "we have Him and will not be lost."[1]

III. Assessment

The picture which emerges from this survey of Staupitz's doctrine of election is clear. On the one hand, Staupitz rejected the nominalist doctrine of predestination with its stress on the role of divine foreknowledge and its excessive and unwarranted confidence in the natural powers of man. On the other hand, he could not bring himself to assert the full Augustinian doctrine of predestination, as had the famous doctor of the Augustinian Order, Gregory of Rimini. He sought, like Thomas and Scotus before him, a middle way between the extremes, in which both the mercy and justice of God could be proclaimed with equal forcefulness and vigor.[2]

Nevertheless, it is not correct to assert, as Erich Seeberg does, that Staupitz is a *Repristinationstheologe*, a disciple of Thomas Aquinas, who believed "...durch Renaissance eines der grossen Meister im Denken aus der Vergangenheit Theologie und Kirche...neu beleben zu können."[3] Staupitz differed with Thomas in four important respects: (1) by stressing the covenantal character of election; (2) by adopting the order first glory, then grace; (3) by redefining *gratia gratum faciens* as the grace which makes God pleasing to man; (4) by emphasizing the fact that predestination is Christocentric. Not only is Staupitz's doctrine of election not a mere repristination of the theology of a single master—whether Thomas or Scotus—but it evidences as well a high degree of systematic originality.

---

[1] "...glauben wir in Christum, so haben wir Christum, werden nicht verloren..." *Glauben* (1525) Kn. 125.

[2] *Libellus* (1517) 20.

[3] Erich Seeberg, *Luthers Theologie in ihren Grundzügen*, 2 ed. (Stuttgart, 1950), p. 16.

CHAPTER FOUR

JUSTIFICATION

I. Facere quod in se est and the Question of a Proper Disposition

In spite of the doctrine of the moral impotence of fallen man and of gratuitous election *ante praevisa merita*, Staupitz affirms the necessity of a proper disposition for the reception of grace. To insist on such a disposition is not in itself remarkable, since this doctrine is a commonplace of scholastic theology. The decisive question is whether this disposition is instilled in man through the gracious activity of God or whether it is dependent on the *praemotio physica* alone.

According to the doctrine of *praemotio physica* the will of man is powerless to act until it is acted upon by the divine will. The power of movement is imparted to all second causes through the prior motion of the First Cause.[1] Acting under this purely natural influence, man has the power to run, to sleep, to eat, to see—indeed, to exercise any of his natural faculties. The nominalists believe that this natural power, which they describe by the term *concursus dei generalis*, is all the assistance which man needs in order to dispose himself for the reception of grace.[2] Staupitz strongly disagrees with them.

To be sure, he admits that there is such a general divine assistance and that all human activity is dependent upon it. But while the doctrine of *praemotio physica* provides an adequate explanation for natural human activity, it is not adequate to explain the life of grace or what disposes the soul for the reception of grace.[3] Even the damned in hell will be moved by purely natural impulses. Only gracious

---

[1] "Nam agens secundum non agit, nisi simul influat primum agens, nec agere potest, nisi motum fuerit..." *Hiob* (1497–8) 29.222.39–40. See *Hiob* (1497–8) 13. 125.13–20; 29.223.2–3. Cf. Thomas Aquinas, *De Potentia* q.3 a.7; q.3 a.7 ad 4, 7, 9; *De Malo* 3.3; III *Summa contra Gentiles* 88; *Summa Theologiae* I q.105 a.5.

[2] Gabriel Biel, II *Sent.* d.28 q.1 a.1 nota 2; II *Sent.* d.27 q.1 a.3 dub. 30.

[3] "Sed gratuitum amorem dicimus inclinacionem sequentem graciam a deo infusam vel sequentem mocionem a deo in mente factam, non mocionem divinam, ut solum operatur generaliter in operibus naturae, quia sic non differret ab amore naturali, sed ut specialiter operatur in his, quae sunt graciae vel quae disponunt ad graciam." *Hiob* (1497–8) 12.113.19–24.

impulses over and above these merely natural movements of the soul
are sufficient to dispose it for the reception of grace.[1] The *praemotio
physica* enables a man to select his clothing for the day; it does not
enable him to turn from idols to serve the living and the true God.

Staupitz does not mean to imply that the natural gifts of man are
not used by God to dispose the soul for grace. The will of man, which
has psychological if not ontological freedom, is moved by God in
such a way that the spontaneity of the will is at all times preserved.[2]
The freedom of choice is not obliterated by prevenient grace. Grace
does not compel men to be converted. Nevertheless, Staupitz does not
lose sight of the fact that it is grace—or perhaps one should say,
certain gratuitous gifts of God—which must be added to the free will
before it can be disposed for the reception of sanctifying grace.
Staupitz does not say what these prevenient gifts of God may be—
save to identify one with the preaching of Word of God and one with
tribulation and temptation.[3]

Under the impact of the gratuitous gifts of God, the sinner is
enabled to do what is in him *(facere quod in se est)*.[4] To those who do

---

[1] "Tercius effectus est, ut praedicator misericordiam dei praedicet secundum
divinam sapienciam, secundum quale et quantum in effectu demonstrandum ordi-
natum ita, ut tempus miserendi certa mensura comprehensum sit. Est autem tempus miserendi, quamdiu deus impulsibus interioribus animam ad bonum facien-
dum et malum declinandum gratuite movet. Non loquimur hic de impulsibus
omnino naturalibus, qui certe et in inferno manent, sed de illis mocionibus, quae
fiunt ad graciam acquirendam iam praedicacionibus iam aliis modis secundum
divinam sapienciam ordinatis." *Hiob* (1497-8) 20.169.1-9.

[2] "Respondet autem dominus ad cor meditantis animae, quod, quamvis bene-
dixi i.e. graciam gratum facientem dedi, libertatem tamen eius non coegi. Habet
enim quandam libertatem, quae sequitur naturam, quae extendit ad bonum et ad
malum eciam post receptam graciam nec involuntarium ad graciam compuli, sed
volenti dedi." *Hiob* (1497-8) 15.134.41-135.3.

[3] In calling man to penance and to acquiring grace, God uses preaching, *Hiob*
(1497-8) 20.169.1-9; and temptation, *Hiob* (1497-8) 12.108.7-12. In the *Libellus*
(1517) St. speaks of a general call "... per lumen quod super nos signatum est, per
legem, per prophetas, per dona, per tribulationes, per apostolos et predicatores
fidei..." *Libellus* (1517) 24. Yet none of these exterior means are efficacious unless
God speaks directly to the heart. *Libellus* (1517) 24. God can speak to the heart
apart from, as well as through, preaching, temptation, and Scripture. *Nachfolgung*
(1515) Kn. 83; *Lieb gottes* (1518) Kn. 106, 108-9.

[4] H. A. Oberman argues that the doctrine of *facere quod in se est* is used by
Robert Holcot, O.P. (ob. 1349) not only on the level of free will and grace, but
also on the level of the relation of reason and revelation. According to Oberman
"...Holcot does not reject the possibility to acquire *de congruo* the articles of faith
which are necessary for salvation. Man can and therefore has to do his very best
in going halfway in his search for God; thus he will receive enlightenment."
Heiko A. Oberman, "'Facientibus Quod In Se Est Deus Non Denegat Gratiam.'

what is in them, Staupitz affirms, God will not deny His grace.[1] The meaning of this statement, which on the face of it sounds very similar to certain statements made by the nominalists, is not instantly apparent. It is clear that Staupitz admits the possibility of cooperation between the will of man and prevenient grace prior to the infusion of *gratia gratum faciens* and that this cooperation disposes the soul for the reception of grace.[2] However, the force of this admission is vitiated, when Staupitz specifically denies that human activity prior to the infusion of *charitas* is either meritorious or, indeed, even morally good.[3] Hearing the call to repentance (inward as well as outward), the

Robert Holcot, O.P., and the Beginnings of Luther's Theology," *HTR* 55 (1962), p. 329. After examining Luther's earliest writings, Oberman concludes "...that Luther at the end of 1509 has become independent of the nominalistic tradition as regards the relation of faith and reason, while retaining till 1515–1516 the doctrine of the *facere quod in se est* in its application to the relation of will and grace." *Ibid.*, p. 333. Staupitz does not apply *facere quod in se est* to the relation of faith and reason, but solely to the relation of will and grace. In the sermons on Job, Staupitz argues that faith is *supra racionem* and insists that the *viator* cannot know God in this present life by means of natural knowledge but needs *fides, spes* and *caritas*. *Hiob* (1497–8) 9.70.16–21; 10.75.24–29. In the *Libellus* (1517) Staupitz teaches that the knowledge of God which the elect needs to praise God is impossible *extra Christum*. *Libellus* (1517) 8, 9, 13, 14. On the other hand, while Luther has abandoned *facere quod in se est* by 1517, there is evidence that Staupitz still retains it in its application to the relation of will and grace. *Von ainer waren rechten rew* (1517) Kn. 19.

[1] *Hiob* (1497–8) 5.30.15–19; 5.32.1–9; 5.32.13–24; 20.168.39–169.1.
[2] Staupitz cites Gerson, "De Vita Spiritualis Animae," pp. 114–5. "Ita enim videmus in naturali generacione animalis, plurima procedunt ad disposicionem, quae formam invehit materiae. Istas disposiciones appellant theologi in adultis operaciones informes, quibus peccatrix anima intendit facere, quod in se est. Se disponit ad vitam, non quod ista disposicio sufficiat, utpote quae longinqua est et nihil de vita graciae habens in se, sed quia nihil interim anima maius habet, quod faciat, quam ut bene utatur suis naturalibus et donis quibusdam gratuitis licet non vivificatis." *Hiob* (1497–8) 189.6–13.
[3] Staupitz quotes Gerson, "De Vita", pp. 120–1, 124 to show that both virtue and merit are dependent upon divine acceptation: "Sic de iusticiis nostris quae sunt sicut pannus menstruatae absente gracia. Hoc est, quod S. Paulus in omnibus epistolis suis fere praedicavit, ne in operibus, sed gracia iustificari credamus.... Ideo, certe opus nostrum et meritum nostrum quantum ex nobis est, vilificari debet, neque enim improbabile est nullum actum creaturae de per se et intrinsece esse bonum bonitate moris aut meriti nisi per respectum ad divinam racionem et voluntatem, quia videlicet divina voluntas et racio dignificat hominem pro tali actu. Immo sine actu quocunque posset dignificare creaturam, si attendatur dominantissima dei virtus respectus suae creaturae." *Hiob* (1497–8) 22.186.32–187.3. Compare Gerson, "De Vita", p. 124: "Et juxta hoc consequenter habetur facilis manuductio ad vivendum quomodo nihil est malum nisi quia prohibitum, et nihil bonum nisi quia Deo acceptum; et Deus non ideo actus nostros vult et approbat quia boni sunt, sed ideo boni sunt quia approbat." with *Hiob* (1497–8) 15.134.37–8: "Neque enim tibi placeant hominum facta, quia bona sunt, sed pocius ideo sunt

sinner may take himself to the confessional booth where the grace of
God is freely offered through the sacrament of penance. Nevertheless,
by doing so, the sinner does not merit justification, though his penitent
response to the preached Word is certainly a preparation for the reception of justifying grace.

Unlike the nominalists, Staupitz uses the doctrine of *facere quod in
se est* to emphasize the moral impotence of man. He denies that the
sinner, aided only by the *concursus dei*, can bring forth an act of supreme
love for God by the exercise of his own natural powers.[1] His thesis,
rather, is that the sinner, moved from without by the work of Christ
on his behalf and from within by the prevenient activity of the Spirit,
still fails to love God perfectly. Doing his very best means that he still
falls far short of the divine standard. He has not learned to love what
is good; at best he has joylessly shunned what is evil.[2] The doctrine of
facere quod in se est does not extoll the natural powers of man, but rather
emphasizes his moral bankruptcy.

Thus, when Staupitz speaks, of *facere quod in se est* and of a disposition to receive grace, as he does especially in the sermons on Job,
he must not be thought to be speaking of the possibility of meriting
justifying grace *de congruo*, as the nominalists wish to maintain. Apart
from the fact that the phrase *meritum de congruo* nowhere occurs in
these sermons, Staupitz explicitly denies that first grace (i.e., *gratia
gratum faciens*) can be merited.[3] The *viator* may—and, indeed, must—

---

bona, quia tibi placent." On the impossibility of good works apart from grace see
Von der nachvolg Cristi (1517) Kn. 28; *Libellus* (1517) 19, 33, 230; *Salzburger Predigten*
(1523) No. 5, Aumüller, p. 126.

[1] "Darauss sich beschliesslich ervolgt, das got uber alle ding lieben ein pur
lauttere gnad ist, uber alle unsere kunst und vermogen, uber alle unsere werck
und verdienen." *Lieb gottes* (1518) Kn. 103.

[2] "Fugisti malum per determinacionem, sequitur tristicia, quia non satis feceris.
Fugisti per declinacionem, tristatur animus tuus, quia non sis bonum amplexatus,
sed tantum a malo declinaveris. Fugisti per consensum in motum boni, tristaris,
quia non potuisti desiderare et velle, sicut optabas. Dixi superius, quod hi, qui
seipsos determinant, bonum per intellectum voluntati proponunt et quia sine
delectacione fecerunt, timent, quia minus dilecti sunt eo, quod scriptum est 'Hila-
rem datorem diligit deus' 2. ad co. ix. [2 Cor. 9:7] Sed scire debent, quod in hac
parte equaliter apud deum veneratur tristicia mali sicut delectacio boni, praesup-
posito semper, quod fecit, quod in se fuit. Verissimum signum est deum susce-
pisse pro sufficienti, cum homo ipse tristatur de insufficiencia facti." *Hiob* (1497–8)
5.32.13–24. Cf. *Hiob* (1497–8) 5.30.15–19; 5.31.1ff.; 5.32.1–9.

[3] "Ego enim et si primam graciam gratis do, augmentum tamen illius posui sub
merito. Nam qui habet graciam, meretur agendo secundum et per graciam eiusdem
gracie augmentum." *Hiob* (1497–8) 15.135.30–33. *Prima gratia* is used by Staupitz
in the sermons on Job to designate *gratia gratum faciens*. In the *Libellus* (1517) it is
used to designate God's decree of eternal election. Cf. *Libellus* (1517) 21.

merit the increase of grace, and can even earn eternal life (i.e., *beati-tudo*), but he cannot merit justifying grace. Justifying grace is a gratuitous gift of God which antedates all merit and makes it possible. It may be given to any *viator*, but it is owed only to the elect.[1]

II. The Context of Justification

The doctrine of penance rather than the doctrine of baptism provides the principal context in which the medieval theologians considered the doctrine of justification. Justifying grace is, of course, first infused in the *viator* through baptism.[2] No one can become a Christian without experiencing the purifying effect of the waters of baptism. But since, on the one hand, every adult Christian can be presumed to fall from time to time back into mortal sin and since, on the other hand, the sacrament of baptism cannot be repeatedly administered, it is necessary for the Christian to receive through another sacrament a renewal of the grace first granted him in baptism.[3] To this end the sacrament of penance has been divinely instituted.

According to the tradition of the Church the doctrine of penance is composed of three elements: *contritio cordis*, *confessio oris*, and *satisfactio operis*.[4] In the early Church the third element in the doctrine of penance, satisfaction, was given prominence. By the twelfth century, however, the accent had shifted from the third element to the first, from satisfaction to contrition. The cause, or better said, the *causa sine qua non*

---

[1] One should keep in mind (a) that through His decree of eternal election God makes Christ a *debitor salutis* to the elect and that justification is owed to the elect as a consequence of this decree *ex debito gratie*. *Libellus* (1517) 22, 26, 27, 33; *Lieb gottes* (1518) Kn. 111. (b) The elect are dear to God through eternal election; God becomes dear to the elect through *gratia gratum faciens*. *Libellus* (1517) 36, 40, 86, 131, 152. (c) The elect have the merits of Christ as their *possessio* through union with Him in a spiritual marriage. *Libellus* (1517) 56, 62, 71, 76, 77.

[2] "'Est autem baptismus iste graciae et aliarum virtutum infusio aspersioque intima animam abluens et reddens ydoneam, cui spiritus sanctus seipsum, vitam et motum et essenciam inspiret et donet.' Ad hanc interiorem ablucionem exterior aquae ablucio quid faciat, magister in quarto videatur et S. doctores una cum ceteris ibi scribentibus." *Hiob* (1497–8) 23.189.23–6. The first sentence is a citation from Gerson, "De Vita," p. 114.

[3] "Justificationem nostram per Sacramenta, in quibus virtus passionis domini nostri Jhesu Cristi agit, recipimus. Inter quae duo principaliter ad culpam delendam instituta atque ordinata sunt: baptismus scilicet et penitencia. Baptismus semel datur dumtaxat et irreiterabiliter. Penitencia vero iterari potest." *Hiob* (1497–8) 11.94.15–19.

[4] For a brief history of the doctrine of penance see especially Gordon J. Spykman, *Attrition and Contrition at the Council of Trent* (Kampen, 1955), pp. 17–89.

of justification was found in the penitent himself. The stress was moved from the achievement of the Christian as a recompense for his sin to the inner compunction and remorse which he feels. Genuine sorrow for sin coupled with a genuine love for God became the pivot on which the doctrine of penance moved.

Peter Abelard maintained, for example, that the forgiveness of sins presupposes nothing more than a sincere contrition of heart.[1] The contrite man will as a general rule confess his sins immediately to a priest. However, such a confession is not a presupposition or precondition of divine forgiveness, but rather a consequence of it. In point of fact, confession is subsumed by Abelard under satisfaction. The eternal punishment for sin is directly remitted by God on the ground of contrition prior to confession, although the temporal punishment is not.[2] The temporal punishment is remitted through works of satisfaction, of which confession is one.[3]

This view of penance made it difficult for the medieval theologian to explain the role of the priest. If the guilt and eternal punishment of sin have already been deleted through the contrition of the sinner, why is it necessary in addition to this to seek the absolution of a priest? Peter Lombard, who agreed with Abelard that contrition is the sole precondition of forgiveness, replied that the priest has merely a declarative function: that is, to indicate publicly to the Church that penitent sinner is already justified.[4] Such a public declaration is necessary in order to readmit the penitent to the eucharist and the full communion of the Church.

Alexander of Hales did not wish to dispute with Lombard that contrition is directly connected with justifying grace or that it is, as Lombard had argued, the necessary disposition for the reception of

---

[1] "Cum hoc autem gemitu et contritione cordis, quam veram poenitentiam dicimus, peccatum non permanet, hoc est contemptus Dei, sive consensus in malum, quia charitas Dei hunc gemitum inspirans, non patitur culpam. In hoc statim gemitu Deo reconciliamur, et praecedentis peccati veniam assequimur..." Peter Abelard, *Ethica*. 19, *PL* 178.664.

[2] "Non enim Deus cum peccatum poenitentibus condonat, omnem poenam eis ignoscit, sed solummodo aeternam." Abelard, *Ethica* 19, *PL* 178.665.

[3] "...in humilitate confessionis magna pars agitur satisfactionis..." Abelard, *Ethica*. 24, *PL* 178.668.

[4] "Non autem hoc sacerdotibus concessit, quibus tamen tribuit potestatem ligandi et solvendi, id est, ostendendi homines ligatos vel solutos—unde et Dominus leprosum prius sanitati per se restituit, deinde ad sacerdotes misit, quorum iudicio ostenderetur mundatus...—quia, etsi aliquis apud Deum sit solutus, non tamen in facie Ecclesiae solutus habetur nisi per sacerdotis iudicium." Peter Lombard, I *Sent*. d.18 c.6 (Quaracchi, 1916).

sacramental absolution. But he wished to give greater scope and emphasis to the role of the priest and of the *confessio oris*. He did so by redefining contrition in such a way as to include the intention to confess to a priest *(propositum confitendi)* as an integral element in the definition of true penance. No one can be really contrite who does not wish to confess his sins to the pastor placed over him by the Church.[1]

The contritionism of Peter Lombard was severely criticized by Duns Scotus. Scotus felt, with good reason, that Lombard had undermined the *ex opere operato* character of the sacrament of penance by reducing sacramental absolution to a declaration of pardon. If the reception of sacramental grace is made dependent on an antecedent disposition of contrition, then it can no longer be said that the sacrament is effective *ex opere operato* (as are the other sacraments of the New Testament) but only *ex opere operantis*.[2] The alternative which Scotus suggested is based on attrition (a repentance for sin springing out of a fear of punishment) rather than on contrition (a repentance rooted in the love of God).[3]

There are two ways open for the sinner to receive justifying grace. On the one hand, he can merit justifying grace *de congruo* by a penitent disposition of attrition which, while not yet contrition, is nevertheless of sufficient quality to be accepted by God. On the other hand, he can receive justifying grace by voluntary participation in the sacrament of penance, even though his disposition is of insufficient quality to merit grace. The first way is extra-sacramental and presupposes a vigorous attitude of attrition. The second way is sacramental and presupposes only the most minimal disposition for the reception of grace *(parum attritus)*. The justifying grace which is given to the *viator* transforms his attrition into contrition.[4]

Gabriel Biel, although he was impressed with the pastoral intention of Scotus' theological formulation, was willing neither to admit that there is an extra-sacramental road of justification nor to surrender the notion of the necessity of contrition as a disposition for the reception of grace.[5] The *viator* is able by the exercise of his own natural powers

---

[1] "...non enim haberet contritio efficaciam in contrito nisi sequeretur confessio sacramentalis, i.e. facta sacerdoti, quia contemptus confitendi vel negligentia simpliciter inefficacem reddit contritionem." Alexander of Hales, IV *Sent*. q.14 m.2 a.1.

[2] Duns Scotus, *Ox*. IV d.1 q.6 nota 10, nota 11.

[3] Duns Scotus, *Ox*. IV d.14 q.4 nota 14.

[4] Duns Scotus, *Ox*. IV d.14 q.2 nota 14.

[5] Gabriel Biel, IV *Sent*. d.14 q.2 a.1 corol. 2–4; a.2 concl. 4 and 6. For Biel see H. A. Oberman, *Harvest*, pp. 146–60.

to bring forth an act of love for God for His own sake *(propter Deum)*. The very instant such an act of contrition, such an inner disposition of love, is present in the *viator*, God rewards it with the infusion of justifying grace. The link with the sacrament of penance is preserved by asserting, after the manner of Alexander of Hales, that the intention to confess to a priest is included in the definition of true contrition.

Staupitz agreed with Biel that the essence of true penance is contrition.[1] There is such a thing as a disposition of minimal attrition or, as Staupitz prefers to say, gallow's penance.[2] Such a disposition is not motivated by a love of God and a chaste desire to maintain His honor at whatever cost, but rather by a servile fear *(timor servilis)*, which, acting wholly in its own self-interest, seeks to flee the impending divine judgment which its own sin has richly merited.[3] In contrast to this, real penance is a genuine sorrow for sin springing out of a love for God.[4]

---

[1] Luther claimed in 1518 that he had learned from Staupitz "...quod poenitentia vera non est, nisi quae ab amore justitiae et Dei incipit, et hoc esse potius principium poenitentiae, quod illis finis et consummatio censetur." "Begleitschreiben zu den resolutiones an Staupitz," *WA* 1.525.7ff. On this point Staupitz disagreed with John of Paltz, O.E.S.A. who was prior at Erfurt in 1505 when Luther began his novitiate. "In uno tantum puncto doctrinae a nobis expositae originalis fuit [John of Paltz], scilicet in quaestione de attritione seu de dolore de peccatis ex motivo timoris servilis et non filialis. Quod nemo affirmare ausus erat firmiter tenuit." Marcus Ferdigg, O.F.M., *De Vita et Operibus et Doctrina Joannis de Paltz, O.E.S.A.*, unpublished dissertation, Pontificium Athenaeum Antonianum (Rome, 1961), p. 317.

[2] "Die erst rew ist diese das der mensch seine begangne missethat dorumb berewt Und In schmerzen bedenckt Das Ime solchs Zu schaden raicht, ain unruwig gewissen macht, zu unern dint, das er sich domit ewiger untodlicher belonung beraubt und ewiger verdamnus tailhafftig gemacht hat. Diese rew... Wirdet auch ainer galgen rew Vergleicht..." *Von ainer waren rechtn rew* (1517) Kn. 16.

[3] "Est enim timoris, ut inquit S. Bona. super 3. Sen. dist. xxxiiii. intueri tria: penam scilicet, ut fugiat, offensionem, ut illam caveat, maiestatem summam, ut illi subiaceat exhibendo reverenciam. Fugit servilis, cavet offendere inicialis, reveretur summam maiestatem resiliendo in propriam parvitatem timor castus et filialis." *Hiob* (1497–8) 4.19.4–9.

[4] "Die ander rew ist diese, das der mensch seiner Volbrachten sundt halben ainen schmerzen und berewung tregt, das er domit got, seinen Schopffer, belaidigt und erzurnt, Und seine gotliche gebot Ubergangen hat. Diese rew, Wiewol sie mit ainem rechten ordenlichen grundt beschicht und stracks In die lieb gottes geplanzet wirdet Ist sie doch zu abwaschung der sunden und ervolgung gotlicher parmherzigkait nit vollig: dann so gros kann des menschen nit rew sein Wo sie nit In die nachfolgen den dritten als sie aller volkomensten genugsamen rew geordent wirdet, das sie ain ainige begangne todsundt ablesch. Wiewol auch solche des menschen berewung geschickt ist lebendig frucht zubringen, wirdet sie doch durch der nachfolgenden schmerzen, rew und trawrigkeit unsers seligmachers allererst angezundet und lebendig gemacht Und dan zu abtilgung Unnser sonden mer dann genungsam." *Von ainer waren rechten rew* (1517) Kn. 16.

The agreement between Staupitz and Biel against Scotus on the importance of contrition is, to say the least, superficial. While Biel is willing to assert that love for God, and therefore contrition, lies within the competence of the natural powers of man, Staupitz, who (as we have already seen) places all love for God within the sphere of grace, grounds contrition in the meritorious sufferings of Christ.[1] The cross is the act of God which, paradoxically, nullifies all human achievement and at the same time makes it possible. The cross reveals the vanity of every human attempt at self-justification and yet, by releasing the power of grace, brings both virtue and merit within the reach of the *viator*. Or, to put the matter differently, the origin of genuine contrition is not the love of the soul for God—an act which in any case the human will under the power of sinful concupiscence is incapable of producing—but rather the love of God for the soul. All human love for God, and therefore all contrition, is a response to the prior love of God, which evokes this devotion and makes it possible.

True penance is more internal than external, more a matter of inner sorrow than of outer expressions of grief.[2] No exterior act can be fruitful unless grounded in an interior work of grace. Confession, penance, works of satisfaction are useless until they are performed by a man in whom faith in Christ has been awakened, a man moved more by the love of God than by the love of heaven or the fear of hell.[3]

---

[1] "Der drit schmertz oder Rew ist der den christus als der Unschuldig ist... Wo wir Unser rew darein ergrunden, Ist zu abwaschung aller unser missethat genungsam..." *Von ainer waren rechten rew* (1517) Kn. 16.

[2] "...wir uber Unser sunden den hochsten schmerzen mer mit den Inwendigen zehern des herzens dann auswendiger bewaynung haben..." *Von ainer waren rechten rew* (1517) Kn. 16.

[3] "...gotlicher lieb, aus der auch diese unser schmertzliche berewung endtlich vlissen sol... und nit aus Ursachen verwurckter ewiger belonung des himels oder verdinter straff der hellen..." *Von ainer waren rechten rew* (1517) Kn. 17. "Hilfft kain Beicht, Hilff kein rew, Hilfft kain menschen werck, man muss in Christum glauben oder in sünden ersterben." *Glauben* (1517) Kn. 126. Keller argues that: "Getreu der deutschen Mystik hatte Staupitz die Scheu vor äusseren Mitteln und Vermittlungen sich trotz der Wiederanknüpfung Luthers an das Prinzip der Gnadenmittel bewahrt. Er kennt eine Heilsvermittlung durch die Kirche auch in diesen Predigten und in seiner letzten Schrift, auf die wir sofort zu sprechen kommen werden, nicht." Ludwig Keller, *Johann von Staupitz und die Anfänge der Reformation* (Leipzig, 1888), p. 172. In the *Salzburger Predigten*, however, Staupitz makes the intention to confess to a priest the precondition of forgiveness. *Salzburger Predigten* (1523), No. 24, Kolde, p. 455; Hs: b II 11, St. Peter (1523), Sermo 11, fol. 93ᵃ. Staupitz does believe that the Church and the sacraments are nothing more than means which God uses to carry out his decree of election in the world. The Church is a

The signs of genuine penitence are unmistakeable. Whoever is seized with the spirit of true penitence is willing to confess his guilt, to justify the sufferings which he is forced to undergo as a consequence of his sin and to mourn the innocent sufferings of Jesus Christ.[1]

Penance is a work of God in the soul and not a self-induced state presented to God as a claim upon His grace. That a man intends to repent at all is itself a gift of God and not a human achievement. *Dolor cordis* is awakened in the soul through divinely sent tribulation;[2] *amor dei* is kindled through the antecedent love of God made concrete in the figure of the suffering Son of God. The initiative in penance as in every step in the justification of the sinner belongs to God. Contrition, confession and satisfaction are only responses to this merciful initiative of a Father, more willing to forgive than eager to condemn.

The possibility of contrition depends on the coincidence of two factors. The objective possibility of repentance, to use language foreign to Staupitz but not foreign to his meaning, is the revelation of the love of God for man through the suffering and crucified Savior. The subjective possibility of repentance depends on the inner activity of the Holy Spirit within the human soul, overcoming the tragic effects of the fall. There is no sorrow for sin and no love for God where these two factors do not coincide.

The suffering love of Jesus Christ awakes in the sinner the answering response of love. Yet this response to the divine initiative, though it is kindled by the cross of Christ and nurtured by the prevenient activity of the Holy Spirit, is nevertheless a weak and imperfect human response. Even repeated confession or sorrow for the weakness and imperfection of the sinner's response may fail to deepen that response appreciably. In spite of this fact, the sinner should not lose heart. God, supplements acting on the basis of the bitter sufferings of Jesus Christ, the deficiencies in human penance.[3] Even though the sinner's peni-

---

function of the *gratia predestinationis*. For Giles of Rome, the grace which makes man pleasing to God is a function of the Church. Cf. Giles of Rome, *De Ecclesiastica Potestate*, ed. Richard Scholz (Leipzig, 1929), pp. 72–3.

[1] "Das sein die drey wartzeichen der rechten ungetichten busse, mit leit erkennen und bekennen sein schult, rechtfertigen sein leiden, und beweinen das unschuldige leiden Christi." *Nachfolgung* (1515) Kn. 70–1.

[2] "Contricio est dolor cordis...nullus ad deum accedere potest sine tribulacione, cum post baptismum iustificacio nostra per solam penitenciam fieri praedicatur, penitencia autem sine tribulacione non est." *Hiob* (1497–8) 11.94.36–42.

[3] "...ob er wol kain Volkomene rew erlangen mag, So sol er doch uber das einen hertzlichen schmertzen und rewen nemen Und haben, das Ime uber sein moglichen Vleis an genungsamer rew mangels Und got den almechtigen abermaln

tence is imperfect, God will not withhold His grace from him. The sinner has done the very best he could.[1]

It is not necessary to enumerate all the sins which have been committed since the last confession in the sacrament of penance. Staupitz recommends only a confession of actual sins against the Ten Commandments or of those relatively minor and trivial sins which, despite their triviality, burden the conscience of the penitent.[2] To ferret out every sin, however venial and inconsequential, would be an endless process. Men should not place their trust in their frequent confessions but in the grace of God, which antedates their repentance and makes it possible.[3]

Staupitz interpreted the power of the keys entrusted to the priest in the traditional way. Through the power of sacramental absolution the priest as the representative of Jesus Christ on earth releases the penitent sinner from his sins.[4] His role is not, as Lombard maintained,

---

ermanen, diesen mangel durch sein pitters leiden Und plutuergiven zuerfullen Und neben seiner geprechenlichen rew ain parmherziger mitwurcker zu sein, bedarff es nit zweiffels, got wil sich an vermogen ains menschen setigen lassen Und diesem rewer sein gnad nit entziehen." *Von ainer waren rechten rew* (1517) Kn. 19.

[1] Once again, twenty years after the sermons on *Hiob*, Staupitz returns to the theme of *facere quod in se est* and the notion that man is a coworker with prevenient grace prior to the infusion of *gratia gratum faciens*. His thesis, however, is not that the sinner, aided only by the *concursus dei*, can bring forth an act of supreme love for God *ex puris naturalibus*. His thesis, rather, is that the sinner, moved from without by the work of Christ on his behalf and from within by the Holy Spirit, still fails to love God perfectly. The doctrine of *facere quod in se est* does not extoll the natural powers of man, but rather emphasizes man's utter impotence. Thus we agree with Wolf when he writes concerning the disposition for grace, that "...Staupitz in diesen Fragen immerhin anders denkt, als die via moderna, wird man zugeben müssen..." Wolf, *Staupitz und Luther*, p. 54.

[2] In this connection see the testimony of Luther, *WATR* 6.6669: "Da ich ein Mönch war, schreib ich Doctor Staupitz oft, und ein Mal schreib ich ihm: O meine Sünde, Sünde, Sünde! Darauf gab er mir diese Antwort: 'Du willt ohne Sünde sein, und hast doch keine rechte Sünde; Christus ist die Vergebung rechtschaffner Sünde, als die Aeltern ermorden, öffentlich lästern, Got verachten, die Ehe brechen etc., das sind die rechten Sünde. Du musst ein Register haben, darinne rechtschaffene Sünde stehen, soll Christus dir helfen; musst nicht mit solchem Humpelwerck und Puppensünden umgehen und aus einem jeglichen Bombart eine Sünde machen!'" Cf. also *WA* 2.721.24ff. and *WA* 8.367.30ff.

[3] "Der mensch sol auch In sein rechten peichten gantz kain vertrawen stellen Sonder allain In die volkommenhait der gnaden und parmherzigkeit gottes, dodurch der sunder allain perectvertigt werden mag..." *Etlich Nutzlich leren* (1517) Kn. 40.

[4] "So sag alles, das dir der gelaubenn und vertrawen zu got verhengt zu sagen, Sag und hiet ich zechen kinder ermört, Ich wolt es gern sagen, das mich grosse mörderin mein gott So genädigkleich wil auffnemen, und mir mein sunt ablegen, Ja auch alle meine guete werch, So ers wolt nach gerechtikait richten mich ver-

simply to declare that the sinner has already been forgiven by God, after the analogy of the Old Testament priest who announced to the people of Israel that a leper had been cleansed of his leprosy. On the contrary, the binding and loosing which the priest's office entails is a real binding and loosing. Sacramental absolution effects a change; it does not merely announce it.

That is not to say, however, that God cannot or will not forgive a man prior to his confession to a priest. In the Salzburg sermons of 1523 Staupitz makes it clear that God can forgive sins before confession.[1] However, like Alexander of Hales, and Thomas Aquinas, Staupitz preserves the link with the sacrament of penance by making the intention to confess to a priest the precondition of forgiveness. The refusal to go to confession is a sure sign of the absence of faith in Christ.[2] There is no way around the sacrament, but only a way through.

This means that indulgences are ineffective without penance.[3] In point of fact, it is specified in the papal bull itself that neither indulgences nor the *klangk* of *guldens* frees the soul from sin without true repentance and confession.[4] There is no cheap way to heaven, no road which does not lead through the sufferings and tribulations undergone by Jesus. Good works and merits cannot be bought and sold. *Beichtgeld* is the devil's invention, not a requirement laid down by the Savior.[1] Discipleship is costly, but the price which it demands cannot be paid with the gold minted in any bank. Discipleship demands a death of self-will and a voluntary following of the sufferings of Jesus. An indulgence is not in itself invalid, but it must not be abused.

---

dampten, und so der priester spricht: 'Ich entpintt dich von dein süntten.' So lass dir sein, Als Xsts selber da stuent und entpunt dich." *Salzburger Predigten*, No. 24, Kolde, p. 455.

[1] "Erstleich wie der himelisch vater, dye sünt so gern und begirleich verzeicht und ee der Mensch peicht, wan er nur gedenckt er wels bekennen, so sein sy im schon vergeben, und lauft jm der himelisch vater entgegen und erzaigt sein vaterleiche trew an jm." Hs: b II 11, St. Peter (1523), Sermo 11, fol. 93ª.

[2] "Aber wer nit gern peicht oder verzweyfeln wil, das ist ain gewiss zaichenn, das der kain glauben, noch hofnung, zu Xsto hat." *Salzburger Predigten*, No. 24, Kolde, p. 455.

[3] "Doraus kompt auch das In alle babstlich Ablas bullen gesetz wirdet, das die des aufgangen ablas sollen vehig und entpfhengklich sein, die warhafft berewt und gepeichtet haben." *Von ainer waren rechten rew* (1517) Kn. 18.

[4] "...dann der klangk des guldens so der In die gelt kisten felt, wirdet den sunder seiner sunden nit entledigen..." *Von ainer waren rechten rew* (1517) Kn. 18.

[1] "Das ist laider yetz darzue kumen, das man dy heiligen Sacrament wil verkauffen. Der tewfel hat das peychtgeld aufpracht das man dye vergebung der sünt umb gelt mues kauffen, Ja man mues schyer das hochwirdig Sacrament kauffen, So ainer ain grosse sünt auf jm wais und sy ist jm laid und er wär jr gern ledig

III. The Primacy of Uncreated Grace

In the sermons on Job, Staupitz defines *gratia gratum faciens* as a *divina mocio* or *gratuitus amor*, infused into the soul and rendering it pleasing to God.[1] Aquinas taught that grace is a power released in the soul which changes the man infused by it, healing his fallen nature and enabling him to perform works which are meritorious *de condigno*.[2] He rejected the position of Peter Lombard, who identified the *caritas* which is infused in the soul through the sacraments with the Holy Spirit. Thomas did not see how he could explain the union of the uncreated Holy Spirit with the created soul of man without endangering the ontological distinction between them[3] or how, on the other hand, he could preserve the notion of the free and meritorious action of man, once such a union of the divine and human is presupposed.[4] Infused love for him is not to be identified with the uncreated Spirit of God (though it is certainly true that God is love and that Christians participate in that love),[5] but is rather a created gift, produced in the soul by God, yet essentially distinguishable from Him. Man loves God and the neighbor by means of a habitual form *(habitus)* which is superadded to this natural powers.[6]

The nominalists weakened the idea of *caritas* as a *habitus* by indicating that the law requiring a *viator* to have a habit of grace is only valid *de potentia ordinata* and by stressing the uncreated gift of the Holy

---

und lauft gen rom, so sagt man, Dw muest fyerzig tucaten geben, so wellen wir dich enpinten, gibstu uns aber nit, so muestu dy sunt behalten. Ach got, ach got, den du mit deim rosenwarben pluet hast gekaucht, den wellen wir dem tewfel umb fiertzig tucaten geben, oder halt oft ain ring gelt. pfü der schantten! Das ist er entzeucht uns dy gnad und gaben der Sacrament. So wir sy also myssprauchen und verkauffen." Hs: b II 11, St. Peter (1523), Sermo 16, fol. 148ᵃ–149ᵃ.

[1] *Hiob* (1497–8) 12.113.19–24. See above footnote 3 for text.
[2] Thomas Aquinas, *Summa Theologiae* Ia IIae q.109 a.9.
[3] Thomas Aquinas, I *Sent* d.17 q.1 a.1.
[4] Thomas Aquinas, IIa IIae q.23 a.2. See further Paul Vignaux, *Luther, commentateur des Sentences* (Paris, 1935), pp. 75–6.
[5] Thomas Aquinas, *Summa Theologiae* IIa IIae q.23 a.2 ad 1.
[6] On grace as *habitus*, see Thomas Bonhoeffer, *Die Gotteslehre des Thomas von Aquin als Sprachproblem*, BHTh 32 (Tübingen, 1961), pp. 87–97. Iserloh summarizes the position of Thomas Aquinas in this way: "Besonders Thomas hatte noch betont, dass das Prinzip des übernatürlichen Handelns dem Menschen innerlich zu eigen sein muss, damit die Handlung freiwillig und verdienstlich ist. Deshalb könne sie nicht vom Heiligen Geist unmittelbar hervorhebracht sein, sondern müsse einer dem Menschen inhärierenden Form entspringen." Erwin Iserloh, *Gnade und Eucharistie in der philosophen Theologie des Wilhelm von Ockham* (Wiesbaden, 1956), p. 81.

Spirit and the divine acceptation of human works.[1] They were joined in their critique of the *habitus* theory by Staupitz, though he went beyond them when in his later writings he rejected the *habitus* doctrine altogether.

In the sermons on Job, Staupitz taught that the infusion of *gratia gratum faciens* is accompanied at the same time *(simul)* by an infusion of the Holy Spirit.[2] The justified sinner receives both a habit of love (the *gratia creata*)[3] and the Holy Spirit (the *gratia increata*).[4] The primacy, however, belongs to the uncreated gift because the motion of the soul toward God is imparted by the indwelling Spirit.[5] Furthermore, the acts of love produced by a man in a state of grace do not in and of themselves have a claim on divine glory. There is no necessity which impels God to accept anything from a creature. The *dignitas* (i.e., the meritoriousness) of works is granted through divine acceptation.[6] God has graciously decreed that he will reward works with a reward which they have not fully merited. The relationship between human behavior and the divine reward rests on a free decision of God. The Spirit is thus the principle both of *sanctificatio* and of *acceptatio*.

In the later sermons and treatises the doctrine of a *habitus* disappears

---

[1] For the nominalist critique of the *habitus* theory see Paul Vignaux, *Luther, commentateur des Sentences*, pp. 45–86; Reinhard Schwarz, *Fides, Spes und Caritas beim jungen Luther*, AKG 34 (Berlin, 1962), pp. 13–40; H. A. Oberman, *Harvest*, pp. 160–84.

[2] "Hoc enim bonum, scilicet gracia, semper dicitur dari racionali cum spiritu sancto iuxta illud apostoli: 'Caritas dei diffusa est in cordibus nostris per spiritum sanctum, qui datus est nobis.' [Rom. 5:5] Simul ergo cum gracia spiritum sanctum recipimus, in quem dyabolus potestatem habere non potest, sed eius potestati per omnia subiectus est." *Hiob* (1497–8) 30.232.36–41.

[3] "Ex habitu, cum delectabiliter ex caritate agit. Signum namque generati habitus est delectacio in opere." *Hiob* (1497–8) 24.197.27–8.

[4] "...tamen illud dicitur gracia omnino specialiter, qua sumus digni deo et per quam sumus grati deo. Magna certe gracia est, quod dedit nobis bona naturalia, sed maior, quando dat, quae per naturam adipisci non possunt, illa autem maxima est, quando dat seipsum et quando nobis graciam gratum facientem, quam habendo sumus deo digni bono increato..." *Hiob* (1497–8) 30.232.17–22. Cf. *Hiob* (1497–8) 23.189.3–6.

[5] *Hiob* (1497–8) 23.189.23–6. See above p. 97, footnote 2 for text.

[6] *Hiob* (1497–8) 22.186.32–187.3. See above p. 95, footnote 3 for text. Gerson is his authority for the doctrine of acceptation. Staupitz may also have heard Paul Scriptoris lecture on the problem. According to Dettloff, Scriptoris has written on this question "...ein sehr sorgfältiger Kommentar, der wie der am meisten bekannte des Franciscus Lychetus immer am Text des Duns Scotus anknüpft und diesem folgt. Er dient dazu, die Lehre des Duns Scotus verständlich zu machen, ohne Neues hinzufügen zu wollen." Werner Dettloff, *Die Entwicklung der Akzeptations- und Verdienstlehre von Duns Scotus bis Luther* (Münster Westf., 1963), p. 348.

entirely. The elect soul in a state of grace is indwelt by God Himself[1]—
or, Staupitz can also say, by *Christus*,[2] by the *Spiritus Sanctus*[3] or by the
Geist Christi.[4] This indwelling Spirit moves man to good works without a created habit of love.[5] He acts on the soul partly through the
impact of the cross from outside and partly through His secret operation from within. Faith, hope and love spring from the fountain of
the Spirit.[6]

At least twice in his writings Staupitz attempted to define the nature
of the love which the Holy Spirit inspires in the Christian and to give
positive meaning to the Latin word: *caritas*. In the sermons on Job
he defined *caritas* as that love which is not self-regarding, as the love
that "seeketh not her own."[7] In the later sermons preached in Nonnberg he does not rescind this definition but expands it by giving it a
concrete Christological content.[8] *Caritas* is the marvelous conde-
scending love of God exemplified in the incarnation and atonement.
It is the suffering love of Christ which submits to pain and death for
the sake of the beloved. It is this kind of love which is showered on
the Christian and which awakens in him the answering response of love.

---

[1] "Derhalbenn ist die erste, die hochste und groste begnadung der ausserwelten
seel, das got sein wonung yn yr macht." *Lieb gottes* (1518) Kn. 98. "O selig, und
mer den selig, ist der mensch, in der der heilig geist von oben herab gestigen, in
dem die selbstendige wesenliche lieb, die got selb ist, yre wonung hat..." *Lieb
gottes* (1518) Kn. 99.

[2] *Libellus* (1517) 179.

[3] *Lieb gottes* (1518) Kn. 99, 102.

[4] *Lieb gottes* (1518) Kn. 98.

[5] "Nymandt kann ainigen guten gedancken, Wort oder Werck haben, Got sey
dann vor mit seiner parmherzigkait und seinen leiden in Ime gewest, damit er Ine
Zu solchem hab bewegt." *Von der nachvolg cristi* (1517) Kn. 28. "O wen der geist
gotz also regirt, würckt und lebentig macht des hertz springt jn freyden, süesser
lieb und danckperkait. In allen dem das jm von seinen lieben got zuefleust, übel
oder guet, darjnn steet seinen willen mit den willen gottes vergleicht und got jst
ain vater aller seiner werck." Hs: b V 8, St. Peter (Lent, 1519), fol. 73[b]. Cf. *Lieb
gottes* (1518) Kn. 99, 102; Hs: b II 11, St. Peter (1523), Sermo 15, fol. 137[b]–138[a].

[6] "Also sichstu tzu dem beschlus, das kein gut werck in uns kompt, der heilig
geist sey den vor darin, wie oben gemelt. Wen er aber in uns ist, so ist er das
lebendig wasser, das do in uns ein springender brun wirdt in das ewig leben,
durch glaub, lieb und hoffnung." *Lieb gottes* (1518) Kn. 102.

[7] "Caritas enim, qua honoratur spiritus sanctus, non quaerit, quae sua sunt, hoc
est: 'communia propriis anteponit,' ut S. Augus., in regula [Augustine, *Regula*. 8,
PL 32.1382] dicit." *Hiob* (1497–8) 21.171.30–32.

[8] "Also hat dy lieb den Sun gotz herausgeryssen von dem marck des vaterlichen
hertzen, herab auf das erdrach jn armuet und ellent. Sy hat in auch gantz zerissen
durch manig gross pein, pis anns kreutz jn den volsmertzenlichisten todt. Das ist
aigentlich dy lieb, dy genent wird Caritas, wann das wart caritas bedeutet mer dan
so man schlechtlich spricht lieb." Hs: 23 E 16, Nonnberg, fol. 67[a].

Parallel to the infusion of grace which heals the soul of man in the present and prepares him for a life of meritorious activity to be actualized in the period of time between his baptism and his death, there is the divine act of remission which disposes of the heritage of actual sin accumulated by the viator in the period of his life prior to his baptism. Using Psalm 32 as the scriptural basis for his argument and calling on the theological resources of Jean Gerson in *De vita spiritualis animae*, Staupitz interpreted this act of remission as an act of non-imputation.[1] The penalty which the *viator's* sins have merited, i.e., eternal death, is commuted by God in penance to a lesser punishment.[2] The actual sins committed by the *viator* are, after the infusion of grace, no longer regarded by God as mortal, but only as venial—no longer punishable in hell, but rather to be expiated in purgatory.[3]

IV. The Effects of Justification

The practical effect of the divine renewal of the nature of man which takes place through justification is, to put it in its simplest form, the undoing of the consequences of the fall. This means, first of all, that the sinner is brought back to a true knowledge of God and is given a glimpse of the divine mercy in all its unfathomable depths. Together with this fresh apprehension of God the sinner is given a clear vision of his own true state vis-à-vis this God.[4] He is made aware of his own sinfulness and weakness, and of his need for that divine mercy which is offered to him in the cross of Christ. God begins His work of renewal by instilling *humilitas* in man.

This new knowledge of God does not begin with the infusion of grace, but antedates it. The rudiments of the knowledge of God are connected, not with the experience of the possession of grace but with the proper disposition for the reception of grace. It is through the preaching of the mercy of God,[1] on the one hand, and the clear

---

[1] "Audi, nullum peccatum potest remitti nisi per hoc, quod deus liberaliter non imputat illud ad peccatum." *Hiob* (1497–8) 23.187.28–30. Cf. Gerson, "De Vita," p. 123.

[2] *Hiob* (1497–8) 23.187.34–188.9. Cf. Gerson, "De Vita," p. 123.

[3] The distinction between mortal and venial sins rests on a free decision of God. All sins are mortal *de possibili*; some sins are venial *de lege statuta*. *Hiob* (1497–8) 23.186.27–32. Cf. Gerson, "De Vita," p. 120.

[4] "Das erst, got ist über treffenleih unbegreiffleich. Dem soltu pegegen mit einer dyenmueting klainmachung und einzwingung alles deins gemüets jn dein hertz jn warhaftig erkantnüs deins nichts." Hs: 26 E 16, Nonnberg, fol. 54ª⁻ᵇ.

delineation of the law of God,[2] on the other, that the sinner is first awakened out of the lethargy imposed on him by the dominion of sinful concupiscence and is brought to a sudden realization of the demands laid on him by God and of the benefits offered to him. This new self-knowledge is a precondition for the reception of grace. The man who is blissfully ignorant of his own true condition will seek to justify himself before God by morally virtuous deeds. He will not gratefully embrace the mercy of God in Christ, because he feels no need of it. The law of God must jar him out of his pitiful state of self-deception, before he will flee to the wounds of Christ for refuge.

Preaching is by no means the only messenger used by God to bring men to a knowledge of the truth. Perhaps no ther means is so extolled by Staupitz as an instrument for dissipating the clouds of misunderstanding and ignorance surrounding the condition of the soul in its relation to God than the instrument of temptation.[3] Under the hammer blows of adversity the sinner is liberated from his delusions and made to confront the truth.

In his sermons and treatises Staupitz wages an unceasing war against a Pharisaical confidence in human righteousness. An overweening confidence in the moral powers of man ignores the indisputable fact that the righteousness of man is impure.[4] Furthermore, to place any confidence in human achievement as an offering which can be presented to God is to lose sight of the true order of priorities.

---

[1] *Hiob* (1497–8) 20.169.1–9. See footnote 4 and 6 above.

[2] For a discussion of Staupitz's understanding of the law see chapter six, section five, "The Inner and the Outer Word." It is not, strictly speaking, the law which condemns man or which brings a knowledge of sin. There is a sense in which the law is itself gospel; i.e., to the extent that it bears witness to Jesus Christ. It is rather the letter of the law which brings man to a realization of his predicament. Cf. *Lieb gottes* (1518) Kn. 97.

[3] "Ideo autem temptacionem miserorum admittit, ut miseros se agnoscant et misericordiam petant aut ad ipsam recipiendam consenciant. O vere nimis necessaria temptacio. Nam et in medio temptacionis nos ipsos negligimus." *Hiob* (1497–8) 16.139.2–5. Cf. footnote 6 above.

[4] "...gedenck ferner, das nymandt gegen gote geschetzt moge gerechtfertiget werden, gedencke das auch die gerechtikeit des menschen unrein ist." *Nachfolgung* (1515) Kn. 69. On the imperfection of human works as a theme in late medieval preaching see Adolar Zumkeller, "Das Ungenügen der menschlichen Werke bei den deutschen Predigern des Spätmittelalters," *ZKTh* 81 (1959), 265–305. After examining representative sermons on the parable of the Pharisee and the Publican, Zumkeller concludes that "...die Fabel von der katholischen Werkheiligkeit wirklich nur Fabel ist." *Ibid.*, p. 305. For a critique of Zumkeller's article, see H. A. Oberman, *Harvest*, p. 181, footnote 112.

Human moral achievement cannot be man's gift to God for the simple reason that it is in fact God's gift to man.[1]

There are, of course, men who pray for long life, not in order to have more time in which to trust in the mercy of God but in order to have more opportunity to fill their days with "fasting, praying, almsgiving and the like."[2] For such a conception of the religious life as a life of continuous achievement time is an indispensable prerequisite. Only a man with many years behind him can hope to have accumulated a creditable record of performance for submission to the divine Judge at the last great assize. Such a legalistic—or as Staupitz says, Jewish[3]— perversion of the relationship which should obtain between God and man is read by Staupitz as one more attempt of fallen man to be wiser than God by presuming to set the terms on which divine mercy may be dispensed.[4] The terms of the relationship between God and man are set by God. No other terms are valid. Whoever serves a God answerable to man in this fashion serves a construct of his own imagi-

---

[1] "Dann dieselben Werck sein nit seine Werck sonder gots werck, der Ime die gnad mittailt, guts zuwurcken, die weil on gots gnad und mitwurckung der mensch kain ainigen guten gedancken, zugeschweigen ain tugentlich werck haben und uben mag." *Etlich nutzlich leren* (1517) Kn. 39.

[2] "Vil leuthe begeren von got langs leben, uff das sie sich bass tzum sterben schicken mogen, fragen aber nicht worynne die ware schickung tzum tode steh, unnd in welchen wartzeichen sie erkendt werde, sunder leben nach iudischer ardt, bawen uff yre werck, uff yre fasten, betten, almussen geben, und der gleichen und halten do fur, yre langleben sey erforderlich tzu ewigen leben, das doch manchem vordamlich gewesen. Es wer besser, der mensch sturbe, eh er wuste, was guter menschen werck weren, dan das er einig vortrawen in sine guten werck setzte, unnd uff seine gerechtickeit etzwas bawete." *Nachfolgung* (1515) Kn. 86.

[3] Giles of Rome considered the position of the Jewish philosopher, Maimonides, to be worse than the position of Pelagius on the question of the relation of free will and grace: "Ulterius erravit circa humanam voluntatem et naturam, ponens quod licet talia a Deo immutari possint, nunquam tamen immutantur, quia tunc frustra esset ammonitio prophetarum; credens hominem per se ipsum absque speciali Dei auxilio posse omnia peccata vitare et omnes monitiones prophetarum implere. Ex qua positione videtur sequi gratiam divinam penitus superfluere. Propter quod haec positio est peior positione Pelagii, secundum quam licet possemus recte vivere sine gratia, non tamen superfluit gratia; quia habendo eam faciliori modo recte vivimus." Giles of Rome, *Errores Philosophorum*, ed. Josef Koch (Milwaukee: Marquette University Press, 1944), p. 64. Perhaps this understanding of Jewish teaching lies behind Staupitz's strictures against a life "nach iudischer ardt."

[4] "O menschliche torheit wiltu sunde wol buessen, so begere der gerechtickeit tzu sterben, wiltu from werden, do begere kain tzeit tzu, thues an allen vortzug, wiltu got gefellig sein, so setze ym keine masse, wie er mit dir handeln solle, gib ym kein tzil, wie lang er dich leben lassen solle, Wie mochstu got hocher geschenden, dan das du yn nicht so weisse hieltest als dich, das du seiner erbarmung nicht mehr gebst dan deinen diensten." *Nachfolgung* (1515) Kn. 86.

nation. The God of the Christian faith is not a God who demands, or even tolerates, placid self-confidence. It is not the righteous, but sinners, who are called by the gospel to salvation.[1]

The sinner does not come to God, then, as one who is already pious; rather he asks to be made pious by the God who takes pity on the Publican and who condemns the Pharisee out of hand.[2] He knows that it is not on the basis of his own goodness, but on the basis of the mercy of God that he is justified.[3] He heeds the admonition to judge himself before he is judged by God.[4] He is willing to confess that he is a sinner, not because the humble acknowledgement of this fact will merit justifying grace for him, but because he knows that God has promised to be gracious to the unselfrighteous. Therefore Staupitz can say in his Salzburg sermons: "Pleibt jr nur sünder, so muess er ewer gerechtmacher sein."[5] Humble acknowledgement of the truth *(humilitas)* belongs to the proper disposition for grace, though it does not merit it. Justifying grace is always a gratuitous gift of God.

Justification is thus connected with the restoration of the knowledge of God and with a clear apprehension of the true condition of the soul. In part this knowledge antedates the actual infusion of grace and as such belongs to the disposition which precedes the reception of *caritas*. In part it follows this infusion and is deepened by it. Those who love God are led into ever deepening knowledge of His ways with men.

The second effect of justification is deliverance from the power of death. This means not merely that the elect will be granted eternal life at the end of their earthly pilgrimage, but that their souls, which are dead to God, will be restored to life *in via*. Man had, as a result of the fall, become liable to a threefold death: of the body *(sein)*, of the soul

---

[1] "Es ist endtlich beschlossen, und vil mals im heilgen evangelio vorkundet, promulgirt, offenbarlichen aussgeruffen, von Christo selb, das got allein sunder, keinen gerechten wolle selickmachen." *Nachfolgung* (1515) Kn. 86.

[2] "Ich kum aber wasch, und vergib, aber und aber und würch dw in mir, dan ich kan werlich nichts guetz tuen, Ja ich sag frey, Ich sag dir auch nit zue frum zu werden, mach dw mich frum mein frumer got." *Salzburger Predigten*, No. 24, Kolde, p. 424.

[3] "Cum ergo homo intelligit, quia non ex suis operibus bonus sit, quod omni penaltati iuste subiectus, ita quod non iustificabitur in conspectu eius omnis vivens, adhuc sperare audet super misericordia, quam sentit ex hoc, quod nullus umquam confidens in ea proiectus sit." *Hiob* (1497-8) 23.188.11-15.

[4] "Attende ergo tibi, o fili mi, et diligenter considera opera tua, discute conscienciam, et cum inveneris culpam, praeveni faciem domini in confessione. Sis tibi ipse iudex, ne forte dominus te iudicet et condempnet." *Hiob* (1497-8) 22.178. 2-5.

[5] *Salzburger Predigten* (1523), No. 2, Aumüller, p. 59.

(recht sein) and of the body and soul together. All three forms of death are overcome for the Christian man, but it is the second form, death of the soul or the loss of *recht sein*, which claims Staupitz's principal attention.

The soul had died to God through disobedience. Death was, so to say, born through disobedience.[1] Therefore death itself must die through a rebirth of obedience, that new life (i.e., *recht sein*) may spring up in its place.[2] This new life is not born out of the moral struggles of man, however well-intentioned or seriously pursued. New life is a gift of God, imparted to those who despair of themselves and who have placed their hope in Christ—the same Christ who dwells by His Spirit in the justified.[3] The will of man is involved in this rebirth of life;[4] no one is compelled to become a Christian.[5] But the role of the will is entirely passive or—if one prefers—wholly receptive. The soul like a bride is passive in its reception of new life.[6] It cannot restore life to itself; it can only accept as a gift from another.

---

[1] "Dorauss sich erfindet, das tzu einem gantzen leben eins menschen muessen got, sele unnd leib voreynet sein, auff das er, wie wil malh gesagt, nicht alleine sey, sunder recht sey, das einem waren menschen tzu gehoreth. Sich erfindet auch, das der todt der selen, der durch ungehorsam geboren, durch gehorsam widerumb sterben moge. Nachfolgendt das kein todt dem menschen ewig sein mag, wann der Todt der selen in ym gestorben." *Nachfolgung* (1515) Kn. 58.

[2] "...wan der bose todt stirbet, muss das gut leben geboren werden..." *Nachfolgung* (1515) Kn. 58.

[3] "Nymandt wirdt new geborn der nicht gestorben ist, Deshalben ist nicht in allen der angeborne todt von Adam gestorben, die Christum bekennen und anruffen, sunder in dene alleine, die in yne gestorben, in Christo leben, die in yrer eignen gerechtigkeit vortzagen, in Christo hoffen, die der gnaden alleine, keiner phflicht warten, gote in allen dingen, sich selb in nichte suchen." *Nachfolgung* (1515) Kn. 59.

[4] "In ista regeneratione sunt pater deus, mater voluntas, semen quo prolificatur merita domini nostri, Jesu Christi." *Libellus* (1517) 35.

[5] *Hiob* (1497–8) 15.134–41–135.3.

[6] "Das weis ich das die andechtige sele brauth ist, weip ist, Ich weis auch das sie des gotlichen ewigen worts entpfenklich ist, Ich weis auch wan in yr das ewige wordt geboren, das sie von gote tzu gleich dem blute Christi new entpfangen, new geborn wirt, Ich halt aber eigentliche, das sie sich in der entpfenknus halte, und halten solle, und musse, wolle sie anders new entpfaen und entpfangen sein, gottes brawt, gottes kindt, and gottes weip werden." *Nachfolgung* (1515) Kn. 78. Though Staupitz does not specify in this passage who is the pattern for the soul in its reception of the *Verbum eternum*, it is clear from other passages that the archetype is Mary. "Das wir aus unsern werchen noch vermügen nichtz künen würchen, das uns ainigerlay zu saligkait müg dyenen. Aber das müessen wir darzue tuen. Wir muessen darem verwilligen. So mag got stat darzue jn uns haben; got wil würchen, wir süllen tragen, und darem verwilligen. Er wil der vater sein der das in und durch uns würcht. Wir süllen und müessen nur dy mueter und tragerin und nererin sein. Es geet eben mit dem werch der feyr zue. Als sich dy sach an-

This restoration of *recht sein* can be interpreted by the use of a different set of categories as the restoration of true freedom.[1] Man the sinner had fallen under the bondage of *amor sui* and had lost the freedom to praise God. Since the psychological spontaneity of the will was preserved, man was unaware that he was in bondage of any kind. He loves the very disobedience which is bringing him to destruction. Nevertheless, the ontological bondage of his will is no less real for being undetected.

The intervention of God brings to man, as we have already seen, knowledge of God and thus of man's true situation. More importantly, it brings release from it.[2] The will is directed by grace back to the true object of its affections. The *Gegenlieb* of man is kindled by the love of God.[3] Man is given the ability to render *laus* to God. He is enabled to delight in choosing and performing the will of God. What once was odious to him has now been made pleasurable. What once was difficult to bear has been lightened. The power of *caritas* (i.e., the Holy Spirit resident in the justified) releases man from his old bondage to sin and takes him up into the free service of his Creator and Redeemer.

Nevertheless, the power of concupiscence is not wholly broken by the infusion of *caritas*. The soul of the Christian man is viewed as a battlefield in which the love of God may overcome the concupiscence which remains after baptism, though not without a struggle and not without the ever present possibility of defeat. The *culpa* of original sin is forgiven in baptism, but concupiscence itself remains as a subterranean power, not sinful in itself, but prompting to sin—a power which can only be neutralized through the counterforce of infused love.[4] Whoever yields to the urges of concupiscence falls back into

---

schlueg mit dem schatz der genaden mit der rainen künigen der mueter gots. Da sy den grues von got durch des engls mund enpfing das dy gesegent frucht, dy frucht jres leibs solt sein, da tet sy nit mer darzue dan das sy darem verwilligt." Hs: b II 11, St. Peter (1523), Sermo 17, fol. 154b-155a.

[1] "Tollit fateor libertatem que constituit servum peccati, et dat illam que nos facit filios dei." *Libellus* (1517) 171.

[2] "Justificatio inquam qua reducatur transgressio ad veram dei obedientiam, quod tunc fit quando per gratiam dei iterum aperiuntur oculi eius ut verum deum cognoscat per fidem. Inflammatur cor eius ut deus sibi placet." *Libellus* (1517) 33.

[3] "Wen aber got denn fels ins hertz des ausserwelten schlecht, so gibt er feuer, als den wirdt die todte kolen lebendig, der schwartz zundter goldfarbe, unnd der kalt brant leuchtend unnd brennend yn lieb, die von gottes lieb entzundet ist. Also entspringet lieb aus lieb, aus der lieb gottes zu uns unser gegen lieb zu gote." *Lieb gottes* (1518) Kn. 103.

[4] *Hiob* (1497–8) 32.247.4-20. Cf. Augustine, *De peccatorum meritis* I.39, *PL* 44. 150.

mortal sin. Whoever resists it through the power of the indwelling Spirit of God increases his own treasury of merit. Concupiscence in the believer thus offers both a danger and an opportunity: the danger of losing everything through mortal sin and the opportunity of gaining still more by struggling and overcoming.

One should not infer from what has been said thus far that sin and grace are evenly matched or that the issue is in doubt between them. Sin can do less harm than grace can do good.[1] Though it is a real and dangerous foe of man, sin lives only by the sufferance of God. Where God has determined to overcome it—as, for example, in the elect—it is overcome. All things, even the sins of the elect, work together for their good.[2]

V. THE MERITORIOUSNESS OF HUMAN WORKS

Staupitz agrees with Thomas Aquinas in affirming the impossibility of meriting either election or justifying grace.[3] Prior to the infusion of *gratia gratum faciens*, the sinner can neither turn from evil nor praise God with his good works, words and thoughts.[4] If a sinner becomes a member of Christ's mystical body at all, it is through grace and not through his own achievement.[5] The Franciscan contention that a sinner can earn first grace *de congruo* by exercising his innate moral powers to the limits of their capacity is rejected summarily. The

---

[1] "Minus ergo potest nocere peccatum quam prodesse gratia." *Libellus* (1517) 32.

[2] *Libellus* (1517) 93. Cf. *Lieb gottes* (1518) Kn. 111.

[3] "Hec est prima gratia, preveniens et naturam et opus, quam certe nemo petiit, nemo meruit, neque prescitis meritis seu previso bono usu rationis futuro, neque exhibitis debetur, sed sola benignissima liberrimaque dei voluntas processit." *Libellus* (1517) 21. Cf. *Hiob.* (1497–8) 15.135.30–33. For Thomas on merit see *Summa Theologiae* Ia IIae q.109 a.5; q.114 a.3. H. A. Oberman summarizes the position of the mature Thomas as follows: "Beim reiferen Thomas allerdings ist das Verhältnis klar: Das meritum de congruo geht der Rechtfertigung zeitlich nicht voran, sondern ist verdienstliche Tat auf Grund freier Willensentscheidung, während er unter meritum de condigno die gleiche Tat versteht, diesmal gesehen als Folge der Gnade." Heiko A. Oberman, "Das tridentinische Rechtfertigungsdekret im Lichte spätmittelalterlicher Theologie," *ZThK* 61 (1964), pp. 257–8.

[4] "Vere honorandus est deus super misericordia sua, qui nec laudari posset nisi praecederet misericordia sua. Dono tuo te laudo, per misericordiam tuam te laudo, inquit Sanctus Augustinus." *Hiob* (1497–8) 1.3.8–10. Cf. *Von der nachfolg cristi* (1517) Kn. 28.

[5] "...O Jesu mein einiger selichmacher, mir bistu geben, mir bistu geboren, gib mir dein leben, dein leiden, dein todt, mache mich dein glid, deinen mit erben, deinen bruder, nicht auss meinem vordienen, der ich keine hab, sunder auss deinen gnaden, von den ich bin was ich bin..." *Nachfolgung* (1515) Kn. 84.

augmentation, but not the infusion, of justifying grace is dependent on human merit. There is, in point of fact, a strong analogy between physical birth and the spiritual rebirth which takes place in baptism.[1] Just as a child is born naked into the world, so the Christian is reborn into new spiritual life without merits or virtues of his own. Justification is given *sine nostris meritis*.[2] Prior to the infusion of sacramental grace—i.e., prior to the union of the justified soul with Christ—neither *meritum de congruo* nor *meritum de condigno* is possible.

Staupitz is, however, far more radical than Thomas in describing the moral capacities of man prior to baptism. Thomas wished to deny the possibility of merit prior to the infusion of grace; he did not wish to cast doubt on the possibility of virtue. Staupitz, on the other hand, is quite willing to deny both.[3] Man's ability to will *(velle)* is a gift of nature and is not, so far as Staupitz gives any positive indication, destroyed by the fall.[4] But this natural capacity of man has been so harmed by the soul's apostasy from God that it can no longer do what is good. Virtue requires grace. Not only are the works performed apart from the influence of grace to be considered as lacking in virtue, they are even regarded by God as sinful.[5] Only those human works which flow out of the gracious activity of God within the human soul are pleasing to the divine Judge. God, in effect, rewards His own

---

[1] "Mater haec est iustificacio gratuita, sicut in baptismo novam parit mater gracia infanciam. Sicut ergo non habui vestem cuiuslibet actualis meriti mei, dicit Job, dum ita spiritualiter renatus sum, quare nec ad virtutes nec ad alia iam amissa, quae multa sint, converti debeo, sic ad deum revertar in nullo opere meorum spem constituens, nudus revertar illuc, quare nequaquam praesumendo aliqua cogito, sed 'dominus dedit, dominus abstulit, sicut domino placuit, ita factum est." *Hiob* (1497–8) 27.211.20-7. The *viator* who has no *vestem* of his own merit, is clothed with the *klaid kristi*, and is thus enabled to do works which please God (because they are God's work in him). "...wir muessen auch gerechtkait haben, das wir mit gerechtkait das Ewangelii halten. Das ist mit der gerechtikait kristi müessen wir angelegt sein und jn dem klaid fur den himelischen vater kömen, so gefelt jm unser werck, Ja gots werch jn seinen ainigen lieben kind." Hs: b II 11, St. Peter (1523), Sermo 15, fol. 138a-b. Compare this description of *duplex iustitia* with *Libellus* (1517) 56, 62, 71, 76, 77.

[2] "...unde aperte concludimus, quod sine nostris meritis ex utero matris ecclesiae progressi sumus." *Hiob* (1497–8) 23.189.41-2.

[3] "Et sic ante mundi constitutionem conclusum fuit neminem sine Christi gratia bene facere posse." *Libellus* (1517) 19. "Siquidem natura destituta nec nosse habet, nec velle, nec facere bonum, cui et deus ipse formidini est." *Libellus* (1517) 33.

[4] "Velle nature est donum. Spirare et facere bonum gratiam requirunt." *Libellus* (1517) 230.

[5] "Ja ich hab gesagt & wills leicht war machn: Sy gefallen jm nit dan wan er jn jn würcht, so gefal es jm selbs, da alles das der got nit würcht, das kan nit guet sein, ja nit allain nit guet, sunder es ist halt sünt."

works.[1] All other works displease Him and are thus considered sinful.

Staupitz does not believe that good works are unnecessary or take merit out of the relationship between God and man. In the sermons on Job of 1497–8 Staupitz opposes the views of Christians who give theological excuses for not doing good works.[2] But it is in his sermons of 1523, preached in the face of the antinomian theology of Agricola,[3] that Staupitz gives the sharpest expression to his position on good works. The teaching that "Christ has done all for me," argues Staupitz, undoubtedly eliminates self-righteousness or any overestimation of man's contribution to his own justification. But, by undercutting the grounds for Pharisaical self-confidence, it does not eliminate the necessity for interior righteousness. Freedom from good works is the devil's freedom; it is not true Christian liberty.[4] *Sola gratia* does not eliminate human merit—except, of course, in the case of very small children who die too soon after baptism to have the use of reason.[5] Adult Christians are called to be *cooperatores* with God.[6]

In medieval theology faith could be considered under two aspects. On the one hand, it is the *fides quae creditur*, the content of faith or the things which are to be believed. On the other hand, it is the *fides qua creditur*, the subjective act of faith itself. The *fides quae* and the *fides qua*

---

[1] "Colligunt sapientes, ex his et multis sententiis aliis deum non premiare nisi sua opera, scientes quod ipse gratiam et gloriam dat." *Libellus* (1517) 38.

[2] *Hiob* (1497–8) 19.159.17–22.

[3] For Staupitz's *Gutachten* against Agricola see N. Paulus, "Johannes von Staupitz," *HJ* 12 (1891) 309–46; 773–777.

[4] "wel man dann nit geistlich petten und mit dem leib auch nichtz thuen, das ist des tewfels freyhait und all zu schimpfleich gehandelt. Ja, sagt man, hat doch Christus alle ding für mich getan, sein doch meinen werch nichtz. Ja, dw tuest recht, das dw glaubst das Christus alle ding für dich hat tan und solt auch nichtz von deinen werchen halten. Aber dy werch gots soltu dw alzeit jn dir lassen gefallen. Was sein dy werch gots? Alles das das aus gelaub, lieb und hofnung geschiecht, das tuet got alles. Das ist der wyl und das werch, das jm der himelisch vater empfolchen hat und nach dem Christus hunger und durst hat, das er uns sälig mach und sein werch jn uns müg volbringen." Hs: b II 11, St. Peter (1523), Sermo 14, fol. 129ᵇ–130ᵃ.

[5] *Hiob* (1497–8) 27.214.26–32; *Etlich Nutzlich leren* (1517) Kn. 40.

[6] *Hiob* (1497–8) 27.214.32–37; *Libellus* (1517) 50. In this cooperation, it is the Holy Spirit who takes the initiative and man who follows. "In ainen stäten, vesten glauben, das dw auch glaubst, das dir got dein sundt well vergeben und dir halten wil alles, das er dir versprochen hat. Dann wurcht got, der heilig geist, jn dir mit dir alle deine werch. In den werchen mag sich der mensch erfrewen, wann sein werch gent nit jnn wint, sunder nur uber sich, er schlaff oder er wach, So feyert der heylich geist nycht, der mit jm jn jm würcht." Hs: b V 8, St. Peter (Advent, 1518), fol. 62ᵇ–63ᵃ.

are the objective and subjective poles of what was envisioned as one integral and unified act.

Both elements can be found in Staupitz's description of faith. There are certain rudiments of Christian belief, certain minimum essentials which even children are expected to know and give assent to. They are, more or less, the doctrines found in the first and second articles of the Apostles' Creed.[1] Not even the most learned Christian can fully understand the doctrines of the faith—or master the rudimentary doctrines of the Creed. The Christian is called to believe implicitly on the basis of divine authority what he does not yet fully understand.[2] What God has spoken cannot be false. Faith is no vaguely directed trust, no object-less commitment. Its object is divine truth.

The object of faith is not merely a set of propositions, though there are in the nature of the case propositions to be believed. Faith is not simply concerned with truth about God but is directed toward the God who is the Truth. Therefore Staupitz speaks of faith in God or of faith in Christ as an act of personal trust.[3] Faith is a reliance on the trustworthiness of the promises extended to the Christian.

The later writings emphasize the character of faith as an act of trust, as a subjective response to the promise of God.[4] This faith, according

---

[1] *Hiob* (1497–8) 10.76.7–18.

[2] "Aber gottes wort sol und muss menigklich glauben, umb das sie die warhait selbs sint, der billich aller verstandt gefangen, all hertzen zufallen sollen, Und sein die sachen wie hoch sie sein mogen, uber unsern verstand, ist doch sie zu glauben genug, das es Got gesagt hat, Und bedarff kainer weytern frag. Das ist des glaubens anfang, on welchen niemandt Got gefallen mag." *Glauben* (1525) Kn. 122. Cf. *Hiob* (1497–8) 10.75.31–4.

[3] "Kain mensch (als ich verhoff) ist so dunckels verstands, das jm nit ein klare sach sey, einem yegklichen menschen der unbetrieglichen warhayt, die Got selbs ist, zu glauben verpflicht sein." *Glauben* (1525) Kn. 121–2.

[4] The notion of faith as trust in the divine promises is not absent from the sermons on *Hiob*: "Sed quomodo resurgit iustus? profecto per penitenciam ponens lacrimas in conspecut dei, sperans in promissione eius." *Hiob* (1497–8) 11.94.33–4. But it is given far greater emphasis in the later writings. God is faithful not only to His decrees (i.e., His eternal decision concerning the elect) but also to His promises (i.e., the revelation of His will and purpose to the elect). "In ainen stäten, vesten glauben, das dw auch glaubst, das dir got dein sundt well vergeben und dir halten wil alles, das er dir versprochen hat." Hs: b V 8, St. Peter (Advent, 1518), fol. 62ᵇ–63ᵃ. "Söliches vertrawen fleusst auss der erkanten lieb Gottes zu uns, wirdt in uns durch unser hytzige lieb zu God für und für erhebt, und in dem wort Gottes von tag zu tag gesterckt, Sy wirdt in der gedult bewerdt, im todt bestetet, darumb das es allain in Gottes versprechung gegründt ist, die unwandelbar, unbeweglich, ewig, stett steet, und vestigklich beleybt, dann der versprecher ist almechtig, der raicher und darbieter ist die warhait, der tröster ist der heylig geyst." *Glauben* (1525) 133–4.

to Staupitz, justifies the sinner apart from the works of the law and is, in fact, the one thing needed to obtain eternal blessedness.[1] Indeed, when asked whether it is permissible to speak of justification by faith alone, Staupitz replied that it is, provided it is understood that it is the living faith which produces good works[2]—what he terms in the *Libellus* (1517) the *fides operans per dilectionem*.[3] In opposing antinomianism, however, he re-asserts the medieval position that good works are "meritorious" *(verdienstlich)*[4] and "necessary to salvation" *(nöt zur Seligkait)*.[5]

With this view of faith as a *fides operans per dilectionem*, Staupitz attributes to it many of the qualities which he had previously attributed to *caritas*. Like *caritas* faith is a gift of God which antedates human works and merits, and without which it is impossible to please God.[6] Like *caritas* faith is the source from which both virtue and merit flow.[7] Faith is not reducible to *fiducia* or *Vertrauen*, though *fiducia* has its place within the larger framework provided by the doctrine of infused grace. There is no opposition in Staupitz's theology between faith— even faith interpreted as *sola fides*—and merit.

---

[1] "In dem glauben wirdt man selig, auch on die werck des gesatz. Davon kumbt, das unns nichts nottigers ist, als im glauben zu üben." *Glauben* (1525) Kn. 126. "Das gott nit mer von uns wil habenn zu unserr säligkait dan allain den glauben. Das mügen, süllen und müessen wir jm geben. Das ander als wil und muess er selbs tuen und uns erkücken. Allain glaub dw jm das er dir versprochen hab, das well er dir halten. Setz all dein hofnung und vertrauen allain gantz jn jn." Hs: b II 11, St. Peter (1523), Sermo 19, fol. 181[b]–182[a].

[2] "Nun möchtestu sagen, Ey lieber got solt es den alles genueg sein mit dem gelauben, Ja freylich ist es genueg, gelaubt nur frey Er kan nit an frucht und werch der lieb sein ist er anders lebentig." *Salzburger Predigten*, No. 24, Kolde, p. 453.

[3] "Ubi ista conveniunt, nascitur filius dei, iustificatus vivificatusque per fidem operantem per dilectionem, operantem inquam per ignem dilectionis nostre, accensum ab igne dilectionis sue, qui solus est ignis perpetuus de celo exiens." *Libellus* (1517) 36.

[4] "Christenliche werck sein die allain, die auss Christlichen Glauben her fliessen, die selbigen sein eynig gut, eynig verdienstlich, eynig unnd kain anndere von Got gebotten." *Glauben* (1525) Kn. 135. Cf. *Glauben* (1525) Kn. 127–8.

[5] "Der werck aber, die in der gehorsam der hymlischen gebot, im glauben und lieb geschehen, hat er nie ubel gedacht, von jnen nicht dann das beste geredt, Ja sie zu der seligkait nöt und nütz verkündet und geprediget." *Glauben* (1525) Kn. 132.

[6] *Libellus* (1517) 15.

[7] "Wir wissen, das niemandt umb Got etwas verdienen mag, etwas guts thun, er sey dann vom vater in Christum gepflantz, das nicht in ander weyss geschicht, als durch den glauben in Christum..." *Glauben* (1525) Kn. 127–8. "...ausserhalb des glaubens in Christum ist kain tugent, kain rechte vernunfft, kain gutte mainung." *Glauben* (1525) Kn. 128.

It is clear from what has been said so far that neither *meritum de condigno* nor *meritum de congruo* is possible prior to the infusion of justifying grace. The idea of Gabriel Biel that a sinner can merit justification by the exercise of his own natural powers is categorically denied. Only works performed in a state of grace are meritorious. Yet are even these works, when measured by the strictest standards of divine justice, fully meritorious? Staupitz does not think so.

There are two standards by which human works may be judged. On the one hand, they may be viewed from the perspective of divine justice *(nach seiner strenger gerechtikeit)*;[1] on the other hand, they may be examined from the viewpoint of divine mercy *(aus seiner ubertreffen-lichen parmherzigkait)*.[2] If human works are judged according to the first standard—i.e., according to the codes of divine righteousness— no human work will survive the divine sentence. Apart from the assistance of divine grace, men can only sin and merit eternal punishment. Merit *nach gerechtikeit* is impossible; only merit *aus parmherzikait* is a viable option for man as a victim of the fall.

This means that no meritorious work—not even one performed in a state of grace—is, properly speaking, a merit of condignity. There is a disproportion between the value of the moral accomplishment of the *viator* and the value of the gift with which he is rewarded.[3] According to strict justice a finite work should receive a finite reward. There should be a rigidly equitable balance between the deed done and the blessing granted. But that kind of balance is precisely what does not obtain in the relationship between man and God. God gives infinite rewards for finite works.[4] He has mercifully decreed to accept the finite works of man. There is no way to rationalize this over-flowing bounty of God according to a scheme of strict justice. The superabounding grace of God makes all such schemes irrelevant.

---

[1] "Und wann got nach seiner strenger gerechtikeit wolt richten und, ob dw auch aller heiligen guete werch, dy sy aus in selbs und aus jrer natur haben, tatzt, so möcht dich got mit recht verdamen." Hs: b V 8, St. Peter (Lent, 1519), fol. 73ᵇ.

[2] "...got hat die straff unser verschuldung, auch die belonung unsers verdinens nie gleich furgenomen Sonder aus seiner ubertreffenlichen parmherzigkait die sunden zu yden mal geringer gestrafft dann wir verwurckt, auch die guten Wurc-kungen reichlicher belont dann wir verdint haben." *Von ainer waren rechten rew* (1517) Kn. 18.

[3] "Nemo minus recipit quam meruit, magis autem plerumque." *Libellus* (1517) 37.

[4] "Ex quo huiusmodi opera persone finite, natura finita sunt, ergo non potest super eis fundari iustitia infiniti meriti, cui debeatur infinitum premium; si autem deus se pro talibus dare decrevit,gratia est, non iustitia." *Libellus* (1517) 43.

Moreover, a relationship of condignity implies a high degree of autonomy on the part of the man who wishes to earn a reward. It is assumed that the achievement which he presents and by which he hopes to lay claim on the divine reward is, in the fullest sense of the word, his own achievement. It is certainly not fair to demand full payment for something which he has only partly done or which he has achieved by dint of the assistance of someone else. But that is exactly what a Christian does. He claims payment for something which has been made possible through the achievement of another. It is the work of Christ in atonement, and not his own merits, which forms the basis of his reconciliation to God.[1] And it is this reconciliation, wholly the work of another, which first enables him to earn merits of his own. The Christian must possess the merits of Christ through union with Him in marriage before he can cooperate with grace in producing good works. Divine mercy makes human merit possible and not the other way around.

Furthermore, the Christian's good works cannot be *merita de condigno* because they are in fact the work of Christ in and through him.[2] It is Christ in the Christian who is the source from whom good works flow and the end to whom they return. Or, as Staupitz says elsewhere, it is the Holy Spirit who renews the Christian and gives him the power to serve and please God. The human agency is not obliterated in this process, but it is clearly subordinated to the inner renewing activity of the indwelling Christ.

The conclusion which follows from this is that only the works of Jesus Christ, regarded as a historical personage and not as a power within the Christian, are meritorious *de condigno*.[3] Staupitz does not

---

[1] "So gelaubet er doch, got geb jm, was jm zu Saligkait seiner sel dynen. Darumb ein solicher gelasner mensch wirt nichtz verzigen. Er stet gantz mit seinen willen jn dem willen gotz. Membt lere. Aber der mensch sol nit darauf gäntzleich setzen, das er ain kindt gotz ist, nit auf sein geduld, nit auf seine guete werch, nit auf sein leyden und wider wärtikait, aber auf den todt seins gotz." Hs: 23 E 16, Nonnberg, fol. 76ᵇ.

[2] "Alia habet deus opera in nobis, opera inquam fidei formate, que per dilectionem operatur et viva est. Ista opera sunt magis sua... Omnia igitur opera que sequentur hunc ignem a Christo exeunt et in Christum vadunt, eapropter sunt opera Christi dicta specialius sed in homine formaliter sunt et non nisi extrinseca denominatione dei sunt et finita sunt." *Libellus* (1517) 40.

[3] "Insuper sublimiora sunt propria merita Christi, actiones scilicet, passiones et mors eius, qui natura fuit et est filius dei, quae et nobis ita donata sunt ut nostra sint. In istis fundamus collocamusque firmam spem, seu certe fundamentum cognoscimus. Et in his tantum meritum condigni locum habet, ipsaque sola sufficiunt saluti universe christianitatis, immo totius mundi. In eis parvuli salvantur,

take the next logical step and affirm, together with John Wyclif, that the merits of the Christian man are only *merita de congruo*.[1] That is, however, the direction in which his theology tends. Good works are regarded as essential to living faith, but they are reduced in significance to the status of half-merits, dependent, on the one hand, on the infused gift of the Holy Spirit who is the principle of sanctification in the Christian and, on the other hand, on the act of divine acceptance. Grace as the *Spiritus inhabitans* and the *Deus acceptans* is the beginning and the end, the alpha and the omega of the divine-human relationship.

The meritoriousness of a good work may be measured in proportion to the resistance encountered by the *viator* in bringing a good act to completion. There is, for example, more merit in suffering than in joy, more merit in poverty than in riches.[2] In fact, those people whose works are highly meritorious are precisely those people who patiently bear the sufferings laid on them by their heavenly Father and who are more eager to vindicate God than to exculpate themselves. [3]Such men despise temporal gain for the sake of eternal reward. The highest level of such meritorious discipleship is found in Christians who voluntarily undergo death as a direct response to the voluntary death of Jesus Christ on their behalf.[4] No witness could be more authentic, no act

---

et nonnunquam in utero sanctificantur. In eisdem solvuntur culpe, relexantur ac remittuntur pene." *Libellus* (1517) 51. Cf. 42.

[1] "Est duplex meritum, scilicet de congruo et de condigno: de congruo quando aliquis meretur de pura gratia praemiantis, ut puta, quando praemians praevenit cooperando omne meritum merentis...; de condigno autem dicitur quis mereri, quando meretur de pura iustitia ab aliquo praemiante, quod fuit quando praemians non gratiose coagit cum illo..." John Wyclif, *De Scientia Dei*, fol. 61v^a–v^b, cited by J. A. Robson, *Wyclif and the Oxford Schools* (Cambridge, 1961), footnote 1. Oberman comments on this passage as follows: "Diese ungewöhnliche Definition des meritum de condigno zwingt Wyclif, merita de condigno sämtlich zu verwerfen, da Gott überall gratiose wirksam ist. Alle merita sind Belohnung de pura gratia und darum immer de congruo." H. A. Oberman, "Das tridentinische Rechtfertigungsdekret," p. 258. Cf. Jan Hus, II *Sent.* d.27 q.5 (*Opera omnia*, II, ed. V. Flajšhans, Prague, 1905, 307–8).

[2] "Weyl den nun mer verdienst ist in armut, den in reichtumhern, mer in leyden, den in wirckenn, mehr in weinen, den in lachen, mer in hunger, den in settigung, mer in gemeinschafft des leydens, den in gemeinschafft des trostes, erzeigt die lieb gotes hie grosser zu uns, wen sy uns klag, iammer, und leyden tzuschickt, den wen sy uns suesset." *Lieb gottes* (1518) Kn. 110.

[3] "Solchen leuten geschicht das sie hocher beschweret yrer feind sunde, dan yr eigne pein, sorgen mehr wie sie Christum rechtfertigen, dan sich selb entschuldigen, tzeitlichs leben vorachten, dann wie sie es behalthen, den kumbt der tod in begirde und sterben inn gewin...Im werden alle werck hochvordinstlich..." *Nachfolgung* (1515) Kn. 71.

[4] "...wilt du gerne vil dienen, es ist kein vordienstlicher werck dan umb gottes willen willig sterben, wiltu gote sunder wolgefallen, begere umb seinen willen tzu

more meritorious, than a willing submission to suffering and death for the sake of Jesus Christ. Obedience to Jesus Christ—even though it is the fruit and not the presupposition of grace—is nevertheless costly to the Christian. Grace does not relieve him from the necessity of facing grief and disappointment. Rather it enables him to triumph over it.

VI. CERTITUDE OF SALVATION

The problem of the certitude of salvation was one of the most difficult problems which the medieval theologian faced. The fundamental text from which he processed in discussing this issue was Ecclesiastes 9:1, a text which underscores in its bleakest form the dreadful uncertainty of grace. In the Vulgate translation the Latin words assert that "...nescit homo utrum amore an odio dignus sit." The judgments of God are hidden from the *viator*.[1] No one knows himself to be just apart from special revelation; which is, for all practical purposes, tantamount to saying that no one can be certain that his name is written in the Book of Life until after death.[2] The most one can hope for in this life is a conjectural certainty. While there is ground for hope in this kind of suppositional certitude, there is no room for foolish presumption.

The problem is complicated further by the fact that certitude about the present possession of grace is not the same thing as certitude of election.[3]

---

sterben, als er umb deinen willen begirlich gestorben ist..." *Nachfolgung* (1515) Kn. 86–7.

[1] "Currit in factis humanis tam absconditum iudicium dei ut nemo sciat an amore dei odiove dignus sit." *Libellus* (1517) 142. "Sed quia securus nemo est testante Scriptura, quia 'nemo scit, an amore vel odio dei dignus est,' [Eccles. 9:1] satis ostenditur, quod illi hic iusti dicuntur, qui se tales reputant, quae quidem reputacio non sine omni peccator esse potest j.io.j. [I John 1:8] 'Si dixerimus, quoniam peccatum non habemus, ipsi nos seducimus' etc." *Hiob* (1497–8) 26.205. 40–206.2.

[2] "Nemo novit absque revelationem se esse iustum." *Libellus* (1517) 143. Cf. *Salzburger Predigten* (1523) No. 1, Aumüller, p. 52: "...wiewol wir all darnach achten & all darumb arbaiten damit wir westen ob wir jn das gothleich puech wärn geschriben. Aber es ist ain verlorene arbait. es sol auch nit sein, dann für wen wär uns der glauben & dy hoffnung? so wir des gewis wärn, so wär d'glauben vergebens & dy hoffnung eytel. hoffen & gelauben süllen wir das all, das wir von got erwelt sein durch XPM, unsern herrn. aber dy gewisshait kümbt erst wan sel & leib ist von ainander schaiden."

[3] "Sanguine itaque Cristi renati non sumus amplius terra ista dyabolo tradita comedenda, sed possessores celi sumus, etsi terram inhabitamus. Neque enim hodie imprudenter beatos vocamus, quos videmus iuste ac pie cum spe futurae

Grace can be lost;[1] the justified sinner can in a moment of weakness or temptation fall back into mortal sin.[2] The presumption is, indeed, that he will tumble in this fashion into mortal sin several times before his death. For this reason the sacrament of penance has been instituted as an ever present means of restoration for the fallen. Even the elect will be caught up in the cycle of repeated failure and repeated restoration. The difference between the elect and the reprobate, however, lies in the fact that the elect will die in a state of grace, while the reprobate will not. The elect have a *ius ad celum* based on the decree of God which makes Christ a debtor of salvation to them.[3]

The basic uncertainty of grace was not simply an intellectual problem engaged by the academic theologian in the classroom; it was an existential problem encountered by the pastor in the parish. In his sermons of 1523 Staupitz sketches the pastoral dimensions of the problem of certitude. Men may know that they are sinners and yet find no way to move from this knowledge to the comfort which the gospel affords. The contemplation of the divine majesty strikes them

---

immortalitatis hanc vitam ducere sine crimine vastante conscienciam, facile impetrantes peccatis huius infirmitatis divinam misericordiam, qui licet de suo perseverancie praemio certi sint, de ipsa tamen perseverancia sua reperiuntur incerti." *Hiob* (1497–8) 26.208.8–14.

[1] "Neque enim hominis gracia sicut angeli in primo actu stabiliri meruit. Sed manet in hac vita libertas cum promptitudine ad casum." *Hiob* (1497–8) 12.107. 12–14. Cf. *Hiob* (1497–8) 12.108.4–12; 12.115.3–9.

[2] Staupitz rejects the position of those who maintain *caritas* cannot be lost. "Fuerunt, qui dicerent caritatem et ideo graciam, non posse amitti, quos magister xxxj. dis. iij. sen. reprobat. Non enim potest dici opinio, sed nec racionabilis sentencia, immo error et insania pocius est dicenda, quia repugnat sacrae scripturae [cites I Cor. 10:12, Rev. 2:4; and the examples of Saul, I Kings 9:2, and David, I Kings 13:14], repugnat experimento nostrae fidei [example of baptized infants who become sinners], repugnat nihilominus recta racioni... Recta eciam racio dictat, quod caritas viae a libertate arbitrii vertibilitatem non tollit ad malum, sicut nec cupiditas tollit habilitatem ad bonum. Simul ergo stant vertibilitas et caritas. Sed ubi est vertibilitas, ibi potest esse culpa, et culpa non potest, ibi gracia potest abesse." *Hiob* (1497–8) 12.107.14ff.

[3] In the *Libellus* (1517) Staupitz no longer speaks of a *praemium perseverantie* or of the amissability of *caritas*. Kolde notes that the "...Frage nach dem Beharren des Gerechtfertigten löst Staupitz sehr einfach, ohne ein donum perseverantiae anzunehmen." Kolde, *Augustiner-Congregation*, p. 290. As was already noted in an earlier chapter, Staupitz has restricted the focus of his discussion in such a way as to make the treatment of this subject unnecessary. He is no longer concerned to describe the experience of all *viatores*, elect and reprobate alike. He begins, rather, with the eternal decree of election and explains how that decree is brought to fruition in the experience of the elect. Thus in the later writings he can use *iustus* or, even more surprisingly, *Christglaubiger* as a synonym for *electus*. Cf. *Glauben* (1525) Kn. 126 with *Libellus* (1517) 86, 90, 93 and *Lieb gottes* (1518) Kn. 111.

with fear and shame.[1] No sooner do they confess their sins to a priest than they fall once again into sin. Finally, the idea insinuates itself into their minds that they have an ungracious God.[2] A truly gracious God would take their bent toward sinning away from them. Therefore they are overcome with despair.

The picture which Staupitz paints, while strikingly similar to the portrait of Luther prior to his discovery of the Reformation doctrine of certitude, is—it must be supposed—not untypical, especially in the monastic circles in which Staupitz preached. The conscientious struggle for perfection, beset as it is on every hand by uncertainty, can easilt lead the sensitive soul into despair. Is it possible for the Christian prior to his death to have any certitude at all concerning his election? Staupitz believed that it is.

There is, of course, the objective certitude that none of the elect will die in mortal sin.[3] The ground of this confidence is not based on the stability of the free will of the sinner, who still has the possibility, even when indwelt by the Holy Spirit, of falling back into the very sin out of which he has been redeemed. It is based rather on the unswerving faithfulness of God to His own purposes for the elect.[4] God disciplines His chosen people when they sin and brings them

---

[1] "So ist auch ain armer man, ain ellender sünder, der voll geswer ist, wo er sich hin wendt. So ist er kranck und unrain, und stinckt sych selber an wie ain as. Er er kent sych selb fur ain sünder, ja fur ain solichn sünder, das er erzytart, wan er nur gedenckt an got. Er fürcht und schambtt sych vor got und allen heiligen. Seinen engst darf er nit anriiessen. Zu den lieben heilig darf er sich nicht wenden, dan er stynckt und ist innen und aussen voller geswer und kranck. Er kan nit gedencken das er den himel pesygen sol. Sein hertz ist vol trübsals und angsten. So er an dy gotleich Mayestat gedenckt also ist er gantz erschrocken und forchtsam und ligt vor des reichen thür unnd pegert nur dy prosame dy von dem tisch vallen. Aber man gibt jm nur dy rynten." Hs: b II 11, St. Peter (1523), Sermo 9, fol. 75ᵇ–76ᵇ.

[2] "Nun möchstu sagen, Ja lieber gott es ist alles verlorn, So ich schon peichtt, So pin ich noch vol sünten, Ich bin rächig, hassig, fleyschleich, und hab all pös zuenaigung zum sünten und kans nit recht peichten, darumb hab ich ain ungnädigen got, Ach nayn meine liebe kindt got hat dir wol versprochenn. Er wöl dy sunt von dir nemen, er hat aber nit gesagt, das er den süntsack wöl von dir nemen, zu den sünten, dw hörst nit auf pis das sel und leib von einander schaiden." *Salzburger Predigten*, No. 24, Kolde, pp. 454–5.

[3] "Modo stante predestinatione, consequens est, peccatum predestinati esse temporale et non perpetuum." *Libellus* (1517) 90.

[4] "Mein zusag wil ich halten, sie halten jr pflicht oder haltens nicht. Ich wil warhafft beleyben, sie besteen oder besteen nicht, dann was ein mal auss Got geboren ist, wirdt weder sünden noch sünden mögen zum todt, jr sündt werden allzeyt lesslich, allzeyt vergeblich, allzeyt abtilglich sein..." *Glauben* (1525) Kn. 127.

back into a state of grace.[1] Step follows step in the *ordo salutis*, not by a *necessitas consequentis*, the absolute necessity which governs the natural processes of creation, but by a *necessitas consequentie*, the conditional necessity which is grounded in the commitment of God to His own decrees.[2] Staupitz affirms that salvation is owed to the elect, not because they have merited it, but in order to fulfil the saving intention of God directed toward them in predestination.[3]

This objective knowledge about the faithfulness of God toward the elect does not comfort the *viator* unless he has some reason to believe that he himself is numbered among this company. If absolute certainty is not, barring an act of special revelation, accessible to the Christian in this life—and it is not—some form of conjectural certitude is. Furthermore, because Staupitz increasingly emphasizes the close link between justification and predestination, he draws almost no distinction between *Rechtfertigungsgewissheit* and *Heilsgewissheit*,[4] though it is clear from the sermons on Job that he does believe in the amissability of grace. There are for Staupitz five grounds on which the suppositional certitude of the *viator* is based.

1. There is, first of all, the nature of God as a merciful Father which the Christian must consider when he contemplates his own salvation. God is no more likely to abandon the Christian in moments of stress and temptation than an earthly father is likely to abandon his own child.[5] Of course, the quality of the Christian's faith is always suspect to doubt; of course, his sins are heinous and frightening.[6] But it is

---

[1] "Wiewol auch der Christglaubige in sünde felt, die götlichen gebot ubertrit, und villeicht mermals, als der nit glaubt, so hat doch der in Christum glaubt diesen vortayl, das jm sein sündt nit zu ewigern verdamnuss zu gemessen werden, das Got darumb nicht von jm ziehen wil sein barmhertzigkait, sunder sein sündt mit veterlicher straff hyn nemen." *Glauben* (1525) Kn. 126.

[2] "Cui data est illa gratia prima cetere sequentur singule necessitate consequentie, et Christus factus est ei debitor salutis. *Libellus* (1517) 22.

[3] "Sicut enim consequens est omnes predestinatos debito vocari, ita vocati debent iustificari, non quidem ex nature sed gratie, debito." *Libellus* (1517) 26: "Quapropter electis non modo vocatio, verum et iustificatio debetur." *Libellus* (1517) 33. Cf. *Lieb gottes* (1518) Kn. 111.

[4] That is, between the certitude that one is in a state of grace and the certitude that one is elect.

[5] "Ist moglich, sprecht got, das eyn vatter sein kyndt hasse, ader das eyne mutter yres seuglings, den sie in yrem leybe getragen, vorgesse, Unnd ab es die selbygen vorgessen mochten, dennoch werde ich dein nicht vorgessen, Nyme war, in meinen handten hab ich dich angeschriben..." *Nachfolgung* (1515) Kn. 67–8.

[6] "Ach gelaubt & vertraut, meine kint. Ja sagstu, ich kan aber nit recht gelaubn, wan ich sünt für & für, sagt doch Jacobus: der gelaub an [ohne] dy werch sey todt, darumb furcht ich mich vor jm. Ach mein liebs kindt, warumb fürchstu dich

foolish for the Christian to fear that his sins are greater than God's mercy.[1] The Christian's confidence is grounded, not in the quality of his own achievement, not in the depth of his own love for God, but rather in the enduring character of the work of God in him, in the unmeasured depths of the love of God for him.[2] God will be faithful to His own decrees.

2. This love is evidenced concretely for the Christian in the work of Christ crucified. Jesus Christ is, to use a metaphor borrowed from the Apocalypse, the Book of Life in which the name of the Christian is written.[3] The true Christian knows that he is lost in himself.[4] Solely through the meritorious sufferings of Jesus, through the wounds inflicted on the cross, is salvation offered to him.[5] There is no point in directing the gaze forever at the soul with all its wavering inconsistency. Whoever has Christ, whoever believes in Him has all that is necessary for salvation.[6]

3. Nevertheless, it is legitimate to look at oneself when searching for certitude. To some extent at least conclusions drawn on the basis

---

vor jm, nun ist er doch gantz freuntleich." *Salzburger Predigten* (1523), No. 4, Aumüller, p. 121.

[1] "Also wirdet auch ain yder sunder billich nit fur christenlich Sonder ainen thorn gehalten So er die grosse und manigfaltigkait seiner sunden grosser und ubertreffenlicher dann die gots parmherzigkait achten wolt." *Wie der mensch durch ain Vertrewlich gemute* (1517) Kn. 24.

[2] "Demnach grundet sich die hoffnung in keinem weg auf die lieb die wir zu got haben, auff die werck die wir gote thuen, Sonder sy grund sich auf die lieb sie got zu uns hat, auff die werck die got in uns wirckt." *Lieb gottes* (1518) Kn. 101.

[3] "Nun hin für sol das creutz ain ere sein und kain schandt mer. Was predigen wir nun mer dann XPM den gekkreutzygten, er yst das puech des leben. Andachtige sel, erlis dich wol yn diesem puech, wil es dir nit smecken, wirf die plätel her umb, reis auf die wunden, nyt yn pein weis als die juden, sunder jn lieb, das dw her aus wellest ziechen die süessichait der gotthayt." Hs: b V 8, St. Peter (1512), Sermo 12, fol. 58ᵃ.

[4] "das sind dy rechten christen dye des evangelii leben & dye erkennen das sy warlich aus jn selber v'dambt aber jm leyden XPI. ganz saelig & gross sint." *Salzburger Predigten* (1523), No. 1, Aumüller, p. 53.

[5] "Was ist das puech, darein wir sein geschribn? Meine kindt, das ist dy haut IHS. XPI. das ist das edel pergyme, das ist das rot leder das geferbt ist mit dem rosenfarben pluet IHS. XPI; darein wir uns selbs nit mügen schreiben...den das leydn XPI & er selbs ist eben das puech des lebens darein er uns selber mit seinem pluet & mit der hoechsten lieb aufgeschriben, ja gar gemalt hat." *Salzburger Predigten* (1523), No. 1, Aumüller, pp. 51–2.

[6] "Venemum anime est quod eam mortificat, quod ipsam in peccatum trahit. Et a tali veneno liber est qui perfecte in Christum credit, de cuius manu nemo rapere potest. Siquidem Christianus nec gratia, nec doctrina eget, habet enim Christum, ergo quicquid saluti sue necessarium est." *Libellus* (1517) 237.

of *parallelismus practicus* are possible.[1] A man who is indwelt by God is, needless to say, a changed man. The work of grace within him has resulted in a transformation of his character. When a Christian discovers such a transformation in his own personality, he is justified in assuming that he is indwelt by the Spirit. Since the possession of grace is more a sign of election for Staupitz than it is, say, for Augustine, who sharply separates predestination from the gift of perseverance, the Christian may regard the present possession of grace as a sign that he is elect. He may argue from effect to cause, from a heart that seeks the glory of God alone to the work of grace which liberated that heart.[2]

The contemplation of oneself, however, generally has a more negative function in the quest for certitude.[3] The sinner realizes, when examining himself, that he cannot hope to base his salvation on his own works or merits or even on his own confession to a priest.[4] The ground for his salvation and therefore the ground for his confidence lies outside himself in the work of another. Indeed, Staupitz identifies this salutary self-knowledge with the witness of the Spirit, spoken of by St. Paul in Romans 8:16.[5] Whoever knows the truth about himself and has abandoned all forms of self-justifying piety has taken an important step toward the acquisition of subjective certitude.

4. The sacraments form a fourth ground on which the subjective

---

[1] "Aus den allen volgt, das uns unsere werck nicht den trost geben, das wir durch sy die hoffnung uberkommen, sy geben aber ein trostlich vermuten das die hoffnung in uns sey, Gleicher weis wy ein igliche frucht yrn baum zeigt, davon sy herkommen ist." *Lieb gottes* (1518) Kn. 101.

[2] "Wen sich aber der mensch sein selbst und aller creaturen ledig findt, seins lebens, seins verdienens, seines heils vergist, unnd nichtz den gottes ere suecht, des willen ym eynig gefallen lest, es reich auch tzu seinem frummen oder schaden, sich selbst teglich verdambt, und uber nyemandt als uber sich urteylt, So ist on allen tzweyfel got in ym, und er stecket voller got." *Lieb gottes* (1518) Kn. 101.

[3] "Aber ich wil euch aines lernen dapey jr mügt wissen, das jr in das lebntig puech seyt geschriben & ist eben das: merckt auf, so jr in ewr selbserkantnus geslagen werd & warlich befint das jr nichtz seyt, nichtz habt, nichtz künt, dann sünten & zum teufel gen, auch so jr schon gern etwas guetz tät redt oder gedacht, so seit jr so hert das yr es nit mügt tan & schwer so jr nit fast darnach fecht." *Salzburger Predigten* (1523), No. 1, Aumüller, p. 52.

[4] "Der mensch sol auch In sein rechten peichten gantz kain vertrawen stellen Sonder allain In di volkomenhait der gnaden und parmherzigkait gottes, dodurch der sunder allain gerechtvertigt werden mag..." *Etlich Nutzlich leren* (1517) Kn. 40.

[5] "Wan yre geist haben gezeugnus vom heiligenn geist, das sy kind gotes sein, gotes erben, miterben unsers herren Jesu Christi, wer das getzeugnus hat, der kent seine werck nit sein, sonder des heiligen geist sein, dem zu sunden unmuglichen ist, und darumb nymbt er sich gantz der natur, unnd bekent sich der gnadenn kindt." *Lieb gottes* (1518) Kn. 107.

certitude of the viator may be based. It was a settled question in
medieval theology since the Fourth Lateran Council in 1215 that the
sacraments confer grace *ex opere operato*. The exterior rite, when
performed by an administrant who has the proper intention and
received by a candidate who interposes no obstacle to the reception
of the grace conveyed by the rite, is thoroughly efficacious. Grace is
objectively offered through the sacrament on the basis of the performance of the rite. The efficacy of the sacrament is not qualified by
the interior disposition of either the priest or the lay communicant.
It is, in other words, objectively certain that baptism confers grace on
the baptized.

It is therefore possible for the *viator* to take comfort from the
knowledge that baptism, apart from any merit on his own part, has
unfailingly conferred grace on him.[1] And not only baptism! Each of
the six sacraments offered to the layman—baptism, confirmation,
eucharist, penance, marriage and extreme unction—provide some new
grace to assist him on his way to the heavenly Jerusalem.[2] None of the
sacraments depends on the mutable free will of man for its validity.
There is no reason for the *viator* to doubt that he receives grace by
participating in one or all of the sacraments, or to question the ade-
quacy of the divine resources to see him on his journey. That he can
fail and die in mortal sin is undisputed; that he need not is the new
and exciting possibility offered to him in the sacraments.

5. The final ground for subjective certitude is found in temptation.
Staupitz cannot imagine a life of grace unassailed by temptation. In-

---

[1] "aber nun in Zeit der genaden ist uns ain lindes liepleichs, sues warzaichn
aufgelegt. Ey, sagt main frumer Jesus, nym nur ain rain wässerl & lass uber dich
laufn, hab ich doch schon dy Wort daryne gelernt: Ich tauf dich jm nach [namen?]
des vaters & des sun & des heilign geist: so pis gewis das ich dy sel auch schon
gewaschn hab, das pluet ist nun schon vergossen, es ist schon für, dy warheit hat
dy figur schon erfült. Glaub nur & wirt tauft, so pist du ganz mein aigntum."
Salzburger Predigten (1523) No. 4, Aumüller, pp. 119–20.

[2] "Et quamvis non possit homo sua inquisitione certitudinem habere an dei
odio amoreve dignus sit, potest tamen per infallibilia signa ad hoc instituta certam
facere spem et eiicere desperationem, quae maxima tribulatio anime est, quae
inititur questioni de sui electioni. [Tribulationes cordis removet spes] per baptismum. Angustias temptationum fugat spe maioris gratie per confirmationem.
Famem eterni cibi spes removet per sacram Eukaristiam. Nuda per defectum iusticie spes repellit per veram absolutionem. In periculum ex defectu meriti spes
tollit per hostiam oblatam. Persecutionem carnis spes subprimit per sanctum ma-
trimonium. Gladium passionis et mortis spes lenit per extremam unctionem."
Libellus (1517) 238–9. I am indebted to H. A. Oberman for the conjectured
omission. See *Libellus* (1517) 240.

deed, the sorrow of heart *(dolor cordis)* which is the indispensable
ingredient of contrition is caused by temptation and tribulation.[1] And
without contrition there is no vocation and, consequently, no justification.[2] Therefore, temptation, so far from being proof that one is
irrevocably bound to his sins, is actually positive evidence to the
contrary. Only the *viator* who is in a state of grace or who is being led
into such a state experiences the fierce struggles of temptation. There
is no grace and no disposition for the reception of grace without
temptation. That is a fixed law of the spiritual life.

The certitude which Staupitz describes is by no means absolute.
Like Gabriel Biel, the great nominalist theologian, Staupitz can offer
no more than a conjectural certitude to the *viator*. No one can know
with final certainty that he belongs to the elect company of the redeemed before his death, unless, of course, God specially reveals it to
him. Apostasy is an ever present danger. Not to recognize this fact is
to indulge in foolish presumption. Nevertheless, even though Biel
and Staupitz share a common frame of reference on the question of
certitude, there are significant differences between them within that
common framework.

Biel considers the work of Christ under two aspects: the *opus spei*,
the historical work of Christ as Redeemer, and the *opus iusticie*, the
continuing work of Christ as Judge.[3] He attempts to balance these
two aspects of the work of Christ in order to guard against presumption on the one hand and despair on the other. The road to the heavenly Jerusalem is a middle course between the extremes. Goaded on
alternately by *misericordia* and *iusticia*, the viator treads the path before
him, oscillating between hope and fear.

This theoretical balance, however, is not maintained in fact. From
the viewpoint of the *viator* the work of Christ as Redeemer lies largely
in the past. The present and future are filled with the work of Christ
as Judge. Ever since the Ascension Christ is absorbed in the task of

---

[1] "Cum enim deus quos praedestinavit, vocavit, et quos vocavit, iustificavit,
iustificacio autem per penitenciam in hac miseria fit post eam, quam per baptismum suscepimus. Non est praedestinatus, quem tribulacio nulla tangit, quoniam
non est sine contricione iustificacio, quae dolor est cordis. Ideo apertissime sequitur, quod non est fugienda temptacio, sed cum timore amplectenda in spe trium-
phi." *Hiob* (1497–8) 11.95.5–11.

[2] "Cognoscimus inde satis aperte non esse divinam vocacionem sine omni tribulacione." *Hiob* (1497–8) 11.94.10–11.

[3] Gabriel Biel, *Sermones dominicales de tempore* (Hagenau, 1510) 4 A; *Sermones de
festivitatibus christi* (Hagenau, 1510) 12 E. For a discussion of Biel see H. A.
Oberman, *Harvest*, pp. 217–35.

scrutinizing the *viatores* to see whether they are making use of the
benefits offered to them through the past work of reconciliation. This
means that, quite apart from the avowed intention of Biel to hew a
middle line between extremes, "…the psychological impact of the
future judgment weighs heavier than the psychological impact of the
past."[1] Or, to put the same matter in different words, there is a strong
eschatological emphasis in the theology of Biel. The Christian life is
a life lived in the shadow of the last judgment.

For Staupitz this marked eschatological emphasis is missing. He did
not doubt for a moment the inexorable coming of the last day of
reckoning. But the emphasis in his theology falls not on the second
advent but on the first, not on the work of Christ as Judge but on the
work of Christ as Judged. The past is filled with the work of Christ as
Redeemer and the present with the work of Christ as Sanctifier. The
Christian life was not for him so much a life lived in anticipation of a
coming event as a life lived out of the past and present resources of
Christus crucifixus and *Christus inhabitans*. His gaze is directed for the
most part away from the soul and its fitness to stand the last judgment
—a judgment which the *viator* is impotent to endure apart from his
union to Christ in a spiritual marriage—and toward the finished work
of Christ effected on the cross and made his *possessio* as the bride of
Christ. To use the distinction made by Biel, Staupitz stresses the *opus
spei* and not the *opus iusticie*. Mercy and not justice stands at the center
of his proclamation.

Joined to this differing emphasis on the two aspects of the work of
Christ is a differing estimate of the capabilities of the natural powers
of the soul to prepare a man for final scrutiny by the divine Judge.
Biel is convinced that a *viator* can bring forth an act of love for God
super omnia by the exercise of his own natural powers;[2] Staupitz is
convinced that he cannot.[3] The focus of Biel's doctrine of justification
is the semi-autonomous soul, which, aided only by the *concursus dei
generalis*, is able to merit justifying grace. The focus of Staupitz's
doctrine of justification, on the other hand, is the impotent soul,
which, even assisted by the *praemotio physica*, can do nothing more
than sin and merit damnation. This is to say that the focus of Staupitz's
theology is not the soul at all, but rather the Other who comes to the
aid of the soul and rescues it from its predicament. The conjectural

[1] H. A. Oberman, *Harvest*, p. 228.
[2] Gabriel Biel, II *Sent.* d.27 q.1 a.3 dub.5.
[3] *Lieb gottes* (1518) Kn. 103.

certainty offered by Biel is concerned with the love of the soul for God and is therefore subject to a high degree of change and fluctuation. The conjectural certitude offered by Staupitz is concerned with the love of God for the soul and is therefore anchored in a reality which remains constant. The contrast is not absolute, but it is real and should not be underestimated.

VII. ASSESSMENT

In outlining a doctrine of justification Staupitz rejected both the extremes of antinomianism on the one hand and nominalist theology on the other. On the question of the necessity of merit, the certitude of salvation, and the role of sacramental absolution, Staupitz remained within the framework of medieval Catholic theology. Within this framework, however, he took positions which were often antithetical to those taken by Biel, whose trust in the natural abilities of fallen man ran counter to Staupitz's Augustinian convictions.

Staupitz's opposition to Biel's anthropology is not in itself proof that Staupitz embraced a Thomistic alternative to the nominalist doctrine of justification. Indeed, in his critique of the *habitus* theory, his emphasis on the primacy of uncreated grace and his stress on the doctrine of acceptation, he showed himself to be an ally of Biel against Thomas. He adopted a more radical position than Biel, however, when he rejected the *habitus* theory entirely.

Though Staupitz agreed with Thomas that no merit is possible prior to the infusion of *gratia gratum faciens*, he differed with him when he affirmed that virtue apart from grace is equally impossible. Furthermore, Staupitz's rejection of the *meritum de condigno* as an appropriate description of merits performed in a state of grace and his devotion to Augustine on the question of the relation of virtue and grace not only separates him radically from Biel, but even differentiates him from Thomas. Like Gregory of Rimini, though without conscious dependence upon him, Staupitz sought to preserve the Augustinian heritage in theology against the Pelagian inroads made by Biel. Grace and not nature, mercy and not justice, hope and not fear were the constant themes of his message.

CHAPTER FIVE

CHRISTOLOGY AND MARIOLOGY

I. The Mystery of the Incarnation

The medieval theologian was the heir not only of the rich theological traditions of the Western Church, but also of the subtle Christological theories of the East. The decisions of the councils of Nicea and Chalcedon were no less a part of his patrimony than the *Enchiridion* of St. Augustine or the *Moralia* of Gregory the Great. Nevertheless, while Latin theologians were quick to embrace the orthodox Christological opinions of the East, they were by comparison much slower to understand them. It was only by a process of trial and error, of statement and restatement, that the Western Church was able to absorb the heritage of Chalcedon and make it its own.

At the beginning of the thirteenth century there were three major interpretations of the union of God and man in the incarnation which were current in theological circles in the West. These opinions were summarized by Peter Lombard in the third book of the *Sentences*, distinction six, in which form they were transmitted to the later generations of theologians who used the *Sentences* as a text. Modern commentators, acting in response to a suggestion by Bernhard Barth, generally classify these three interpretations as the *habitus*, the *assumptus* and the subsistence theories.[1]

The *habitus* theory is based on the doctrine of the immutability of God. If God is truly unchangeable, argued the theologians who supported this view, then He could not have changed in any fundamental way in the incarnation. The humanity of Jesus is not something which is essential or substantial at all. Indeed, it is little more than a cloak or mantle in which the divine Logos clothed Himself. Naturally, the

---

[1] Bernhard Barth, O.S.B., "Ein neues Dokument zur Geschichte der frühscholastischen Christologie," *ThQ* 100 (1919) 409–26; 101 (1920) 235–62. Cf. Also Ludwig Ott, "Das Konzil von Chalkedon in der Frühscholastik," in *Das Konzil von Chalkedon: Geschichte und Gegenwart*, Vol. II, *Entscheidung um Chalkedon*, ed. Aloys Grillmeier, S.J., and Heinrich Bacht, S.J. (Würzburg, 1953), pp. 873–922; Ignaz Backes, "Die christologische Problematik der Hochscholastik und ihre Beziehung zu Chalkedon," *Das Konzil von Chalkedon*, II, pp. 923–39.

union which is effected in this way between the divine and the human in the incarnate Lord is at best external. In point of fact, the divine Logos assumed the soul and body of Jesus separately, before they were united and therefore before a human personality had been constituted.[1]

This opinion was rejected by Pope Alexander III in 1177.[2] It thereafter ceased to be a living option for the major theologians of the thirteenth century, who were content for the most part to view the *habitus* theory as a Nestorian aberration. Thomas Aquinas, for example, argued that the *habitus* theory has two principal defects, when viewed from the standpoint of Chalcedonian theology. On the one hand, by comparing the incarnation to the putting on of a garment, the *habitus* theory reduces the hypostatic union to an accidental relationship between divinity and humanity. On the other hand, by stressing the idea that the soul and the body of Jesus were separately assumed by the Logos, it endangers the true humanity of the Son.[3] Either defect, Thomas concluded, is sufficiently serious to warrant categorical rejection of this theory.

The *assumptus* theory proved to be scarcely more acceptable. According to this interpretation it is not human nature or *humanitas* which was assumed by the Logos in the incarnation, but rather a complete human being *(homo)*. The advocates of this position hoped that, by arguing in this way, they could avoid the error of the defenders of the *habitus* theory, who had asserted that the soul and body of Jesus were separately assumed and who had thereby fallen under papal condemnation. To some extent at least, their efforts were rewarded. For a time after the discrediting of the *habitus* theory, the *assumptus* theory gained in popularity as a basis for Christological discussion. But its inner deficiencies as an explanation of the mystery of the incarnation did not remain unnoticed.

The chief opponent of the *assumptus* theory in the thirteenth century was Thomas Aquinas.[4] Thomas maintained that the *assumptus* theory, if taken seriously, forces one to assert that the two natures of Christ

---

[1] Thomas Aquinas, *Compendium Theologiae*, 209.

[2] "Cum Christus perfectus Deus perfectus sit homo, mirum est, qua temeritate quisquam audet dicere, quod 'Christus non sit aliquid secundum quod homo.'" *Denz.*[31] 393.

[3] Thomas Aquinas, *Compendium Theologiae*, 209.

[4] "Haec positio (duas hypostases vel due supposita esse in una persona christi) de necessitate in errorem Nestorii dilabitur." Thomas Aquinas, IV *Summa contra Gentiles* 38; cf. *Summa Theologiae* III q.2 a.6.

are carried by two separate and distinct hypostases or *supposita*. Thomas did not believe that one could save the intention of the Chalcedonian formula by finding the unity of the divine and human in Jesus Christ in His *persona* rather than in His *suppositum*. It is impossible, when speaking of rational creatures, to distinguish between *suppositum* and *persona*, since the two terms are virtually identical. The *suppositum* of a human being is his *persona*. Thus the formula *duo supposita in una persona* is in reality equivalent to an assertion of *duae personae in Christo*. The *assumptus* theory is, to put the matter bluntly, no less Nestorian than the *habitus* theory which it attempts to supercede. That two natures were united in Christ is affirmed; that two persons were so united is resoundingly denied.

The interpretation of the incarnation which became standard for orthodox theology in the West was the subsistence theory. The advocates of this theory maintained that the proper interpretation of Chalcedon involves a rejection of the errors of the other two theories. Against the defenders of the *habitus* theory, the supporters of the subsistence theory asserted that the humanity assumed by the divine Logos was perfect—i.e., that it consisted of a rational soul and of human flesh. Against the proponents of the *assumptus* theory they argued that the two natures of Christ were borne by only one carrier *(suppositum)*. It was not, in other words, a complete human being who was taken up by the Second Person of the Trinity in the incarnation, but rather human nature—not *homo* but *humanitas*. Thomas Aquinas summarized the viewpoint of this school of interpretation when he asserted that the mystery of the incarnation is the mystery of *una persona subsistens in pluribus naturis*.[1]

Staupitz's comments on the nature of the incarnation are scattered and unsystematic. Yet there is enough evidence in his writings to indicate that his Christological views were orthodox and fitted generally within the framework of the subsistence theory. The Son as the divine Second Person of the Trinity is the source of His own being and of all created being.[2] He is eternal and therefore did not have, as

---

[1] Thomas Aquinas, IV *Summa contra Gentiles* 39.

[2] "Jhesus antburt, ych pins. Ich pin alain das wesen von jm selbs hat und allen andern dingen wesen gibt." Hs: b V 8, St. Peter (1512), Sermo 4, fol. 17ᵇ. We have already noted that Christology is dealt with in many contexts in the writings of Staupitz and qualifies doctrines such as creation, predestination and justification. We do not intend in this chapter to repeat what we have already said in other chapters. We are concerned here with Christology in its narrower, rather

the Arians had wrongly argued, a beginning in time. The relation between the Father and the Son is not a relationship of creation but of generation. The eternal Logos was begotten by the Father; and from the Father and the Son the Holy Spirit proceeds.[1]

The assumption of human nature by the divine Logos was a voluntary act, which brought the impassible God within the realm of weakness and suffering.[2] The human nature which was assumed consisted both of a human soul and of human flesh. To be sure, the flesh which was assumed was sinless. That is not to say that Staupitz places the locus of sin in matter as the Manicheans had done. The locus of sin is, as we have already seen, in the will. But the humanity which was assumed was unfallen humanity. Therefore Staupitz feels it necessary to assert that the incarnation was not *in carne peccati* but rather *in similitudinem carnis peccati*.[3] The humanity assumed by the Logos was real humanity, but it had not fallen under the power and dominion of sinful concupiscence.

The hypostatic union is not a union of two hypostases or *supposita*, as the advocates of the *assumptus* theory had argued. On the contrary, there is only one *suppositum* or carrier in the man Jesus Christ. But in this one *suppositum* two natures are united.[4] Staupitz joins with Aquinas in rejecting the Nestorian heresies of the twelfth century. *Duae naturae in uno supposito* is the formula to which he subscribes.

The doctrine of the hypostatic union forms the basis for the doctrine of the communication of attributes *(communicatio idiomatum)*. According to Thomas Aquinas, whose teaching on this point represents a broad medieval consensus, it is possible to attribute to the concrete person, Jesus Christ, qualities which, properly speaking, belong only to one nature or the other. One cannot say, however, that the divine nature has the qualities of the human or that the human nature has the qualities of the divine. It is possible, in other words,

---

than in its broader context. Thus we have limited discussion in this chapter to the work of Christ *extra nos* and *pro nobis*.

[1] "...ja ich sag also das der himelisch vater seinen aingepornen sun, das ewig wort, in ain solichen hertzn gepirt & der vater & der sun lassen von jn aus den heilign geist." *Salzburger Predigten* (1523) No. 3, Aumüller, p. 114.

[2] "Habemus ergo ex humana infirmitate huiusmodi motus animi, non autem ita dominus Jhesus, cuius et infirmitas fuit es potestate, ita ut, cum voluit, suscepit animo humano, ut, cum volu't, factus est homo." *Hiob* (1497–8) 33.251.32–4.

[3] "Immediate superius intellexisti peccata Christiani in Christum transponi et Christi fieri qui venit non in carne peccati sed in similitudinem carnis peccati." *Libellus* (1517) 78.

[4] "...scientes quod unum suppositum est deus et homo." *Libellus* 44.

to affirm that the Son of God suffered, but not that the divine nature suffered. The divine and human natures are not to be commingled or confused. Nevertheless, their unity in the person, Jesus Christ, makes an attribution of the qualities of both natures to the common carrier possible. What is forbidden to the theologian *in abstracto* is permitted *in concreto*.[1]

It is in line with this counsel that Staupitz attributes to the incarnate Lord qualities which belong clearly to one nature or the other. He can speak, therefore, at great length of the sufferings of Jesus Christ and of the temptations and hardships to which the incarnate Word was exposed, without compromising belief in His deity.[2] By the same token, he can predicate qualities to the historical person, Jesus of Nazareth, which clearly belong to deity.[3] The union of two natures in one *suppositum* makes such a mutual predication of attributes possible—or perhaps better said, inescapable.

Nevertheless, it is not the how of the incarnation, but rather its meaning and significance which claims Staupitz's principal attention. Why has the eternal Logos, the divine Second Person of the Trinity, joined Himself to human nature and become incarnate? What purpose is served by this amazing condescension of God? What mysterious intention motivated it?

For Staupitz the answer to these questions is clear and unambiguous. The Son of God has become man in order to rescue mankind out of the frightful predicament into which sin has plunged it.[4] The force which motivated God to take this radical step is nothing other than His own inexplicable and unfathomable mercy.[5] Nothing forced Him

---

[1] Thomas Aquinas, *Summa Theologiae* III q.16 a.5.

[2] See especially the section below on the atonement. Staupitz's lenten sermons are particularly rich in descriptive detail concerning the sufferings of Jesus Christ.

[3] See p. 134, footnote 2 above as an example of this.

[4] "Ach, mein gott sey dir lob und danck, das dw mir zu hilf pist kömen, dann Jhesus ist uns geparn, Jhesus hatt uns gelytten, Jhesus ist uns gestorben, Jhesus ist uns erstanden..." *Salzburger Predigten*, No. 24, Kolde, p. 454. This passage is vaguely reminiscent of Luther's Christmas hymn of 1524: "Gelobet seiest du, Jesu Christ, dass du Mensch geboren bist... Er ist auf Erden kommen arm, dass er unser sich erbarm..." Staupitz is clearly opposed to the thesis of Duns Scotus that the incarnation would have taken place even if man had not sinned; i.e., that Christ had been chosen by God to acquire glory by becoming a man and living a life of obedience to the Father as a *viator*, wholly apart from all consideration of the fall of Adam. Cf. Scotus, *Ox*. III d.1 q.3 n.3.

[5] "Als der mensch jn der unschuld staint jm paradeis, das wär geschehen aus lieb. Aber das ist dy übersteigung der lieb mit ungemessner lieb, das got nach dem val den sterbleichen menschen an genomen hat, und hat gelitten, gestarben, be-

to do it—not even the lamentable plight of fallen man. The terms of logical or dialectical necessity cannot be superimposed upon this decision. It was a free and uncoerced act on the part of One who is subject to no necessity, save, of course, the necessity of the law of non-contradiction. The mystery of the incarnation consists for Staupitz, not so much in the union of two natures within one hypostasis—though that is certainly remarkable—as in the spontaneous conde-scension of divine mercy in its encounter with human need.[1]

II. TEACHER AND EXAMPLE

Staupitz's reflections on the work of Christ *extra nos* focus especially on two aspects of that work; namely, on His function as a Teacher who enlightens men about the divine will and as a Mediator who restores men to harmony with it. Staupitz's understanding of the work of Christ is not, of course, limited to these two functions. The activity of Christ as a divine Judge who condemns the evil deeds of men is recognized by Staupitz, though it is not emphasized. But while the manifold activity of Jesus Christ cannot be summarized completely under His work as Teacher and as Mediator, these roles nevertheless provide the two principal foci upon which Staupitz concentrates his attention.

The relation to Jesus Christ to the will of God exemplified in the Law is threefold. First of all, He is the Legislator, *der ewig gesetz geber*, who by virtue of His status within the divine Trinity had given the Torah to Israel.[2] Indeed, as Staupitz ironically noted, the very com-

---

graben, abgefarn zunn hellen, und erstanden wolten annemen als warn got und menschen." Hs: 23 E 16, Nonnberg, fol. 58a-b. "Got ist mensch warden aus un-gemessner lieb. Nit allain aus lieb, sunder aus übersteigung der lieb. Darumb, das wir jm veraint wurden durch dy vermächlung und den kus der lieb." Hs: 23 E 16, Nonnberg, fol. 56b.

[1] "Admirantur Theologi unionem ypostaticam divine nature cum humana, im-mortalitatis cum morte, impassibilitatis cum dolore; ego admiror coniunctionem summe misericordie cum summa miseria. Admiror, inquam, et gratias ago quia inde venit salus peccatori; inde processit gloria maxima salvatoris. Inde deus suavis nobis factus est; inde peccator deo acceptus. Gratias igitur habeo et miseri-cordias domini in eternum cantabo." *Libellus* (1517) 64.

[2] "Pistus, mein herr, der ewig gesetz geber, der yst dem gesetz nit untertänig. Jst von den menschen verklagt warden ein precher des gesetzt. Merck, der mensch, der sich treulich fleist des willen gotz, yst nit müglich, das er ain gesetzt ubertreter sey, die weil das hertz zu got gerict yst, yst nit müglich den willen und pot gotz übertret, dar umb vil mer der mensch, der das gesetz selber geben hat, kan das nyt übertreten...mit dem götlichen willen, ja mit der gothait also veraint, der kan nit

mandments under which Jesus was falsely arraigned before the Sanhedrin were commandments of which He Himself was the divine Author. The will of God is, in the profoundest sense imaginable, identical with the will of Jesus Christ.

Jesus is not only the divine Law-giver; He is the Interpreter of the Law as well. He is, to use a phrase which Staupitz employed, the *magister veritatis*.[1] All that God commanded Him to speak, He taught His disciples. He was the promised Messiah to whom God had entrusted His message and who in obedience to that commission transmitted the message to others.[2] The Church, at least in part, received its understanding of the will of God *ab ore Christi*.

The last relationship of Jesus to the will of God is the most important relationship of all, the relationship of One who by all His words and deeds perfectly fulfilled it.[3] In spite of the fact that Jesus Christ was exposed to the greatest temptations ever endured by any man, He remained faithful to the will of His Father.[4] All His life long He conducted Himself as an obedient Son in His Father's house, voluntarily choosing and joyfully performing the obligations which His Father laid upon Him.

There are three results of this steadfast obedience of the Son to the will of the Father. In the first place, Jesus became by His obedience a mirror of true humanity.[3] All that God intended man to be when He created him, all that man failed to be when he apostasized from the will of God through His own disobedience, is perfectly realized in the man, Christ Jesus. He is the *exemplum vivendi*, the living *Vorbild* to

---

noch mag noch sünten noch das gesetz übertreten." Hs: b V 8, St. Peter (1512), Sermo 8, fol. 35ª. In contrast to Staupitz, Luther denied that Jesus Christ was a Legislator: "Christus autem definitive non est Legislator, sed Propitiator et Salvator." *WA* 40 I.232.29–30.

[1] "Christus, quem pater dedit nobis magistrum veritatis et vivendi exemplum, cum convivium ageret, gratias egit, discrete distribuit, eternae retribucionis expectacionem insinuavit." *Hiob* (1497–8) 9.63.37–40.

[2] "Sie haben Christum den versprochen Messiam, in welchen Got sein wort gesetzt hat, der jn sagt alles, das jm Got gebotten hat..." *Glauben* (1525) Kn. 124–5.

[3] "Faceamus interim de aliis et videamus an possit de peccato suo convinci, qui natura impeccabilis est." *Libellus* (1517) 74.

[4] "Dan das ist nicht moglich, das einem sterbenden menschen ein anfechtigung komme, die nicht in Christus sterben uberwunden, des anfechtigung uff erden die allergrosten, wie auch aller sein leiden das groste gewesen..." *Nachfolgung* (1515) Kn. 63.

[5] "...des haben wir an cristo unserm erloser In seiner arbeit, mueseligkait und widerwertigkait, die er weil uff erdrich gangen ist gehabt hat, ainen offenwarn spigel." *Wie ein mensch ainen gegrundten ordenlichen fursatz* (1517) Kn. 21.

whose discipleship the baptized Christian in a state of grace is called.[1] It is not merely the will of God codified in the law of Moses—or even in the words of Jesus—which the Christian is summoned to obey. Rather it is the life of Christ which is the Christian's chief instruction; it is His incarnate Person which is the *regula et mensura fratrum*.[2]

Secondly, through His obedience the mercy and love of God are revealed in all their fullness. The proper knowledge of God has, so far as Staupitz is concerned, a Christological center.[3] That is not to say that all knowledge of God in the sense of information about Him is referred to a Christological starting point. But proper knowledge —i.e., the knowledge which springs from faith, is motivated by love, and issues in praise—is impossible *extra Christum*. The reasons for this are twofold.

First of all, the objective possibility of such knowledge depends upon divine revelation.[4] Relying heavily on quotations from the Gospel of John, Staupitz argues that the revelation of the Father takes place through the Son, all of whose works reflect His deity and whose sufferings reveal love alone.[5] Whoever wishes to know the mercy of God in its sublimity must contemplate that mercy as revealed both in the active and passive obedience of Christ.[6] The search for the objective revelation of the nature of God leads through the sufferings of

---

[1] See above, p. 138, footnote 1.

[2] "Et in primis, si attendimus vitam Christi, quae nostra est instruccio, si apostolorum et aliorum sanctorum exempla cogitamus, perspicuum esse debebit apud Christianum id, quod dicimus." *Hiob* (1497–8) 19.158.29–31. "Christus filius dei vivus est primus in multis fratribus, ergo est regula et mensura fratrum." *Hiob* (1497–8) 11.91.32–3.

[3] "Ex ante dictis satis, ut estimo, apparuit deum absque notitia et delectione sui laudari non posse, nec digne laudari absque certissima notitia, quam, sine Christi fide, nemo consequit." *Libellus* (1517) 14. "Ex his omnibus consequens est deum, pro sua debita laude, non esse cognitum, ignoto Christo." *Libellus* (1517) 13.

[4] "Quod enim Christus filius dei creditur, cognoscitur et colitur non revelatione carnis et sanquinis sed revelatione celestis Patris venit, cui credentes iam spe salvi facti." *Libellus* (1517) 9.

[5] "Cum autem nemo novit patrem nisi filius et cui revelare voluerit filius, non potest rite laudare deum qui non Christum verum dei filium credit, et confitetur. Quem qui videt, is patrem videt quia pater in filio et filius in patre est. Videt, inquam, fide nunc, demum spe, sicuti et ipse visus est." *Libellus* (1517) 8. Cf. Matt. 11: 27; John 14 :9; John 5 :19; 10 :38; 14:10; 14:11; 17 :21. "Recht was ist anders jn dem pitern leydn dan klare lieb." *Salzburger Predigten* (1523) No. 5, Aumüller, p. 125. "Contemplemur ergo opera que facit, que testimonium perhibent quod ipse vere sit deus, non ista precise que miracula appellamus, sed universa que facit." *Libellus* (1517) 95.

[6] "Presertim quia sublimitas misericordie extra Christum nec visa est nec videri potuit." *Libellus* (1517) 13.

Christ.[1] In this man alone the dimensions of divine *Barmherzigkeit* are first clearly set forth. He who sees the Son, sees the Father. That is the basis on which Staupitz builds.

No less important than the objective possibility of such knowledge is its subjective ground. The experiential knowledge of God depends on the work of grace begun in baptism and continued in the other sacraments. And this interior work of grace rests in turn on the external work of reconciliation brought to fruition by the incarnate Lord Jesus Christ. The knowledge of God, the love of God, the praise of God are all dependent upon an interior renewal, which is unthinkable apart from Jesus Christ. The Spirit who renews man is, as Staupitz has already pointed out, the Spirit of the Son. All that God has to give to man is given in Christ, through Him and for His sake.[2]

III. MEDIATOR

The third result of the obedience of Christ is that it issues in the atonement. Staupitz did not himself work out a carefully reasoned or closely argued theory of the atonement. Yet motifs from all three of the major interpretations of the meaning of the atonement—the Patristic, the Anselmian and the Abelardian—can be found in his discussion of the problem.

The weakest of the three motifs—and by far the least significant for Staupitz's theology—is the *Patristic* or *Christus Victor* motif, the theme of the triumph of God over the enemies (namely, sin, death and devil)

---

[1] "...war aus kümbt, als ich warlich glaub, das der mensch, der got warlich suecht, nymmermer kain rechtz traurygs hertz hab. Tring dich durch das leiden, far ein auf dem wasser des mitleiden, far ein jn das bekümert gemüet, jn das hertz gotz, tring hin ein durch den durchmarterten, durchwunten und durchlöcherten leid und durch die tugentsam sel unaussprechlicher geduld und gelassenhait und hör nit auf pis dw kümbst jn die aller süessist gothait..." Hs: b V 8, St. Peter (1512), Sermo 6, fol. 28[a-b].

[2] "Der Götliche segen ist zugesagt und in Christo gewiss gemacht und volzogen..." *Glauben* (1525) Kn. 123. "Darumb zu empfahen gottes gaben, wie die namen haben, ist der glaub in Christum nötig, darinnen du vergwisst bist aller zusagung Gottes, glaub das Christus der sun gottes sey und zweyffel in nichte, in jm, durch jn, umb seinen willen geschech dir alles guts. Glaub in jn, vertraw in jn, ist er doch das wort Gottes, ist er doch die warhait, müst er doch sich selbs lassen, solt er dich verlassen, ja sein auch verlangenen, wo er dir die versprechung seines vaters nit wurde halten." *Glauben* (1525) Kn. 122. As we have already noted on page 117, footnote 4. Staupitz teaches that God is faithful not only to His decrees (i.e., His eternal decision concerning the elect) but also to His promises (i.e., the revelation of His will and purposes to the elect).

which oppress man and hold him in bondage. The *Überwindung* or victory celebrated by Staupitz is the victory over the enemies of man —sin, death, hell and suffering.[1] The death of Christ was, as we have already noted in an earlier chapter, the death of death.[2] By submitting to the power of the enemies of man, Jesus triumphed over them and broke their bondage for the elect.

Far more significant for Staupitz is the Abelardian motif, the notion that the love of God demonstrated in the cross of Christ can awaken an answering response of love on the part of the sinner. This theme occurs again and again in Staupitz's writings. The fire of divine love centered in the cross kindles an anwering flame of love in the heart of the believer.[3] Or, to change the metaphor, the fountain of divine *Barmherzigkeit* releases a stream of grace which flows through the sufferings of Christ and into the human heart.[4] Divine initiative and

---

[1] "Misericordia assentit veritati et offert modum quo stante veritate nihilominus salus peccatoris sit possibilis; quando, scilicet, mors peccatoris solvitur per mortem innocentis, mors hominis per mortem dei [Note Staupitz's use of the *communicatio idiomatum*], ignis inferni per ignem celi, passio hominis per passionem dei omnipotentis." *Libellus* (1517) 102. For Staupitz, however, who differs from the Fathers, the victory over the enemies of man took place on Good Friday rather than on Easter—i.e., through the cross rather than through the resurrection. Staupitz evidences very little interest in the resurrection, ascension or third advent. For Staupitz the period between the resurrection and the third advent is filled with the work of *Christus inhabitans* or the *Geist Christi* in the Church here on earth. He emphasizes the role of Christ as a present Sanctifier rather than as an ascended Intercessor. The work of intercession seems to be reserved principally for Mary, though Staupitz never separates mercy from Jesus Christ.

[2] "...in seinem sterben stirbt der todt, dann do ist der tod vorschlickt ader vorschwunden in der uberwindung, recht do ist der todt gestorben, do das leben am holtze starb." *Nachfolgung* (1515) Kn. 58.

[3] "Wen aber got denn fels ins hertz des ausserwelten schlecht, so gibt er feur, als den wirdt die todte kolen lebendig, der schwartz zundter goldtfarbe, unnd der kalt brant leuchtend unnd brennend yn lieb, doe von gottes lieb entzundet ist. Also entspringet lieb aus lieb, aus der lieb gottes zu uns unser gegen lieb zu gote." *Lieb gottes* (1518) Kn. 105. One should see this Abelardian motif in its relation to Staupitz's redefinition of *gratia gratum faciens* as the grace which makes God pleasing to man.

[4] "Der fels gibt auch nit wasser, den mit der rueten moysi geschlagen, Christus wirt nit gnaden flussig, auffs hochst lieblich, und freuntlich, in dem das ehr gegeissel, gekront, verspottet, und gekreutziget ist, Sonder in dem, das er in der barmhertzig got, der rechte moyses, der das gesetz der lieb gegeben hat, aus lautter lieb zu uns geschlagen hat, auff das nichtz, den lieb auss ym flies, und unsere hertzen durchflies, durch den heiligen geist, die selbstendige wesenliche lieb, die got selbst ist, und uns vor allen gnaden und gaben an aller unser gerechtigkeit gegeben ist." *Lieb gottes* (1518) Kn. 103. "So videstu, das das leiden des leibs und dy gehorsam der sel fliessen her aus dem prunn der parmhertzykait gotz. O mein got, nun sych ich dein lib, dein genad und dein parmhertzikait erkenn ych, wann da ych dein veint was, da hastu das getan. Wer yst ye gebesen, der für sein feindt

human response, *Lieb* and *Gegenlieb* are centered in the crucifixion of the Savior.

Staupitz is not satisfied to discuss the atonement solely within the framework of the justice of God or to view it simply as a transaction which took place in the relationship between the Father and the Son.[1] God the Father was not merely the the offended party who needed to be appeased and whose justice was satisfied by the death of His Son. He is Himself the compassionate source of all grace and reconciliation. The death of Christ was not the cause of divine mercy, but its effect. It is not God, but fallen man, who needs to be pursued.

Nevertheless, Staupitz did not doubt for a moment that the atonement was, as St. Anselm had argued, an act of satisfaction. By virtue of His human nature, Jesus Christ was capable of rendering satisfaction for the sins of the human race.[2] By virtue of His divine nature, He was capable of condemning and destroying sin.[3] Therefore, God laid on Him the guilt *(culpa)* and punishment *(pena)* of sin, in order that through His innocent sufferings He might pay the debt owed by fallen man to his Creator and bring the elect to final salvation.[4]

The death of Christ is not isolated from the life of active obedience which preceded it. Indeed, the *kenosis* of the Son is interpreted by Staupitz as a kind of *Gelassenheit*, an abandonment of everything which

---

den tod hiet geliten, wer mocht das umb dich verdienen, so wir all dein veint warn? Da fleust es heraus, da yst nichtz dann parmhertzikait..." Hs: b V 8, St. Peter (1512), Sermo 1, fol. 3ª. Cf. *Lieb gottes* (1518) Kn. 117–8.

[1] "So wil ych [Jesus] alain auf dise nacht also leiden, das ich nit alain der gerechtikait genueg wil tain, sunder auch der parmhertzikait genueg thue. Das leiden, das die parmhertzikait warcht, yst tausentmal grösser gebesen, dann das leiden, das die gerechtikait warcht, wann nach der gerechtikait, so wär genug gebesen das leyden, das der herr an dem mynsten gelid erliten hat. Ain ainyg leiden der parmhertzikait yst grosser dann alle leyden der pein oder marter. Darumb sprichstu: Jch will leyden nit alain das der gerechtikait genueg gechich, sunder auch der parmhertzykait." Hs: b V 8, St. Peter (1512), Sermo 3, fol. 12ª.

[2] "Propter similitudinem carnis capax est satisfactionis; potest enim ieiunare, orare, elemosynam dare, sese sacrificium deo offerre. Et illas penitentias omnes et singulas omnium electorum imposuit dominus capiti suo." *Libellus* (1517) 80.

[3] "Propter equalitatem cum deo potest damnare, tollere, delere, extinguere, omnia delicta et peccata. Ipse siquidem deus fecit omnium peccata sua per impositionem penitentie pro omnibus. Et ipse homo patiens et moriens satisfecit pro omnibus." *Libellus* (1517) 80.

[4] "...ipse dei filius dolores nostros portavit, ut reduceret culpam nostram per rectitudinem penae innocentis ad ordinem virtutis, ergo magis reducet nos per penam suam et nostram ad ordinem gloriae in ecclesia triumphante, sic reduxit sua pena ad graciam in ecclesia militante." *Hiob* (1497–8) 1.5.24–8. "...mein praut, ich muess als bezalen was dw verschult hast..." Hs: b V 8, St. Peter (1512), Sermo 5, fol. 20ᵇ.

stood in the way of the fulfillment of the will of God.[1] In becoming
man the Second Person of the Trinity surrendered His divine honor
and lordship, His innocence and comfort, and eventually temporal life
itself. No price was too high to pay in order to bring the will of God
for the redemption of the world to fruition. By this singleness of
purpose He left an example for the Christian man to follow.

Nevertheless, no matter how strongly Staupitz emphasized the importance of the life of Christ, he did not regard the death of Christ as
something incidental or secondary. The fiercest penalties which Jesus
underwent for the sake of the sinner were endured by Him on the
cross. The cross was not only the place where Jesus abandoned all
that He had, including His own life, in obedience to the will of God
—though it was certainly that. Far more importantly, the cross was
the place where Jesus Himself was abandoned by the Father.[2] No
penalty is more severe than the penalty of divine abandonment.[3]

Staupitz attempted to make it clear that the abandonment of Jesus
Christ by the Father was a vicarious act. That is to say, Christ was
abandoned in order that sinful man might not be.[4] The sufferings
of Christ were not gratuitous nor was the crucifixion simply a tragic
event in the religious history of man. Christ is the Lamb of God, who

---

[1] "Sich nue du krancker mensch deinen got, der dy hochste ere gehabt, hat sie
gelassen, unnd die schmach des creutz erlidten…Was ist das anders, dann unnser
got hat ere, nutz, lust, gebendeyunge, bedeckung, herschafft, unschuld, gerechtickeit, das tzeitlich leben, weisheit, gewaldt, reinickeit, sehen, horen, richen,
schmercken, fulen, tugende und alles tzeitlich, uber das alles denn gott aussgetzogen, unnd gelassen worden, Mein got, sprich er, mein gotte, wie hastu mich
vorlassen. Hie sollen wir lernen gelassen sein in dem wenige das wir haben, und
sein umb des willen, der alles gewesen, der alle ding gehabt, unnd umb unnsern
willen gelassen hat." *Nachfolgung* (1515) Kn. 80–1.

[2] "O gelassenheit, wie gar einig ist dein werck, wie gar gross ist deine frucht,
Es kan nicht anders sein, wer es alles lest der vorleurt keins, dennoch bleibt die
gelassenheit Christi einig, von dem geschriben [Matt. 27 : 46], 'mein got, mein got,
wie hastu mich vorlassen,' das mag nymant sprech, dann er alleine, derhalben ist
er nicht allein von unsern wegen gelassen, sunder auch vorlassen gewesen." *Nachfolgung* (1515) Kn. 81.

[3] "Das viert: Mein himlischer vater hat mich [Jesus] vil herter peinygt dann
die juden. Alle hellische pein oder leyden haben heint mein hertz töd also. O frey
dich des pluet, truck all parmhertzikait heraus, da wirstu sechen ainen frumen got,
ainen armen got, ainen reichen got. O wie gar ain unaussprechliche puess yst das,
da sych der aller liebst got von jm selbs hat geschiden, da Jhesus allain yst gebesen
und wolt würchen das hail aller menschen, das erfordert, das sich got von jm selbs
schied und gab seinen leib jn pein, sein sel jn trawern, da der gantz mensch zw
got soll werden." Hs: b V 8, St. Peter (1512), Sermo 3, fol. 12a-b.

[4] "…umb unsern willen ist er vorlassen gewesen, domit wir nicht vorlassen
werden, umb unsern willen hat er den got aussgetzogen, auff das wir yne alle tzeit
antzyhen…" *Nachfolgung* (1515) Kn. 81.

bore the sin of the world on His shoulders, and who, by dying, expiated it.[1] No one enters into a renewed relationship with God apart from Jesus Christ.[2] No possibility exists for fallen man to reconstitute his broken relationship with God by exercising the gifts granted to him in creation. The children of Adam are redeemed through the expiatory sacrifice of Jesus Christ or they are not redeemed at all: "Dan ausserhalb Jhesu ist kain genad."[3]

Because of the salutary effect of the sufferings of Christ for the elect, Staupitz finds it impossible to view them solely as an unmixed evil. To be sure, he acknowledges the tragic dimensions of the death of Christ and comments ironically on the topsy-turvey values of a world which considers the violation of the Passover a greater sin than the execution of the Son of God.[4] Nevertheless, he insists that it is sweet to contemplate the sufferings of Christ, since in these sufferings the mercy of God for the reconciliation of the world is revealed.[5]

The death of Christ is sufficient as a sacrifice to atone for the sins of all men.[6] The mere fact that baptized infants may be saved without any merits of their own is in itself evidence adequate to establish the sufficiency of the atoning death of Christ.[7] This

---

[1] "Kain mensch mag seiner sündt ledig werden, dann allain im glauben in Christum, der das lamb Gottes ist, das der welt sündt hynwegk nimbt, auff jn sind unser aller sündt gelegt, und er ist der Bock, der aller welt sündt in die wüste tregt, Ausserhalb sein ist kain erlöser." *Glauben* (1525) Kn. 125–6.

[2] "Hec ist plenissima restitutio interne pacis, quam extra Christum qui est pax nostra nemo invenit. Sed sine pace vult pacem, qui extra Christum querit quietum." *Libellus* (1517) 106. "Christus gehort on alle mittel gote zu, wir durch Christum." *Lieb gottes* (1518) Kn. 111.

[3] Hs: b II 11, St. Peter (1523), Sermo 21, fol. 201[b].

[4] "Das sibent, das got also gesmacht yst worden und seyn tod also geryng geacht, das dy juden ringer geacht haben, das hail der welt zw tötten dann in das haus pilati zu geen. Da hin yst es kömen, das got so gering geschätzt ist worden, das kain sündt klainer yst geacht worden dann dye sündt, das man Christum tödt oder der tod Christi." Hs: b V 8, St. Peter (1512), Sermo 1, fol. 2[b].

[5] "Ach meine lieben kindt, uebt euch in der allersuessisten petrachtung des pitern leidens XPI. Ich sage euch zue ye lenger jr euch daryn üebt, ye mer werd jr darin suessen gesmack vinden." *Salzburger Predigten* (1523), No. 1, Aumüller, p. 54. "Kain saliger ding ist auf erden dann das leiden Christi wann alle salichait liegt dar an." Hs: b V 8, St. Peter (1512), Sermo 1, fol. 2[b].

[6] "Hoc etiam ne praetereas quod passio filii dei sufficiens est pro omnibus..." *Libellus* (1517) 84.

[7] "Tercium principii est satisfacere debiti, quamvis dominus noster Jhesus Christus dignatus est pro nobis satisfacere et utique sufficienter fecit pro tanto, ut eciam sine nostris meritis salvari possimus, cuius manifestum signum habemus in parvulis noviter baptizatis, qui si moriuntur, priusquam peccandi potenciam habent, salvantur continuo. Quare? solo merito Cristi, neque enim benefacere possunt, quando adhuc male facere nequeunt." *Hiob* (1497–8) 27.214.26–32.

sufficiency, however, is not unlimited. The limitations are twofold.

On the one hand, the atonement is limited in its effect to the remission of the sins of the elect. Christ did not lay down His life for all men, Staupitz noted, but only for many *(non pro omnibus sed pro multis)*.[1] Staupitz did not believe that the atonement was inherently inadequate to expiate the sins of the whole world, but rather that it was not intended to do so. It is not a question of inadequacy, but of intention. The atonement is delimited and defined by divine election.

On the other hand, the atoning death of Christ is limited by the divine decision to make men partners *(cooperatores)* with God.[2] Penance changes eternal guilt into temporal, but it does not eliminate it altogether. The *pena* which remains after penance is to be remitted through works of satisfaction performed by the justified sinner himself. The sacrifice of Christ does not do away with human cooperation, but rather makes it possible. The *conformitas Christi* for which fallen man was created and to which he is recalled can only be regained through the work of Christ, who in His dual office as *Vorbild* and *Mittler* shows man the way to God and places him on it.

IV. MARY, THE VIRGIN MOTHER OF GOD

A. *Immaculate conception.* The doctrine of the immaculate conception, which was defended and advocated by Duns Scotus against Thomas Aquinas, was at first opposed by the leading doctors of the Augustinian Order, who sided with the Dominicans against the Franciscans. The maculist position in the Augustinian Order was represented by such important theologians as Giles of Rome,[3] Albert of Padua,[4] Augustinus Triumphus of Ancona[5] and Gregory of Rimini.[6] Beginning, however, with John of Basel,[7] Henry of

---

[1] "Hoc etiam ne praetereas quod passio filii dei sufficiens est pro omnibus, licet non pro omnibus sed pro multis effusus sit eius sanguis." *Libellus* (1517) 84.

[2] "Voluit tamen nos habere cooperatores, et ideo in aliis sacramentis post baptismum non datur ita plenitudo graciae, sicut in baptismo ad omnem culpae satisfaccionem, sed aliquid nobis agendum relinquitur post satisfaccionem, quod utique penosum est. Ita eciam de penalitatibus senciendum est, quod per eas satisfacimus debito, etsi, pro quo fiat, ignoramus." *Hiob* (1497–8) 27.214.32–7.

[3] X. Le Bachelet, "Immaculée Conception," *DThC* 7 (Paris, 1922), col. 1055.

[4] H. A. Oberman, *Harvest*, p. 288.

[5] E. Dublanchy, "Marie: Les privilèges essentiels de la Vierge Marie," *DThC* 9 (Paris, 1927), col. 2385.

[6] Gregory of Rimini, II *Sent.* d.30–33 q.2 a.1. See especially fol. 114 M, O, P, Q; 115 C, F, H. Cf. H. A. Oberman, *Harvest*, pp. 286–92.

[7] H. A. Oberman, *Harvest*, p. 288, footnote 21.

Friemar[1] and Thomas of Strassburg[2] in the middle of the fourteenth century, prominent Augustinians began to take up the standard of the immaculists. Thus the fact that Jacobus Perez of Valencia,[3] John of Paltz[4] and Johannes von Staupitz argued for the doctrine of the immaculate conception in the late fifteenth and early sixteenth centuries is not a sign of a limited rebellion on the part of a few doctors against the teaching authority of Giles of Rome, but is rather symptomatic of a change of mind within the Order as a whole, as opposition to the immaculate conception gradually disintegrated.[5]

The usual arguments for the immaculate conception are not discussed by Staupitz, who treats Mariology in the context of preaching and is interested therefore in its edifying rather than in its purely dogmatic aspects. He does indicate that Mary was preserved from original sin by the special power of God.[6] This preservation is wholly gratuitous and not—if one may argue from silence—based on any foreseen merit whatever. She is preserved from sin in order that she might be the Church on earth in the brief period between the cruci-

---

[1] Wilfrid Werbeck, *Jacobus Perez von Valencia, Untersuchungen zu seinem Psalmenkommentar, BHTh* 28 (Tübingen, 1959), pp. 214–5, footnote 1.

[2] Werbeck, *Perez*, pp. 214–5, footnote 1.

[3] Werbeck, *Perez*, pp. 214–5.

[4] R. Weijenborg, O.F.M., "Doctrina de Immaculata Conceptione apud Ioannem de Paltz, O.E.S.A., Magistrum Lutheri Novitii," *Virgo Immaculata*, Vol. XIV, *De Immaculata Conceptione apud varias Nationes* (Rome: Academia Mariana Internationalis, 1957), pp. 160–83. Weijenborg surmises that "...Paltz dependeat a traditione immaculatistica sui Ordinis, praesertim auctorum germanicorum." *Ibid.*, pp. 175–6.

[5] According to Eduard Stakemeier, Luther affirmed the "...immaculatam conceptionem pluries...et deinde non quidem negavit, sed potius in Scripturis non formaliter et expresse edoctam, ideoque nec necessario credendam putavit." Eduard Stakemeier, "De Beata Maria Virgine Eiusque Cultu Iuxta Reformatores," *De Mariologia et Oecumenismo* (Rome: Pontificia Academia Mariana Internationalis, 1962), p. 450. Since Staupitz stands in the immaculist tradition of the Augustinian Order, he is a theological ally on this point with Biel and Gerson, who are also defenders of the doctrine of the immaculate conception. For Gerson's Mariology, see André Combes, "La doctrine mariale du chancelier Jean Gerson," *Maria: Etudes sur la sainte Vierge* 2 (Paris, 1952), 865ff. For Biel, see Oberman, *Harvest*, pp. 281–322.

[6] "So doch der heilig sagt, er wär nicht ain sünder gewesen, der betrug sich selbs und dy warhait war nit jn jm. An allain dy schatzkamer aller genaden, Maria, von der wir hie nichtz reden. All heiligen sindt gefallen und all auserwelt fallen noch täglich, aber sy fallen nit zum tod." Hs: b II 11, St. Peter (1523), Sermo 19, fol. 181a-b. "Es wirt nit ain mensch auf der gantzen welt sein, das sy wochen nit tödleich und verdämleich wert fallen. Allain dy zart rain künigin, Maria, dy mueter gotz, dy auch nur aus der gewaltigen und mächtigen genad gots enthalten davon ist warden." Hs: b II 11, St. Peter (1523), Sermo 22, fol. 220a.

fixion and the resurrection.[1] During these three days Mary was not merely a type of the Church (a role which is also hers); she was, when all fled, the Church itself. The immaculate conception is connected with a kind of remnant theology. Mary is preserved from original sin in order that faith may not die out on the earth.[2]

B. *The Maternity of Mary*. God chose Mary to become the Mother of Jesus Christ. The second Adam is not created from the dust of the earth as was the first Adam. Rather the Logos joins himself to human flesh in the body of Mary,[3] who is the second Eve and the fulfilment of the prophecy of Genesis 3:15.[4] That is not to say, of course, that Mary has in herself the possibility of becoming the Mother of God. She has no natural possibility as a Virgin of becoming the Mother of

----

[1] "Der heilig gelauben und das Ewangelij ist an dem tag des leiden Christi als gar aus geloschen. Das nit mer dan ain ainiger mensch jn der gantzen welt ist gewesen darjnn das liecht hat geprunnen. Das ist dy aller heiligist mueter gots Maria gewesen, dy got auch aus seiner sunderleicher gewaltigen kraft und gnad enthalten hat vor dem vall, das das liecht jn jr nye geswecht ist warden. Aber sunst ist es jn allen menschen als gar aus geloschen, das nit ain fünckel da war peliben." Hs: b II 11, St. Peter (1523), Sermo 19, fol. 178b–179a.

[2] This theme is found throughout Staupitz's writings, beginning with his earliest sermons on Job: "Et ut multa paucis referam, omnes apostoli domini fugerunt et a Cristo et a fide. Judas quoque Jhesum tradidit. Maria Magdalena viventem inter mortuos quaesivit. Sed quia multa? unicam spem nostram virginem et matrem absume: ceteri peccaverunt in Christi passione omnes scandalizati. Et nos miseri nonne merito timemus existentes in gracia et donis imperfecciores." *Hiob* (1497–8) 12.115.40–116.3. "...der [Jesus] ist also von den menschen verlassen warden, das nyemants auf erd pey jm peliben ist jm glauben, dann allain Maria, sein raine mueter." Hs: b V 8, St. Peter (1512), Sermo 2, fol. 9b. Cf. *De Compassione Gloriose Virginis Marie* (1517) Kn. 35; Hs: b II 11, St. Peter (1523), Sermo 19, Fol. 178b–179a. See footnote 1 above.

[3] "...das ist aus der rainen junckfrawn Maria in der der heilig geist Christum empfangn hat & hat aus jrm rainen fleysch & pluet das allersauberist & allerunvermayligist genommen & hat daraus gewürcht den rainen leib Jesu Christi, hat darein gossn dy heilig sel dy er am kreutz um unsern willn gelassen hat, damit veraint dy gotheit, also das alle drey natur jn der rainen künigen Maria gewant habn dy aus Davit geschlächt ist gewesn." Staupitz, *Salzburger Predigten* (1523), No. 3., Aumüller, p. 115.

[4] "Weib yst das freuntlichist wort. Do der herr das wort sprach da gedacht er an das weib Eva das jn yn das leyden pracht her. Das weib eva yst gebesen ain verderberin des gantzen menschlichen geschlächt. Herwiderumb, das weib maria hat zuknüscht der schlangen yr haubt. [Cf. Gen. 3:15] Dw pist das weib dar ynn behalten yst die genad und all tugent der propheten. Dw pist das edlist weib, dw pist das rainyst weib, dw pist das weib das mans pluet nie permackelt hat... O weib, weib, aus dir schreyen all propheten, küm, küm, dw pist das weib das mich myt yren prüsten gespeist hat, dw pist das weib die mich ernept und erzogen hat, dw pist das weib das mir mein fleish und mein pluet von den yren geben hat und albey mein trost gebesen yst und noch yn dem lesten mir pey steckt." Hs: b V b, St. Peter (1512), Sermo 11, fol. 50a.

any child, much less the Mother of the Savior. But God creates a
possibility where no human possibility exists.[1] The child is conceived
by the Holy Spirit.

There is a sense, however, in which Mary cooperates with God in
becoming the Mother of Jesus Christ. She does not merit this honor
—either *de congruo* or *de condigno*.[2] But neither does the Holy Spirit use
her as the potter uses the clay. She accepts the message of the angel in
the Annunciation. By her own *fiat* she cooperates with God.[3]

Mary is thus a type of the Church and an example which the
Christian is enjoined to follow. In himself the Christian cannot find
the resources to earn his salvation from God. Everything is offered
to him as a gracious gift. The Spirit will work in and through him.
But he must agree to let the Spirit work. He is urged to utter the *fiat*
to the will of God. The God who speaks to the heart of man by
prevenient grace will do the rest.

C. *Cooperation in Redemption.* Mary at the cross is no longer viewed
by Staupitz primarily as the Mother of God, but as the Bride of Christ.
She stands, thus, not above Him or below Him, but beside Him,
sharing His sorrows in this moment of His utter abandonment by God.
On the cross Jesus calls His mother *Weib*, not because she is no longer
His mother, but because the love of a man for his bride is even

---

[1] "...da die iunckfraw fraget wie man tragend wurd, und von wem, wen die
ordenung der natur nit gehaltenn wurdt, ward yr unnd allen heiligen seelen die
unterricht: Der heilig geist wirt von oben herab in dich kommen, und die kraft
des allerhochsten wirdt dich umbschettigen, [Luke 1:35] als sprach er: Ein kind
gottes wirt nit aus den plutenn, nit aus fleyschlicher begyr, nit aus dem wilen des
mannes, sonder allein aus gote geporn [John 1:13]." *Lieb gottes* (1518) Kn. 98–9.

[2] Bonaventura and Thomas Aquinas teach that Mary's merits are only *merita
de congruo*. Bonaventura, III *Sent.* d.4 q.4; Thomas Aquinas, *Summa Theologiae* III
q.2 a.11 ad 3. According to Laurentin, "...Marie mérite sa maternité, non certes
d'un mérite de justice *(de condigno)* fondé sur l'égalité entre l'oeuvre accomplie et
la récompense, mais d'un mérite de convenance *(de congruo)* fondé sur la délicatesse
et l'amitié." René Laurentin, *Court Traité de Théologie Mariale* (Paris, 1953), p. 77.
Staupitz gives no indication whatever that he considers Mary's cooperation to be
meritorious. God's choice of Mary to be the *Theotokos* is wholly gracious.

[3] "Das wir aus unsern werchen noch vermügen nichtz künen würchen, das uns
ainigerlay zu saligkait müg dyenen. Aber das muessen wir darzue tuen. Wir
muessen darem verwilligen. So mag got stat darzue jn uns haben; got wil würchen,
wir süllen tragen, und darem verwilligen. Er wil der vater sein der das in und
durch uns würcht. Wir süllen und müessen nur dy mueter und tragerin und nererin sein. Es geet eben mit dem werch der feyr zue. Als sich dy sach anschlueg mit
dem schatz der genaden, mit der rainen künigen, der mueter gots. Da sy den
grues von got durch des engls mund enpfing das dy gesegent frucht, dy frucht
jres leibs solt sein, da tet sy nit mer darzue dan das sy darem verwilligt." Hs: b II
11, St. Peter (1523), Sermo 17, fol. 154ᵇ–155ᵃ.

tenderer than the love of a son for his mother.[1] The depth of Jesus'
compassion for Mary can therefore only be expressed by the word,
Weib.

Yet there is more to this transposition from *Mutter* to *Weib* than
simply a device for expressing the depth of the tender feelings of Jesus
for His aged mother. At the cross Mary shares in the sacrifice of Son.
Her sufferings, while not caused by the physical agony of her own
cross, are nevertheless intense.[2] For the sake of that other *Braut*, the
Church, or, perhaps one should say, the elect soul, Mary suffers
abandonment by her Son.[3] However, these sufferings, like the sufferings of Jesus Christ, are fruitful. As the Bride of Christ she becomes
the Mother of the Church.[4] This child is born, not in her womb, but
in her heart.[5] Indeed, so intimately are the sufferings of Jesus Christ

---

[1] "...weip, spricht er, worumb weip, und nicht mutter, uff das vorstanden
wurde, das Maria yne mehr tzu barmhertzickeit bewegte, als seine brauth, dan als
seine muter. Etzliche sagen es were hertzlicher gesprochen, mutter dan weip, ist
nicht war, die eh hat yr geeigent das wortlein weip, und als die liebe tzum weibe
ubertrifft dy liebe tzu vater und mutter, wo sie anderst gantz, war und guet ist,
also ist vil freundlicher gesprochen weip dan mutter, nichts mynner ist es beides,
dy einige gebererin gotes Maria nach dem buchstaben, die das allerliebste weip,
die allerliebste mutter gottes ist." *Nachfolgung* (1515) Kn. 77.

[2] "Ich waiss nit wol wie gross oder wie man aussprechen sol das dass laid Maria
gebesen sey kain leiden konig martier wie als gros gebesen als maria leiden.... O
mein süesser Jhesus gib deiner mueter ain tröstung." Hs: b V 8, St. Peter (1512),
Sermo 1, fol. 5ᵃ.

[3] "...umb des weibs willen hab ich meinen vater ym himml verlassen und wil
und mues auch dich, mein muter auf der erd, verlassen, das ist die gelaubig kristen-
lich sel, die ych mir vermächelt hab und wils nyt lassen, so ich auch des tods
sterben. Ayn ee jst zwischen geist und geist wie zwischen man und weib. Aber das
gezimt sich, das sich die sel verain mit mir. O mein mueter, die zeit yst hie, ych
mues peyligen und wann mir die praut angelegt wirt nit auf einen senften petlein,
sunder nackent ann das kreutz, es mues also sein...." Hs: b V 8, St. Peter (1512),
Sermo 1, fol. 5ᵇ.

[4] "O himlischer vater, sprich aus ob nyt recht sey das das weib, meyn mueter,
auch ain mueter sey der gantzen kristenlichen kirchen oder aller der für die ych so
pitterlichen leid und ob nit recht sey das das weib das meyn praut sey, sey auch ain
mueter aller meiner kynder. Den sententz hat der himlisch vater geben, das pillich
und recht yst das Christus unser vater und Maria unser mueter yst." Hs: b V 8,
St. Peter (1512), Sermo 11, fol. 50ᵇ–51ᵃ.

[5] "Weyb und nymer myeter, dw wirst nun nyt mer meyn müeter sein, sunder
so mir mein hertz pricht, wirstu mein praut sein. Ich pin der vater, dw solt die
praut seyn, dar aus alle welt geporn wirt. Dw tregst ainen andern sun, das gantz
menschlich geschlächt, dw wirst pald peren, dw tregst so vil kinder, dir möcht
das hertz prechen. Dw tregst nit jm pauch, sunder jm hertzen." Hs: b V 8, St.
Peter (1512), Sermo 11, fol. 50ᵃ⁻ᵇ. The term, bride of Christ, is used by Staupitz
as a designation for Mary, the Church, and the individual soul of the Christian
man. Cf. *Hiob* (1497–8) 1.3.19–31; 2.8.7–9; *Libellus* (1517) 56, 112, 353. Out of the

and the sufferings of Mary intertwined in the redemption of the Church, that Staupitz can affirm that there is no child of Christ who is not a child of Mary.[1]

D. *Intercessor*. It is clear from Staupitz's writings that Mary serves as an intercessor for the elect.[2] She is referred to as the "noble Queen,"[3] "the Treasury of graces,"[4] "the Mother of mercy,"[5] "the Mistress of temptation,"[6] and "our only Hope."[7] No one becomes blessed without her assistance.[8] Yet Staupitz is not very specific in explaining what these titles mean or in what way Mary renders aid to the struggling *viator* here on earth. Unlike Biel, however, Staupitz does not turn to Mary as *purus homo* for compassion and understanding rather than to Jesus Christ the *deus homo*;[9] neither does he assign the realm of mercy

---

spiritual union of Christ and Mary the Church is born. There is a sense also in which the Church is the Mother of the faithful. *Hiob* (1497–8) 23.189.41–2. Out of the spiritual union of Christ and the Christian the *laus dei* is born.

[1] "...sie [Mary] ist bey dem creutze des meisters bestanden, unnd wirdt nicht fluchtig vom creutze des jungers, dere wil dich Christus am creutze bevolen haben, und also bevolen, wirstu yr kindt nicht sein, so saltu auch sein kindt nicht sein. Sie ist das weip, das Cristen tregt, sie ist die mutter, die sie seugth, etzet, unnd trencketh, hab sie liebe, lieber hab sie lieb, ader got hath dich nicht lieb." *Nachfolgung* (1515) Kn. 78.

[2] "Derwegen ruffen wir alle, Maria muter der gnaden, muter der barmhertzickeit, beschirm uns vor dem feint in tots notten, vorlass uns nicht, dir seyn wir geben, dir seyn wir am creutz bevolen, mit schmertzen hastu uns geboren, du bist unsser rechte mutter, in dir ist alle mutterliche trew befunden, dan du bist alweg den tzu hylff kommen, die dich in warheit treulich angeruffen haben, uns armen sundern erwirbstu vorgebung, dene wolvordienten die ewige belonunge, du bringst dem nichthaben den genuge, dem leidenden, gedult, dem streyter uberwindunge..." *Nachfolgung* (1515) Kn. 77.

[3] "...Maria der adeln kunygin..." Hs: b V 8, St. Peter (1512), Sermo 1, fol. 3b.

[4] "...dy schatzkamer aller genaden, dy rain künigin, Maria." Hs: b II 11, St. Peter (1523), Sermo 19, fol. 178b.

[5] "...Maria muter der gnaden, muter der barmhertzickeit..." *Nachfolgung* (1515) Kn. 77.

[6] "...Maria...ein maisterin über all anfechtung..." Hs: b V 8, St. Peter (Lent, 1518), fol. 70b.

[7] "...unicam spem nostram virginem et matrem..." *Hiob* (1497–8) 12.115.40. 116.3.

[8] "In der wart da er zwm Johannes sprach, nym war dein mueter, und zw der Maria, weib nym war dein sun, etc., [John 19:26–27] da hat er yr auch gebalt geben das sy ist ein maisterin über all anfechtung, das ist die mueter aller genaden und parmhertzykeit, das ist die müter dy nit pitre wart aus gibt, das yst die müter von der all auserbelt erleucht werden, das ist die mueter die aller pet gebert wirt für wen sy pitt, das ist die mueter von der all auserbelt und ain yeder yn sunderhait von irer verdienen begey sälichait und freyd entpfächt und kainer mag an yr hilf sälig werden." Hs: b V 8, St. Peter (Lent, 1518), fol. 70b–71a.

[9] H. A. Oberman, *Harvest*, pp. 313–322. Cf. Heiko A. Oberman, "The Virgin Mary in Evangelical Perspective," *JES* 1 (1964), pp. 287–8.

to Mary and the realm of justice to Jesus Christ.[1] Though Staupitz is willing to speak of Jesus Christ as a Legislator, he does not emphasize His role as Judge.

What is striking about Staupitz's Mariology in view of parallel late medieval developments is the way in which he has attempted to minimize the dangers of Pelagianism in discussing the role of the Virgin Mary. Her preservation from grace, her faithfulness at the cross were not due to any merit of her own—not even a *meritum de congruo*—but solely to the grace of God, Though Mary cooperates with grace, her cooperation is clearly a response to the prior action of God and not in any sense its cause. Her participation in bringing the Church to birth is of a non-meritorious and passive nature. She does not offer her Son to the Father; He is taken from her. Only in heaven is she assigned an active role in the redemption of the elect. The significance of this fact is heightened when one reflects that Staupitz shows little interest in the work of the ascended Christ.

To sum up then: at the center of Staupitz's *kerygma* is a message about Jesus Christ, the God-man. The mystery of the incarnation is the mystery of the amazing condescension of God, who freely assumes the likeness of sinful flesh in order to rescue man from the frightful predicament in which sin has entangled him. In His dual office as Teacher and as Mediator, Jesus Christ points the way to the heavenly Jerusalem and provides man with everything necessary for his journey. In redeeming man, Jesus Christ was not utterly abandoned by the Church. In Mary the Church found its sole representative at the cross. Man cooperates with God in his salvation, but his cooperation is utterly dependent upon grace.

---

[1] H. A. Oberman, *Harvest*, pp. 310–13. Cf. Oberman, "Virgin Mary," *JES* 1 (1964), pp. 286–7.

CHAPTER SIX

LIFE IN THE SPIRIT

I. The State of Scholarship
on Staupitz's Mystical Theology

Staupitz's mystical theology has been discussed and debated by a succession of scholars from Geuder in the early nineteenth century to Strohl in the mid-twentieth. There is general agreement among these scholars that Staupitz maintains a metaphysical discontinuity between creature and Creator and that he shuns the kind of speculation which is characteristic of Dionysian mysticism. But there is agreement on little else. Staupitz's name is linked in traditional scholarship with Bernard, Tauler, Gerson, and Thomas à Kempis. Keller classified him with the Friends of God.[1] Boehmer, on the other hand, felt it more appropriate to describe Staupitz as a representative of the *devotio moderna* in Germany.[2] Lau argued that Staupitz introduced Luther to German mysticism,[3] while Strohl placed him in the line of a mysticism "plutôt francais".[4]

The difficulty of classifying Staupitz's mystical thought with any degree of precision is compounded by the fact that the various types of mystical theology are themselves subject to continuous discussion and revision. C. L. W. Grimm, writing in 1837, could speak with impunity of the pantheism of Tauler.[5] More recent scholarship, under

---

[1] Keller did not believe, however, that Staupitz should be seen as pure representative of the Friends of God since "...weit mehr als diese hat er...augustinische und mittelalterlich scholastische Gedanken, die der deutschen Mystik fremd sind, in sein System verwerbt..." Ludwig Keller, *Johann von Staupitz und die Anfänge der Reformation* (Leipzig, 1888), p. 75.

[2] Heinrich Boehmer, *Martin Luther: Road to Reformation* (New York: Meridian Books, 1957), p. 100.

[3] "In Staupitz, Luther encountered the world of German mysticism, the mysticism of the fourteenth and fifteenth centuries." Franz Lau, *Luther* (London: SCM Press, 1963), p. 60.

[4] Henri Strohl, *Luther jusqu'en 1520*, 2nd ed. rev. (Paris, 1962), p. 71, footnote 5.

C. L. W. Grimm, "De Ioanne Staupitio eiusque in sacrorum Christianorum instaurationem meritis," *Zeitschrift für historische Theologie*, N.F. I (1837), 111–15.

the influence of writers such as Denifle,[1] has taken the position that the theology of Eckhart and Tauler is compatible with the orthodox presuppositions of the scholastic theology of Thomas Aquinas.[2] Indeed, Käte Grunewald argues that Tauler is a representative of a voluntaristic mysticism rather than of the *Schaumystik* of Eckhart.[3]

Ernst Wolf discussed briefly the relationship between Staupitz and late medieval mysticism. He agreed with Boehmer that one could discern certain affinities between the theology of Staupitz and of Thomas à Kempis. Both Staupitz and à Kempis taught an ethical mysticism directed toward the will and glory of God and centered on Jesus Christ as an example to be imitated. Neither mystic was inclined to engage in intellectual speculation about the themes of mystical piety. Their approach to the spiritual life was practical rather than theoretical. Thomas à Kempis differed from Staupitz, however, when he stressed the role of an ascetic technique in deepening Christian piety.[4]

Wolf also believed that there was some similarity between the mystical thought of Staupitz and the theories of Eckhart, Tauler and the *Theologia Deutsch*. The emphasis on *Gelassenheit* and on the *resignatio ad infernum* are themes common to all four writers. Nevertheless, the idea of *resignatio ad infernum* emerges in the writings of Tauler and

---

[1] Denifle argued that Protestant historians accused the German mystics of pantheism (a) because they did not understand the Catholic theology of grace which underlies the teaching of the mystics and (b) because they did not realize that the mystics did not explain in detail the dogmatic foundations of their teaching, since they preached to congregations of believers. As a result of this, the Protestant Church historian "...*muss* die katholische Lehre missverstehen, ja er wird wo möglich seinen eigenen protestantischen Begriff hineinlesen." Heinrich Seuse Denifle, O.P., *Die deutschen Mystiker des* 14. *Jahrhunderts* (Freiburg i.d. Schweiz, 1951), p. 229.

[2] Bernd Moeller notes that "...die Tauler-Forschung heute wohl darin einer Meinung ist, dass seine Lehre letzten Endes mit dem orthodoxen Thomismus in Einklang gebracht werden kann..." Moeller himself feels, however, that "...in der Stimmung, in der Methode des Denkens und so im Grunde auch in den Ergebnissen tatsächlich ein tiefer Unterschied zur Scholastik besteht." Bernd Moeller, "Tauler und Luther," *La Mystique Rhenane, Colloque de Strasbourg* 16–19 *mai* 1961 (Paris, 1963), p. 166.

[3] "...Gottes Wille selbst kommt in den Menschen. Aber das geschieht nicht durch ein naturhaftes Hineinsinken des göttlichen Willens in den menschlichen, sondern so, dass der neue Wille des Menschen in 'Einförmigkeit' mit Gottes Willen handelt... Statt einer Schaumystik also eine in diesem neuen Sinne wirklich voluntarische Mystik." Käte Grunewald, *Studien zu Johannes Taulers Frömmigkeit* (Leipzig, 1930), pp. 40–41.

[4] Wolf, *Staupitz und Luther*, p. 97, footnote 5.

Eckhart as a kind of pious exercise.[1] All such exercises or techniques are foreign to the spirit of Staupitz, whose writings are remarkably free of advice concerning the proper method for gaining conformity with Christ.

Wolf proposed a new hypothesis to explain the kind of mystical theology which he found in the writings of Staupitz. Following the lead of Denifle,[2] Grabmann[3] and Karrer,[4] who had studied the mystical thought of Eckhart and Tauler and shown its compatibility with the Thomism of the Dominican Order, Wolf argued that the mysticism of Staupitz was nothing more than the application to the spiritual life of insights gleaned from the theological writings of the Doctor of the Augustinian Order, Giles of Rome. The idea of conformity to Christ is not a motif which Staupitz borrowed from Thomas à Kempis but which he found in the *Sentences Commentary* of Giles of Rome.[5] Staupitz gained the character and reputation of a mystic—to use the words of Denifle—only in his "...Nebenberuf in den Frauenklöstern..."[6] The mystical theology of Staupitz is, if one may put it this way, a kind of preached Egidianism, and Staupitz himself is a "mystic" out of the school of Giles of Rome.[7]

II. PREACHER OF GRACE AND OF THE CROSS

It should be apparent by now from the evidence which we have presented in the preceding chapters that Wolf greatly overestimated the influence of Giles of Rome and Thomas Aquinas[8] on the theo-

---

[1] "Die Auffassung, die Staupitz von der resignatio ad infernum hat, ist derjenigen der Mystik Taulers, Eckharts und auch zum Teil der Deutschtheologia allerdings verwandt... Jedoch tritt in der Auffassung der Mystiker die Betrachtung der resignatio als frommer Übung stärker hervor." Wolf, *Staupitz und Luther*, p. 113.

[2] Heinrich Denifle, *Archiv für Literatur- und Kirchengeschichte des Mittelalters* 2 (1886), p. 647ff. Cited by Wolf, *Staupitz und Luther*, p. xi.

[3] Martin Grabmann, *Mittelalterliches Geistesleben* (Munich, 1926), p. 392ff. Cited by Wolf, *Staupitz und Luther*, p. xi.

[4] O. Karrer, *Meister Eckehart* (Munich, 1926). Cited by Wolf, *Staupitz und Luther*, p. xi.

[5] "...aber bei Staupitz tritt einmal die sog. asketische Technik auffallend zurück und sodann hat er die Grundlage seiner Auffassung der imitatio, den conformitas-Gedanken, aus Ägidius übernommen und weit straffer als etwa Thomas von Kempen durchgeführt. Wolf, *Staupitz und Luther*, p. 97, footnote 5.

[6] Cited by Wolf, *Staupitz und Luther*, p. xi.

[7] "...es sieht so aus, als ob Staupitz in ähnlicher Weise 'Mystiker' sei, 'Mystiker' aus der Schule des Aegidius Romanus." Wolf, *Staupitz und Luther*, p. xi.

[8] Wolf was not alone in his high estimate of the influence of Thomas on Staupitz. Boehmer called Staupitz "...at once a Thomist and a mystic..." and

logical development of Johannes von Staupitz and that he assumed a greater theological continuity within the Augustinian Order than in fact existed. Though scholars believe that the teaching authority of Giles of Rome was always respected, it was not allowed to stifle theological diversity. Augustinian theologians in the early sixteenth century had at their disposal a far wider *corpus* of the writings of St. Augustine than was accessible to Giles of Rome. Indeed, so marked is the difference in familiarity with the Augustinian *corpus* between theologians in the early fourteenth century and theologians in the latter half of the same century that Damasus Trapp can speak of Thomas of Strassburg as the last Augustinian of Giles of Rome and can point to Gregory of Rimini as the first Augustinian of St. Augustine.[1] Moreover, we have already had occasion to notice how the Augustinian Order in the process of its theological evolution had departed from the maculist position of Giles to embrace the immaculist doctrine of the Franciscan Order.[2] There is no evidence to indicate that Staupitz, who cites St. Augustine 163 times from 24 works in his sermons on Job and who defends the doctrine of the immaculate conception, opposed the theological evolution of his Order and advocated a return to a purer form of Egidianism. Rather, Staupitz's own demonstrable preferance for Scotistic-nominalistic solutions to many theological problems over a Thomistic alternative argues against the thesis of Wolf and Seeberg[3] that Staupitz attempted to repristinate the theology of Giles of Rome in his own time. Staupitz's opposition to the

---

noted that "...there is no contradiction between these mystical ideas and the vulgar-Thomistic ideas which Staupitz otherwise advocated." Apart from a concern with how "...one can attain to the saving love of God" the treatise *On Predestination* (1517) is an "...otherwise wholly Thomistic book..." Heinrich Boehmer, *Martin Luther: Road to Reformation*, pp. 99–100.

[1] "Thomas of Strassburg marks the turning point in Augustinian Modern theology. I call him the 'last Augustinian of Aegidius' and Gregory the 'first Augustinian of Augustine'. The two terms are not mutually exclusive. Aegidianism is oldfashioned Augustinianism coupled with the *cognitio universalis*, the Gregorian Augustinianism is 'Modern', is better acquainted with *all* the books of Augustine, not only with his major works, and goes hand in hand with the *cognitio rei particularis*. Aegidius remained the venerated figure of the Augustinian School before and after Gregory, but after Gregory especially more corrective reservations were made in regard to Aegidius." Damascus Trapp, O.E.S.A., "Augustinian Theology of the 14th Century; Notes on Editions, Marginalia, Opinions and Book-lore," *Augustiniana* 6 (1956), p. 181.

[2] See above, Chapter 5, section IV, "Mary, the Virgin Mother of God."

[3] Erich Seeberg, basing his evaluation on the study of Ernst Wolf, characterizes Staupitz as a *Repristinationstheologe*. Erich Seeberg, *Luthers Theologie in ihren Grundzügen*, 2 ed. (Stuttgart, 1950), p. 16.

Pelagian tendencies in the theological anthropology of the nominalists did not make him a Thomist by default. Staupitz is a representative of no single school of theological thought.[1] His theology is a creative amalgam of insights drawn from many sources and graced with certain unique touches all his own.

Nevertheless, even though Wolf's thesis cannot be accepted as it stands, there is an important element of truth in it which should not be overlooked. Staupitz does not analyse the faculties of the soul—as Gerson does—in order to defend the thesis that mystical theology is an affective science,[2] though he agrees with Gerson in *De Mystica Theologia* that the only union which is possible *in via* between God and the Christian is a union of will.[3] He does not elaborate a method or

---

[1] We agree in the main with the judgment of Saarnivaara that "Staupitz cannot be identified with any school of theology." We do not concur, however, when he goes on to say that Staupitz "...was closer to Aquinas than Scotus or Occam." Our research has shown that on a whole series of points—e.g. the concept of *bonitas*, the doctrine of acceptation, the primacy of uncreated grace, among others —the reverse has proved to be the case. Uuras Saarnivaara, *Luther Discovers the Gospel* (St. Louis: Concordia Publishing House, 1951), p. 25, footnote 68.

[2] "...misticam [theologiam] vero reponimus in potentia affectiva, cui pro obiecto bonum assignamus." Jean Gerson, *De Mystica Theologia, Tractatus Primus Speculativus, Consideratio* 29, ed. Andre Combes (Lugano, 1958), p. 73.

[3] "Spiritus ergo noster, cum Deo adheret per intimum amorem, unus spiritus est cum eo per voluntatis conformitatem." Gerson, *De Mystica Theologia, Tractus Primus Speculativus, Consideratio* 40, ed. Combes, p. 104. "Et paucis interpositis concludit: O summa libertas, qua obtenta vix possit homo peccare. Racio: quia derelicto seipso totus adheret deo tamquam suae rectitudinis regulae, unde unus spiritus fit per voluntatis conformacionem, non substanciae ydemptitate." *Hiob* (1497–8) 3.16.14–18. Cf. *Hiob* (1497–8) 3.12.31–39; 3.15.1–3; 3.15.29–31; 24.196.14–22; 24.196.38–197.6; *Nachfolgung* (1515) Kn. 82; *Libellus* (1517) 153; 173; 207; *Tischreden* (1517) Kn. 42; *Lieb Gottes* (1518) Kn. 114. One may legitimately argue that the term "mystical theology" should be applied only to Staupitz's teaching concerning those ecstatic experiences which are a foretaste of heaven and not to his teaching about the spiritual life in general. One would thus distinguish between "mysticism", i.e., spiritual rapture, and "piety", i.e., conformity to Christ through union with the Spirit. If carried to its logical conclusion, this line of reasoning would lead one to conclude that the perfect conformity to the will of God which is gained by a handful of the elect *in via* and which is the highest form of union with God prior to death, is an expression of "piety" and not of "mysticism", since it is not necessarily accompanied by ecstatic experiences. In our opinion, however, mysticism is not to be restricted in this way as a term applicable only to the experience of spiritual ecstasy. Mysticism is, rather, concerned with the experience of union with God in this life, whether this union takes place on the level of the intellect or on the level of the will. Mystical theology is not merely a theory of spiritual rapture—though that may be included as one element in it— but is "...an expression, for the profit of all, of that which can be experienced by everyone." Vladimir Lossky, *The Mystical Theology of the Eastern Church* (London: James Clarke and Co., Ltd., 1957), p. 9.

technique which a spiritual novice may use in order to reach a higher plateau of spiritual experience. His sermons are barren of spiritual exercises and injunctions to a more rigorous asceticism. He does not consciously recommend the teaching of any of the masters of the spiritual life and is remarkably free of that self-preoccupation which is often characteristic of medieval mysticism. His warm-hearted piety nourishes itself on the great doctrines of the Christian creed. It is grace and the cross, the work of *Christus crucifixus* and *Christus inhabitans*, which preoccupies his mind and dominates the center of his mystical teaching. To put it simply, Staupitz's mystical theology is the application to the spiritual life of the principles of his "academic" theology.

All the central doctrines of the Christian faith have an immediate application to the problems of the elect and Staupitz moves easily from the pure exposition of a doctrine to its immediate application. The doctrine of the fidelity of God sustains the Christian in the midst of the fiercest temptations.[1] The doctrine of creation underlines man's absolute dependence upon God[2] and the doctrine of the fall reveals man's inability to reestablish his relationship with God by the exercise of his natural faculties.[3] Staupitz uses the doctrine of election to show that grace is the precondition of mystical union and then interprets justification itself as a kind of mystical union with Christ.[4] Christology[5]

---

[1] "Sed nequaquam nos in temptacione deserit, qui creavit, qui et natus est in mundo, in hoc et ad hoc venit in mundum, ut testimonium perhibeat veritati [John 18:37]." *Hiob* (1497-8) 11.98.28-30. "A die incipit temptacio, quando vel propter Christum directe vel propter eius imitacionem in nos venit. Ideo studeamus Christum imitari toto corde et opere, et impossibile est, ut nos derelinquat in temptacione." *Hiob* (1497-8) 11.100.19-22.

[2] Man is absolutely dependent upon God for the preservation of his being. *Libellus* (1517) 1. When Staupitz stresses the nothingness of the creature, he is confessing man's absolute dependence upon God. *Libellus* (1517) 4, 5, 252, 257. Thus a foundation is laid in the doctrine of creation for the *humilitas* of the creature.

[3] "Et sic ante mundi constitutionem conclusum fuit neminem sine Christi gratia bene facere posse." *Libellus* (1517) 19. Cf. 16, 33, 42.

[4] "Is qui credit in Christum fide viva eiicit demonia et intra se, si dici licet, trahit Christum. Melius autem dicitur Christum ingredi in animam iusti per fidem vivam." *Libellus* (1517) 179. Cf. 45. On the relation of election and justification see *Libellus* (1517) 22, 26, 27, 33. Wolf observes correctly that "zweierlei gilt es noch zum allgemeinen des Gedankens der conformitas Christi zu beachten. Sie ist nicht nur Pflicht der Erwählten, sondern auch nur ihnen allein möglich, darum auch das Zeichen der Erwähltheit schlechthin. Ausserhalb des Gnadenstandes kann sie nicht erzielt werden." Wolf, *Staupitz und Luther*, p. 88.

[5] "Cristus, quem pater dedit nobis magistrum veritatis et vivendi exemplum..." *Hiob* (1497-8) 9.63.37-40.

and Mariology[1] provide him with the two examples to whom he points as models to be imitated. Virtually every doctrine is discussed with a sharp eye to its practical relevance. Thus his theory of the Christian life, insofar as one may isolate elements of a selfconscious theory out of his sermons and treatises, is shaped more by his theological convictions on the principal doctrines of the creed, than it is by his dependence upon the medieval masters of the spiritual life—whom he almost never cites and whose influence is more indirect than immediate.

The fact of the matter is that Staupitz is difficult to classify as a disciple of any of the important late medieval mystics. Like Thomas à Kempis, Staupitz teaches a union of will with God rather than a union of essence and elevates the incarnate Jesus Christ as an example which should be imitated by the Christian in his daily life.[2] Yet in contrast to Thomas, Staupitz holds that conformity to Christ is more than an imitation of Christ. It is, one may say, an imitation of Christ in union with him. The spiritual marriage with Christ effected in baptism or penance is the precondition of imitation, and not vice-versa. The resignation of man to the will of God is not simply a response to the work of Christ on his behalf[3]—though it is that—nor merely a willingness to let the will of God be done in everything[4]— though it is that, too. Man's *Gelassenheit* is the surrender of himself fully to the Spirit resident within him. His cooperation is little more than a *fiat* to the Holy Spirit, who by His unceasing activity in the soul of man prompts an imitation of Christ and produces obedience.[5]

---

[1] Hs: b II 11, St. Peter (1523), Sermo 17, fol. 154b–155a.

[2] Boehmer emphasizes the similarity between Staupitz and Thomas à Kempis: "...he is no longer seriously concerned about the ultimate goal of genuine [sic!] mysticism, the union of the part of God enclosed in the soul with the undivided God-substance. On the contrary, he designates as the highest experience and foretaste of blessedness the nuptial union of the soul with Christ, in which there is only a blending of the will and the feelings, but not a temporary suspension of the essential distinction between God and man." Heinrich Boehmer, *Martin Luther: Road to Reformation*, p. 100.

[3] "Lass dich, edle sele, lass alle ding und dich, umb des willen, der alle ding umb deinen willen gelassen hat, lass tugendt, lass gnade, lass den sterbenden Christum, Und abs gote gefiele, so lass auch den got, so wirstu nymmer gelassen von gote." *Nachfolgung* (1515) Kn. 81.

[4] "Quia placent ei universa que deo placent, displicent singula que deo displicent. Et est semper deo conformis atque ideo rectus mundusque corde, unus spiritus cum deo, cui in omnibus et per omnia vult obedire. Cetera extra se et seipsum non attendens, habet quasi non sit, equale gaudium estimans pati et bene sentire, mori et vivere, salvari et damnari, modo fiant omnia iuxta beneplacitum dei." *Libellus* (1517) 173.

[5] "Das wir aus unsern werchen noch vermügen nichtz künen würchen, das uns

The work of Christ as Teacher and Example becomes significant only for the man in whom the Spirit of Christ dwells as Sanctifier.

Staupitz's relationship to Tauler, Eckhart and the *Theologia Deutsch* is also somewhat problematical. They have, of course, many points in common: a stress on *Gelassenheit* and *resignatio ad infernum*, an emphasis on the Christian life as a way of suffering, a renunciation of self-trust —the themes could be multiplied. Furthermore, if one compares the practical, ethical concern of Tauler with a similar thrust in the preaching of Staupitz, the problem of distinguishing them becomes far more difficult than the scholars in the nineteenth century would have led one to believe. Nevertheless, distinguishing them from one another, while difficult, is certainly not impossible. The principal difference lies in Tauler's doctrine of *Seelengrund*.[1] For Staupitz, man after the fall has no natural resources for the return to fellowship with God, whether these resources are called *synderesis*[2] or *Seelengrund*. There is no natural inclination of the soul to do the will of God *post peccatum*, no knowledge of the first principles of the divine will which survives the death

---

ainigerlay zu saligkait müg dyenen. Aber das müessen wir darzue tuen. Wir muessen darem verwilligen. So mag got stat darzue jn uns haben; got wil würchen, wir süllen tragen, und darem verwilligen. Er wil der vater sein der das in und durch uns würcht. Wir süllen und müessen nur dy mueter und tragerin und nererin sein." Hs: b II 11, St. Peter (1523), Sermo 17, fol. 154[b]. On the work of the Holy Spirit resident in man see *Von der nachvolg cristi* (1517) Kn. 28; *Lieb gottes* (1518) Kn. 99, 102.

[1] On the meaning of *Seelengrund* in Tauler's theology see Paul Wyser, O.P., "Taulers Terminologie vom Seelengrund," *Altdeutsche und Altniederländische Mystik*, ed. Kurt Ruh, *Wege der Forschung* 23 (Darmstadt, 1964), pp. 324–352. The following discussion of Tauler is based on the unpublished study of *Seelengrund* in Tauler and *Syntheresis* in Gerson by Steven E. Ozment. Ozment argues that "...*syntheresis* and the *Gemüt-Grund* are correlative in at least four points. (1) Both designate anthropological resources for relating man to eternal things (first principles of truth and-or of morality); (2) both are expressive of a sensitivity to the congruence of nature and supernature, the rational creature and the Creator, from the side of the creature as well as from the side of the Creator, even *post peccatum*; (3) both are fundamentally definitive of inchoate *homo spiritualis*, man *coram Deo*; and (4) both are confirmed and enhanced by sanctifying grace." Steven E. Ozment, "*Homo Spiritualis*: A Programmatic Essay on the Influences of the Anthropological Analyses of Late Medieval Mysticism, as Summarized by John Tauler and John Gerson, on the Formation of Martin Luther's Theology," unpublished paper submitted to Church History Colloquium, Harvard Divinity School, (February 1, 1966), p. 9.

[2] Gerson defines *syntheresis* in the following manner: "Synderesis est vis anime appetitiva immediate a Deo suscipiens naturalem quamdam inclinationem ad bonum, per quam trahitur insequi motionem boni ex apprehensione simplicis intelligentie sibi presentati." Gerson, *De Mystica Theologia, Tractatus Primus Speculativus, Consideratio* 14, ed. Combes, p. 33.

of man's *recht sein*. God does not search for some apex of the soul, some point of likeness with himself, when he justifies the ungodly. Nor can man, by preparing the ground of his soul, obligate God to indwell him.[1] The justification of the sinner depends upon God's decree of election and not upon the innate capacities of fallen man. There is no uncorrupted kernel in the soul of man. The radicality of Staupitz's Augustinianism sets him apart from Tauler and Gerson.

III. The Covenant and Mystical Experience

Staupitz's mystical teaching is shaped by his understanding of God's covenantal relationship to man. God has placed Himself under obligation to the elect by an eternal decree. He has made Christ a *debitor* of justification to the elect.[2] We have already seen in another context what is involved in this decree of election. All the steps in the *ordo salutis*—vocation, justification, regeneration, glorification—are the gradual unfolding in time of the eternal decree of God. Salvation is owed to the elect, not because they have merited it, but because God is faithful to His own decision. All of the elect are united with Christ in a spiritual marriage and are enabled by the Spirit of Christ dwelling in them to conform their wills to the will of God. The elect live in union with Christ as a result of an eternal decree of God.[3] Such a union is owed to them. It belongs, so to say, to the covenanted mercies of God.

There is a kind of democratization in Staupitz's mystical thought, a leveling process which places all Christians initially on the same plateau. Union with Christ in the Church is a precondition of a life of discipleship. A spiritual marriage with Christ is not the goal of a long process of rigorous spiritual discipline—as it is for Bernard of Clair-

---

[1] Tauler says, for example, in his Christmas sermon, "Am heutigen Tag," on the text Isaiah 9 : 5: "Wenn der Mensch so die Stätte, den Grund bereitet, so muss sonder allen Zweifel Gott ihn ganz und gar ausfüllen, eher bärste der Himmel und erfüllte das Leere. Viel weniger lässt Gott die Dinge leer, es wäre das ganz gegen sein Wesen und seine Gerechtigkeit." *Johannes Tauler, Predigten*, ed. Georg Hofmann (Freiburg i.Br., 1961), p. 17. For Staupitz, however, man cannot place God under obligation by any activity of his own, though he can rely on the covenant obligations God freely assumed. Staupitz rejects, moreover, the implicit assumption that the will of God must conform to standards of justice which are independent of that will itself. The will of the covenanting God is the standard for righteousness, not vice-versa.

[2] *Libellus* (1517) 22, 26, 27, 33; *Lieb gottes* (1518) Kn. 111.

[3] *Libellus* (1517) 56, 62, 71, 76, 77.

vaux.[1] It is not the apex of the Christian life, but its entrance. It is not an experience reserved for a spiritual elite, but the common privilege of all Christians.

It is important at this juncture to draw a distinction which is implicit in Staupitz's writings between the possession of a gift of God and the conscious enjoyment of it. There are experiences of ecstasy, foretastes of heaven, which Staupitz describes in vivid sensual imagery. These experiences of rapture may accompany the spiritual marriage of Christ and the Christian, but they do not do so necessarily. They are not owed to the elect, and their presence or absence, while altering the atmosphere surrounding the justification of the elect, does not materially enhance or diminish the fact of spiritual union.[2] In justification the elect are united to Christ, whether they feel it or not. Union with Christ and conformity to Christ may take place in an emotional desert. Indeed, joy may be withheld from the elect in order that they may earn greater merit by performing the will of God in spiritual dryness.[3] Union and conformity are owed to the elect, not rapture.[4] Christ is the *debitor* of a spiritual marriage; He is the *dator* of conjugal bliss.[5] Joy belongs to the uncovenanted mercies of God.

At every level of his spiritual experience, the justified sinner loves God *super omnia*; i.e., to the limit of his present capacity.[6] However,

---

[1] "The soul that reaches this point is ready for the mystic marriage. She does not reach it without grace, or without long co-operation with grace by her own zeal *(industria)*..." Etienne Gilson, *The Mystical Theology of Saint Bernard*, trans. by A. H. C. Downes (New York: Sheed and Ward, 1940), p. 113. Cf. Hilda Graef, *The Light and the Rainbow* (Westminster, Md.: The Newman Press, 1959), pp. 206–225.

[2] "Nihilominus abundantiore misericordia Christus dominus noster spiritum electe anime rapit in se vel in extasi ponit, ut, solis eternis intenta, futuram dulcidinem pregustet et solido cibo, vel ad morulam, vescatur. Absolutus ab officio anime ita quod, si in corpore vel extra sit, prorsus ignoret. Magna sunt ista, tamen ad salutem non necessaria." *Libellus* (1517) 160–61.

[3] "Ego namque pro certo habeo illa bona sic cum ariditate perfecta nonnumquam maioris esse meriti, quia graviori sunt laboris." *Hiob* (1497–8) 5.30.34–6.

[4] "Decreta est electio et praedestinatio certorum ad conformitatem imaginis filii dei..." *Libellus* (1517) 19. *Conformitas* is included in the original decree of election.

[5] "Magna sunt ista, tamen ad salutem non necessaria. Idcirco non habent Christum debitorem, sed liberalissimum datorem." *Libellus* (1517) 161.

[6] "Got uber alle ding lieben, ist seliglich lieben, wen aber auch in der seligen lieb hoher und nyder, mer und weniger stadt haben. Ist nicht vergebens oder unnutz, eben von der selbigen unterschid zugedencken. Man nennet, als ir vil mals gehort, etzliche in der lieb gottes uber alle ding anfahen, etzliche zunemer, etliche volkommen, untter welchen die ersten weniger, die andern mer, die dritten am meysten got lieben. Doch lieben sy yn alle uber alle andere ding..." *Lieb gottes* (1518) Kn. 103.

the frontiers of his capacities for love, obedience, self-denial, are constantly being expanded by the work of the Spirit resident within him.[1] Staupitz divides Christians in the usual fashion into three groups according to the level of their spiritual attainment: the beginners,[2] the advanced,[3] and the perfect.[4] Every Christian travels the path to perfection. Union with Christ in the Church makes a life of love and obedience possible.[5] Perfection of love—i.e., perfect *Gelassenheit*—is possible in principle in this life.[6] It is doubtful, however—though

---

[1] "Christus muess christus bleyben, got muess als got uber alle ding gliebt werden, das ist das fundament aller lieb unnd gutten begirde, unnd ist allen waren liebhabern gemein. Das aber untterscheid, mer und weniger, hoher und nyderer, geliebt wirt, entspringt auss dem das die liebliche erzeygung gottes wirckt nit in form wie die natur yr hochstes vermogen, sonder mer ader weniger wie der heilig geist wil, unnd wo, unnd wen er wil. Dem nach ist nit allein got uber alle ding liebenn gnad, sonder auch ein ytzlicher grad der lieb gnad." *Lieb gottes* (1518) Kn. 104. Cf. Kn. 107.

[2] "In yn [i.e. der anfaher] ist vermischung forcht mit der lieb, yn yn ist vermengung tzeitlicher und hymelischer begirde, sy lieben neben got vil ding, darumb erhelt sich ire guete nit den in dem, das die lieb gotes, das die hymelischen begirden furdringen, und got wiewol mit andern dingen, doch mehr denn andere ding, geliebt wirt." *Lieb gottes* (1518) Kn. 104.

[3] "Es geschicht etwan weyter, das sich got vonn hymel noch freundlicher yns hertz thuet, und entzundt den willen der massen, das er nicht allein yetzundt yne uber alle ding lieb hat, sonder auch alle andere ding zu gottes lieb brauch, alle ding yn sein lob ordene." *Lieb gottes* (1518) Kn. 105.

[4] "Der wirt volkommen genent, dem sich goth so lieblich, so fruntlich, so sues einbildet, das im wirt, es sey nichtz den got, nichtz lieblich denn got..." *Lieb gottes* (1518) Kn. 106.

[5] In his treatise on *Glauben* (1525), Staupitz speaks of four types of union which God effects among Christians. The first three types of union occur in justification: (1) union of all believers in heart and soul; (2) union in the mystical body of Christ; (3) the marriage of Christ and the Christian. The fourth type of union is begun in justification and is perfected for the great majority of Christians after death. It is the union of will, or *Gelassenheit*, or the perfect surrender of the Christian to God—the terms vary. In union with Christ, the Christian is given the ability to surrender himself wholly to God. "Noch ist ein höhere vereynigung, in welcher Christus, und der in jne glaubt, sich gantz in Got ergeben, das er allain alles in allen dingen sey, alles in allen dingen wurck." *Glauben* (1525) Kn. 130.

[6] Staupitz speaks of the *perfectus Christianus*, who is willing to be damned for the glory of God. See *Libellus* (1517) 253. It is clear that perfection is not deferred to the afterlife, but is possible in principle prior to death. Whether one actually reaches perfection prior to death, depends on the activity of the Holy Spirit. "Die bewegung ist des heiligen geistes, die empfindung ist unser..." *Lieb gottes* (1518) Kn. 105. Time is not a decisive limiting factor for God. "Also geschicht auff disen tag, das got in einer stund, ia in vil kurtzerer zeit, die grad der lieb in uns verandert." *Lieb gottes* (1518) Kn. 109. Staupitz's optimism about perfection is not based on an underestimation of the debilitating effects of the fall. He has a strongly Augustinian doctrine of sin. His optimism is not based on the belief that fallen man *ex puris naturalibus* can love God *super omnia*. It is rather an optimism of grace.

Staupitz is ambiguous on this point—if more than a minority of
Christians, a kind of spiritual elite, will actually reach such a level of
perfection in this life. For the rest, perfect surrender to the will of
God, perfect imitation of Christ, perfect love of God, is an eschatological experience. That is to say, it will take place for them only after
death. The point that should be noted carefully is that it *will* take place,
however variable and uncertain the timetable may be. God intends to
bring all the elect to spiritual perfection. It is part of the covenant
obligation which He has freely assumed.

Just as there are levels of spiritual experience, so, too, there are
levels of spiritual enjoyment. Staupitz uses sensuous imagery drawn
from married life to describe the spiritual rapture which God grants
to some as a foretaste of that perfect enjoyment of God which is
characteristic of the *beati* in heaven. There are three levels on which
spiritual delights occur: the level of the young maidens, the level of
the concubines, and the level of the queens.[1] The fourth and highest
level is reserved for the Virgin Mary, who alone knows "how sweet
Christ is."[2] These levels parallel the levels of spiritual attainment. One
would assume—though Staupitz nowhere makes it clear—that perfect
Christians, if they are granted ecstatic spiritual experiences at all, are
granted them on the level of the queens. However, their spiritual
attainment in no way merits spiritual rapture nor is such a foretaste of
heaven a necessary concomitant of their pilgrimage toward the eternal
Jerusalem. Spiritual perfection belongs to the covenanted mercies of
God; spiritual rapture does not. God is a *debitor* to the elect of conformity to Christ; He is only a *dator* of ecstasy.[3]

God can bring man to perfection. One gets the impression, however, that only a
minority of saints will reach this higher state prior to death.

[1] "Scripture dicunt quadruplices esse animas quas Christus sponsali amore com-
plectitur. Sunt adolescentule iuvenes in fide. Sunt concubine amore divisa, in
quibus nihilominus sponsi amor interna electione precellit. Sunt regino qui pro
sponsi celestis amore spreverunt mundum cum concupiscentiis suis." *Libellus*
(1517) 116.

[2] "In quarto gradu est sola virgo dei genetrix Maria, que sola sapuit quam sit
dulcis." *Libellus* (1517) 121.

[3] *Libellus* (1517) 161. The language which Staupitz uses to describe these mystical experiences is rather erotic. He says, for example, of the queens: "He nude
copulantur nudo. Sapiunt preter Christum non esse dulce... Neque enim potest se
nudus Christus negare nudis..." *Libellus* (1517) 120. Staupitz speaks of the mystical
experiences of Christians as a foretaste of salvation. But he can also speak of the
gratia gratis data, the gifts of the Spirit given to the Church for its benefit, as foretastes of salvation. He has in mind principally the gifts listed in I Cor. 12:8ff. and
Mark 16:17–18. See *Libellus* (1517) 107, 184, 210, 212, 236, 247. Just as Staupitz

Visions occupy a very peripheral position in Staupitz's theology. While he admits that God occasionally grants visions to the faithful, he regards self-proclaimed visionaries with suspicion. In the *Libellus* of 1517 he ridicules: "...certain heralds of their own sanctity who boast in a prophetic manner of having various visions...they see the omnipotent God the Father as a venerable old man with a beard, and innumerable other things which laughter prevents me from reciting."[1] One should seek the face of God, not in the fervent white heat of a private intuition into hidden mysteries, but in works which honor Him.[2] Staupitz does not think highly of visions which do not lead to moral improvement.[3]

IV. LIFE UNDER THE CROSS

The character of a Christian life is defined less by its ecstatic experiences—which are granted occasionally and only to a few—and more by the quality and steadfastness of its obedience to the will of God. To be a Christian is to follow Christ—even if that following is impossible apart from union with Christ in justification. As the incarnate life of Jesus was marked by suffering and temptation, so, too, is the life of His disciples. The servant is not above His Lord.

Cross-bearing is the voluntary activity of a committed disciple.[4]

---

is less interested in mystical experiences than he is in conformity to Christ, so, too, he is less interested in the manifestation of gifts than he is in virtue. "Certum esse predictam eiectionem demonum virtuti non conferre, neque eiusdem esse certum signum." *Libellus* (1517) 184. The ability to cast out demons is not a certain sign of virtue, nor is the *ars incantandi* a gift granted only to the good. See *Libellus* (1517) 212.

[1] "Est itaque res salutaris valde videre Christum, non ut quidam precones proprie sanctitatis visiones varias prophetico more se habere gloriantur... viderunt omnipotentem deum patrem venerabilem senem barbaratum et innumerabilia alia que recitare risus prohibet." *Libellus* (1517) 164.

[2] "Vis videre deum in leticia cordis. Quere ipsum in omnibus operibus tuis. Neque enim potest ita inventus absque leticia videri. Sed quomodo inventus? Plane ut operator tue salutis in te et tecum; non enim sine te deus te salvum faciet, qui te sine te creavit." *Libellus* (1517) 169.

[3] "Euntes igitur per medium hoc certum habemus, quod visio illorum que extra nos fiunt non constituit nos bonos, nec plane nos tales ostendit. Multi nempe Christum viderunt realiter in cruce pendentem, qui tamen perstiterunt in duricia cordis sui... Non ergo istam visionem queras ubi aliquid creaturam sive creatorem ipsum extra te vides, quia per talem visionem non es melior non vidente, sed peior nonnumquam." *Libellus* (1517) 166.

[4] "Adiungitur tamen: 'et sequitur Christum', quia nimirum multi, omnes, velint, nolint, crucem portare compulsi sunt. Se quia multi involuntarie, multi sine fide, plerique autem propter iniquitates et scelera sua cruciantur in hoc mundo,

Not every splinter on the path is a cross nor are involuntary sufferings the mark of a man who is conformed to Christ. God, who is the true Teacher of sanctity,[1] uses the misfortunes of life to temper the Christian, provided that these sufferings are voluntarily borne for the sake of Christ. The Christian's sufferings do not come from the world, but from God.[2] They can be endured, however severe they may be, through the sufferings of Christ.[3] Indeed, the best friends of God often suffer the worst trials.[4] It is a mark of His special favor to be brought through fiery ordeals. The crucible of suffering is more important for Staupitz than the dreams of the visionary. Ecstatic joy may uplift the heart of a Christian for a brief time, but innocent suffering, voluntarily borne, brings him nearer to that perfection which is his birthright as an elect child of God.

Not all sufferings are fruitful. A man may learn to suffer from misfortune, but fruitful suffering is learned only from the sufferings of Christ.[5] It is lovingly borne by the elect as a response to the self-offering of Christ on behalf of the elect.[6] The elect suffer innocently

---

non sequuntur Christum, ideo nec conformes sunt imaginis filii dei nec praedestinati." *Hiob* (1497–8) 11.92.16–20. Wolf correctly notes that "in der Willigkeit des Leidens und Sterbens liegt das Wesen der Gleichförmigkeit, nicht in den Vorgängen selbst..." Wolf, *Staupitz und Luther*, p. 89.

[1] "Hieremias spricht, das die in Christum glauben, kains Lerers bedurffen des glaubens dann Gottes... dann ich [Gott] wirdt mein newes gesetz jnen innerlich einbilden, und in jre hertzen schreyben..." *Glauben* (1525) Kn. 124.

[2] "Aber etleich mainen & sagen, Ja wans gott tät, so wolt ichs gern leiden; aber es tuet mirs nur dye welt, der tewfel und pos mensch. Ach nayn, sy tans warleich nit, got tuet dirs als aus lauterer lieb..." *Salzburger Predigten* (1523), No. 1, Aumüller, p. 54.

[3] "Das ist eben der drit punckt, das ist das uns durch das leyden Christi alle ding träglich wern zu leiden, so wir gedenken, ey es ist nur das joch Christi." *Salzburger Predigten* (1523), No. 1, Aumüller, p. 55. "Willig Und gedultig zuleiden flewst nit aus menschlicher natur, krafft oder Wurckung Sonder allein aus der Wurckung Und crafft des leidens christi..." *Das alles unnser leyden* (1517) Kn. 31.

[4] "Als wies got vil mals umb wend und gibt seinen liebsten freunten und kyndern hie solich leiden, die nur die aller pösisten schelck und puben solten leiden, ja das leiden, das nur den verdambten jn der hell zw gehört...solich leyden werden nur aus sunder grosser lieb gotz und den liebsten und frümisten aufgelegt..." Hs: b V 8, St. Peter (Advent, 1518), fol. 61a-b.

[5] "Zu leyden lernt den menschen ain yglicher Unfal der Ime begegnen und zusteen mag, aber fruchtbarlich zu leiden wirdet allein aus dem leiden christi gelernt, durch nachfolgende anzaigung." *Das alles unnser leyden* (1517) Kn. 30.

[6] "Nun merck, hab flies wan dw betrachten wild das leiden Christi, hab nit aufhören, pis dw findest yn deinen hertzen ain mitleiden oder bewegung deins hertzen. Wenn dw der empfindest, so stee nit stil, gee hin durch zw der sel, und gedenck das ander: O dw aller edliste sel, wie steet es umb dich? dem leib geet es ye werlich übel, was merck ych jn dir? Ain gantze, volkömene gehorsam des him-

for Christ because He suffered innocently for them. They triumph over their sufferings in the power of the grace merited for them in the sufferings of Christ. The Christian does not flagillate himself or attempt to bring upon himself unnecessary pain. Rather he waits to receive from God, what God has to give him, knowing that he can overcome the fiercest trials by his participation in the sufferings of Jesus Christ. He learns to suffer patiently, not in order to shorten purgatory[1] nor in the hope of heavenly reward,[2] but out of the love of God alone.[3]

Temptation like suffering is sent to the Christian from God,[4] even though the immediate instrumentality of temptation is the devil. Life is itself from beginning to end a continuous temptation.[5] In his treatise on *Nachfolgung* of 1515, Staupitz lists nine characteristic temptations which assail man: three of which spring from his sins, three from his virtues, and three from outside him.[6] The first three temptations concern unrepented sin,[7] trust in one's own works,[8] and an inclination to doubt the righteousness of God.[9] Self-trust is itself the most deadly temptation, because it makes victory over all other temp-

---

lischen vater und hast nit aus wellen geen von der pein, sunder pis ynn tod gehorsam wellen sein. O mein got, gib myr das ich dir nach folg mit gehorsam, wie dw wildt, und zu dem stee nit still, tring hin ein durch das leiden der sel und lueg was die gottheit dar zue thue..." Hs: b V 8, St. Peter (1512), Sermo 1, fol. 2b–3a.

[1] "...also nimpt er das leyden dorumb an das er In erstatung der bezalung gemachter sundtlicher schulden dester eher Und on langs pein des fegfeurs zu got komen mag." *Von den Graden* (1517) Kn. 21.

[2] "Der ander grad ist das der mensch das Unschuldig leyden gedultiglich zutragen annimpt, nit dorumb das es Ime ein ablegung der pein des fegfewrs und seiner sunden sein sol Sonder von wegen ainer merung seins Verdinens und belonens In den himeln..." *Von den Graden* (1517) Kn. 22.

[3] "Der drit Grad und der Volkomenste ist der Wann der mensch solch leiden In gedult treg, nit dorumb das er got bit, Ime das fur ein erstatung Verdienter puss und pein seiner sonden zusetzen, oder Ime deshalben das verdinen seiner belonung zu manigfalten, Sonder allein aus lieb gotes und der Ursach des unschuldigen leidens christi..." *Von den Graden* (1517) Kn. 22.

[4] "Sic ergo, fili mi, praepara animam tuam ad temptacionem et audi, quae nobis pastor noster primus Petrus dicat [cites I Peter 1:6]... Quanto enim stipula preciosus est aurum, tanto est virtus in temptacione probata preciosior illa, quam non tetigit manus temptantis. Ideo ergo dominus nos temptari permittit, ut virtus nobilior sit et gloria nobis multiplicetur." *Hiob* (1497–8) 22.178.18–28.

[5] "Kind, spricht der weysse, so du tzu gottes dynste nehen wildt, steh in gerechtickeit und forchte, unnd schick dein sele tzu der anfechtigung. Dann das leben ist vom anfang biss tzum endt anfechtigung." *Nachfolgung* (1515) Kn. 62.

[6] *Nachfolgung* (1515) Kn. 66–7.

[7] *Nachfolgung* (1515) Kn. 63–4.

[8] *Nachfolgung* (1515) Kn. 64.

[9] *Nachfolgung* (1515) Kn. 64.

tation impossible. Victory is possible only when the sinner, realizing his own impotence, surrenders his own will to the Spirit of God who dwells in him.[1] He cannot march to triumph in his own strength, but he can allow himself to be carried.[2] The gospel has to do with this salutary "carrying" by the Spirit. Like the Virgin Mary, who believes that God can create a possibility where no human possibility exists, the Christian utters his own *fiat* to the will of God.[3] He dare not trust himself in the face of temptation. He must rely on the power of Christ. Nowhere is this feeling more evident in the sermons of Staupitz than in the prayers which are often inserted into the exposition. In the sermons on Job, for example, Staupitz prays:

> I, a man about to be tempted, call upon You before I feel temptation present, that You may confer upon me the strength and unchangeable perseverance with which I can conquer the enemy, increase grace, and merit eternal life. This, most merciful Lord and most pious Savior, I now pray with a tranquil heart. For I know myself, know, I say, my infinite imperfections. I have often experienced in myself that, when suffering is present, I judge less correctly concerning Your loving-kindness. Therefore I come before Your face in confession, seeking mercy and grace. I do not ask, most sweet God, I do not ask that You take temptation away from me, which by Your wisdom You have determined. Rather I ask that You comfort me, that You give me aid, lest I succumb.[4]

The Christian is comforted in his temptation by the thought of the fidelity and omnipotence of God.[5] God has committed Himself to aid

---

[1] "Das erst: pestee den veint nit aus aigener kraft zu pestreiten, sunder lauff zu der warhait zu dem mund gotz umb rat. Das vintzt dw klärlich jm dem gesetzt der pot gotz, was der willen deins frumen gotz sey. Dem volig nach in lieb und jn laid mit rechter diemnütiger gelassenhait." Hs: 23 E 16, Nonnberg, fol. 30b–31a. Cf. *Nachfolgung* (1515) Kn. 66.

[2] "Ich kan weder gen noch sten & mag nichts dan nur ymer fallen & darnyderlign. so kumbt dan main got, so er syecht das wir uns erkennen & sagt eben darumb hab ich dirs evangelium gebn das du wist wer du seyst, kanstu nit gen, du kanst dich aber wol tragn lassn. Ey kum her du v'lornes schaf, du armer mensch, auf meinen rucken. ich wais dich wol zu tragn. kum nur zu mir & peleib in dem erkentnus. leg dich gantz jn mich, stirb in mir; wirstu jn mir begrabn, so wirstu naemlich jn mir auch ersten." *Salzburger Predigten* (1523), No. 2, Aumüller, pp. 56–7. To die in Christ is a metaphorical expression used to designate (a) the absolute renunciation of all self-trust in the face of the debilitating effects of the fall; and (b) the confession of absolute dependence on Jesus Christ for pardon from past offenses and the power to live in obedience to the will of God.

[3] See above, footnote 33.

[4] For the Latin text see *Hiob* (1497–8) 11.85.33–42.

[5] See above, footnote 24.

the elect and bring them to final salvation, even though they have good reason to despair of their own abilities to withstand temptation. And He has the power to perform what He has committed Himself to do. All things, even the sins of the elect, work together for good to those who love God.[1] God permits Christians to fall into sin in order to teach them to despair of themselves and to commit their lives unreservedly to God.[2]

Death is the point in the experience of the *viator* in which temptation becomes most intense.[3] In the last moments of life, the Christian must rely as never before on the power of God. Although Staupitz does not elaborate an *ars moriendi*, he does indicate that Christ teaches man how to die.[4] A man may stand in three possible relations to death. He may love his temporal life more than right living.[5] He may love right living more than life, but still adhere too much to this present world.[6] Or he may have advanced to such a state of spiritual maturity that he finds this present life burdensome and longs to be in the presence of God.[7] This last relation to death is the most desirable and is a mark of the surrendered man.

The whole life of the Christian is an imitation of the *Gelassenheit* of Jesus Christ.[8] The locus or center of this imitation is the cross—or,

---

[1] "Got lasst kainen fromen Christenlichen menschen on sonder treffenliche gute ursachen zum fall der sunden komen, dann Wann er dem menschen solchen seinen sundtlichen fal nit zu pesserung, merung der gnaden oder andern nutzbarkait leeren und wenden wolt, So lies er keinen gerechten nymmer mer fallen, als paulus spricht, Diligentibus deum omnia cooperantur in bonum, Den gotforchtenden Werden alle ding, all Ir Ubungen, Ja auch die sunden, spricht die glos, lauter zu Irem nutz und guten bewendt." *Sentencien* (1517) Kn. 27.

[2] "Derhalben enzeucht uns offt got gnediglich auch die lieb der zuenemer, und iagt uns in erkantnus unsers unvermogens in forcht, in vertzweifelung an uns selbst, damit wir wie die kleinen kind zu ym als dem eynigen erloser fliehenn, uns zu nichte, ynn allein gross machen." *Lieb gottes* (1518) Kn. 110.

[3] "Er komme auch mit gewalt, arger list ader bossheit, der halben sollen die menschen alletzeit, sunderlich aber in tods notten auss eignen krefften nicht streiten wider seinen gewalt, list und bossheit." *Nachfolgung* (1515) Kn. 68.

[4] "...wer nicht von Christo sterben lernet, der kans nymmer mer." *Nachfolgung* (1515) Kn. 73.

[5] *Nachfolgung* (1515) Kn. 60.

[6] *Nachfolgung* (1515) Kn. 60.

[7] "Czum letzten sein etzliche die yr tzeitlichs leben Christo in irem hertzen alleine tzu geeygendt, die mit dem geiste gottes regiret, auss in selber kommen, allein gotleidende menschen sein, von den selbigen steht geschriben. Die mit gottes geist gewurckt werden, die sein kindt gottes. Solchen menschen ist das leben beschwarlich, dan der leib der sterblich ist, beschweret die sele und underdrugt den vilden kenden sinn, Es ist in auch vordriesslich, dorumb das es sie vorhindert an dem steten, fursen, wunigklichen ruen in Christo." *Nachfolgung* (1515) Kn. 60–1.

[8] See above, p. 158, footnote 3.

more broadly speaking, the events of Passion Week. The life of the
Christian is a recapitulation of the experience of Christ in Gethsemane,
in which the Christian moves from resistance, to conditional acceptance, to total submission to the will of God.[1] Discipleship is an *imitatio
Christi*, not an *imitatio sanctorum*[2]—though Staupitz makes an ex-
ception for the Virgin Mary, who like her Son is a model for the
Christian. The Christian is gradually brought by the Spirit so to love
the will and justice of God that he is willing to be damned for the
glory of God *(resignatio ad infernum)*.[3] Naked, he follows the naked
Christ.[4] Such a perfection of life, more than anything else, renders
laus and *honor* to God.[5]

With such a strong emphasis on suffering, temptation, and obedience, it is surprising to find so little stress on asceticism.[6] Not all
pleasures in life must be fled.[7] There are licit as well as illicit pleasures,
and the cause of true morality is not advanced by confusing them.
Temporal goods may be loved in their proper order.[8] Indeed, the
sexual act in marriage—so far from being sinful—can even be meri-

---

[1] "Verum sunt quidam gradus in dilectione iusticie. Primus nature ordine est
dum pena simpliciter non assumitur sed resistitur quantum possibile est, salva
obedientia salutari. Secundus quando conditionaliter consentitur in penam propter
expressam voluntatem dei. Si decreta est a te, domine deus, fiat voluntas tua.
Tercius dum nihil aliud desideratur quam ut beneplacitum dei impleatur. Ut ibi
residet dilectio iusticie summa." *Libellus* (1517) 191. Cf. 192–3.

[2] "Wer do wil der lerne von sant Peter sterben ader von andern heilgen, ader
aber sehe, wie die frommen yr leben schliessen, Ich wils von Christo lernen und
nymandts anders. Er ist mir von got ein vorpildt geben, nach dem sal ich wircken,
leyden und sterben..." *Nachfolgung* (1515) Kn. 62.

[3] "Postremo debet perfectus Christianus ex corde sine fictione, tametsi absque
tristicia vix possibile sit, si tamen est possibile in gaudio fieri, gaudens pro gloria
dei; si illa exaltatur magis per eius separationem a deo quam per eius coniunctionem, cedere eterne glorie, resignare deum." *Libellus* (1517) 253. Cf. 252.

[4] "...vil vortreglicher ist es, das wir dem nackenden, dem blossen Jesu nackendt
und bloss nachfolgen und lassen das willig das wir doch willig ader unwillig
lassen muessen." *Nachfolgung* (1515) Kn. 72.

[5] "Non est, quo deus verius quam vitae perfeccione honoratur." *Hiob* (1497–8)
8.57.7.

[6] Speaking of certain forms of asceticism, Staupitz notes: "Illis quoque discre-
tione opus est. Sunt enim huiusmodi aliquando culpe et displicent deo. Sunt non-
unquam pene et penetentie et placent altissimo." *Libellus* (1517) 185.

[7] "Recedere dulcedinibus carnis inordinatis deo placet; non recedere a dulcedinibus licitis deo non displicet." *Libellus* (1517) 188.

[8] "Sed qui non timet te propter te, non timet te virtuose. Ad haec respondet
dominus dicens: dupliciter potest res corporalis diligi, desiderari et eciam delec-
tari. Uno modo in suo gradu sub deo, et sic potest fieri bene. Alio modo supra
deum vel forte equaliter deo et sic fit viciose. Primo modo Job diligit bona tempo
ralia, non secundo." *Hiob* (1497–8) 15.132.12–16.

torious.[1] Moderation, not the removal of pleasure, is the goal.[2] Staupitz frowns on excessive ascetic practices.

At the same time Staupitz places a positive valuation on monastic life—and, in fact, on observant monastic life. In his sermons on Job, Staupitz makes it clear that it is the "reformed" and not the "unreformed" monasteries which have zeal for the honor and glory of God.[3] Nevertheless, the value of monastic life is not to be sought in its ascetic practices, but in the promise of the continual presence of God.[4] Basing his argument on Matthew 18:20, Staupitz asserts that Christ has promised to be present where two or three are assembled in His name. Because a monastery is a perpetual assemblage in the name of Jesus Christ, it has the promise of His perpetual presence.

Staupitz does not believe, however, that the monastic life can guarantee a deeper level of spirituality than secular life. It is very difficult, Staupitz admits wryly, to judge the spirituality of people.[5]

---

[1] "Item tercio actum carnalis copulae in matrimonio non solum bonum, sed et meritorium nonnunquam esse probabo..." *Hiob* (1497–8) 6.38.29ff.

[2] "Jam ergo non pro delactacionum remocione, sed moderacione laboramus." *Hiob* (1497–8) 6.43.2–3.

[3] "Sed econtrario reformati zelose agere consueverunt, quoniam Spiritus sanctus diffusus est in cordibus eorum et qui propter deum sese et sua relinquerunt, propter zelum amicum perdere minus curant, quod utique est divini honoris causa, tantum facile hominem alienum contempno, qui propter deum meipsum abnego." *Hiob* (1497–8) 20.164.28–33. On unreformed monasteries see *Hiob* (1497–8) 20.164. 20–8.

[4] "Wie gar ain gross und sälig ding es ist wo ain samung im namen Christi pey ain ander ist. Den ist got gantz gepunten [N.B. the covenantal language] zu thuen was sy wellen. Darumb seint dy klöster gestyft warden und auf kömen, das wir got darjnn hier mügen dien und pey einander jn aim willen jn aim geist und jn ainer samung wannen jn dem namen Ihesu Christi. Damit er auch albeg pey uns und mytten unter uns mues sein." Hs: b II 11, St. Peter (1523), Sermo 18, fol. 164ᵇ. Unlike John of Paltz, Staupitz does not link his ideal of monastic life with his Mariology. "Vor allem aber zeichnet sich Paltz' Erörterung über das Mönchsideal durch die einzigartige Betonung der Mariologie aus. Maria ist schlechterdings in allem Vorbild für das Mönchtum. Jede auch noch so geringfügige Dienstleistung im Kloster ist nicht als imitatio Christi, sondern als imitatio Mariae zu verstehen: sie wird an Stelle und im Auftrag Marias getan." Bernhard Lohse, *Mönchtum und Reformation, Luthers Auseinandersetzung mit dem Mönchsideal des Mittelalters* (Göttingen, 1963), p. 170.

[5] "Beschwerlich und ergerlich ist es ander lewt Irer fromkait, tugent und gaistlikait halben zuurtailn, denn nymandt Wais Wo got der almechtig wonen, bey Welchem er auch am hochsten gnad wurcken Will und beschicht gar zuvilmalen, das Undter ainer Samaten schauben mere tugent, bestendigkait unnd gots Wurckung, dann unter der kutten Verporgen ligt. Es ist wol war, die gaistlichen In den kutten haben das hoffclaid christi, dorumb man sich auch Vermutet das sie christo zu hoff neher sein, Aber herwiderumb so hat christus auch etlich die er von haus auss bestellet die das hoffclaid nit haben, zu denen stelt er bey weilen mer dann den andern seinen Vertrawen." *Ander personen nit zu urtailen* (1517) Kn. 33.

A layman may be more spiritual than a monk in a cowl. Indeed, the external humility of the monk may mask a subtle and dangerous pride.[1] Life under the cross may be lived outside as well as within a cloister's walls.

V. THE INNER AND THE OUTER WORD

A. *Spirit and Letter.* In his treatise on *The Spirit and the Letter* written in 412 A.D., Augustine expounded his mature doctrine of grace over against the teaching of Pelagius.[2] Augustine agreed with Pelagius that the opposition in II Corinthians 3:6 between the spirit and the letter is not an opposition between the literal and the allegorical interpretation of Scripture. Pelagius, however, in his exposition of Romans 3:28 argued that the "works of the law" from which the Christian is freed refers to the ceremonial rites of Judaism: circumcision, Sabbath observance, etc. Augustine disagreed sharply with him. The law which kills and condemns a man is not the ceremonial law of the Old Testament, but rather the whole system of ethical precepts which exists in the Bible side by side with the ceremonial codes. Man as sinner cannot perform the law of God until the Spirit of God is imparted to him. The law of the Old Testament is written on tables; the law of the New Covenant is written on hearts. Until the Spirit aids man from within, the law can only serve as man's accuser.[3]

Staupitz's successor as dean of the theological faculty of the University of Wittenberg, Andreas Bodenstein von Karlstadt, attempted to reinterpret the Augustinian distinction between letter and Spirit in his commentary on the *Spirit and the Letter* of 1517.[4] Karlstadt, who had studied at Erfurt and Cologne, joined the faculty of Wittenberg in 1505, seven years before Luther's appointment to the same faculity

---

[1] "Gar offt beschicht es das In der grosten diemutigkait die groste hochfart verporgen ligt. Monich mensch erzaigt sich gegen dem andern gantz hohe gedult und diemutigkait mer Zu ainem rum und hochfart, dann aus ubung der tugent, Und dis ist die strafflichst Und ungeschickest hochfart, die auch zuvil malen In der kutten steckt." *Tischreden* (1517) Kn. 42–3.

[2] For a brief introduction to this work see John Burnaby, *Augustine: Later Works*, LCC 8 (Philadelphia: The Westminster Press, 1955) pp. 182–92.

[3] Augustine, *De Spiritu et Littera* 42 (*PL* 44.271).

[4] On the problem of Scripture and Spirit in Karlstadt, see Ernst Kähler, *Karlstadt und Augustin* (Halle, 1952), pp. 40*–42*. See also Gordon Rupp, "Word and Spirit in the First Years of the Reformation," ARG 49 (1958), 13–26; George H. Williams, *The Radical Reformation* (Philadelphia: The Westminster Press, 1962), pp. 821–28.

He began his theological career as a Thomist, earning his theological doctorate in 1510 and a doctorate in canon and civil law in 1516. In January 1517, Karlstadt purchased the works of Augustine. His original purpose in studying Augustine was to test the validity of Luther's interpretation of Augustine. However, under the influence of a theological treatise by Staupitz, probably under the influence of Staupitz's treatise on *Predestination* of 1517, Karlstadt was led to a decisive change in his own theological outlook. Karlstadt had known Staupitz during the years 1505 to 1512, when Staupitz was a professor of theology at Wittenberg and the dean of the theological faculty.[1] But it is not until 1517 that there is evidence of theological influence.

In interpreting Augustine, Karlstadt demonstrates in a more extreme form a spiritualism which one also finds in the theology of Staupitz. Augustine's contrast between law and Spirit became for Karlstadt a contrast between the external Word and the Spirit. The preacher can reach the ear, the letter can inform the eyes, but only God can touch the heart.[2] The true Word of God is an inner illumination of the Spirit. The inner illumination precedes the external

---

[1] On the relation of Staupitz and Karlstadt, see Kähler, *Karlstadt*, pp. 2*-8*. "Von Luthers ständigem Hinweis auf Augustin gedrängt, hat K. dann auf einer Reise nach Leipzig im Januar 1517 die Werke Augustins erworben und unmittelbar darauf sie durchzuarbeiten begonnen. Die Frage, mit der er, historisch gesehen, an Augustin heranging, war einfach die, ob Luthers Berufung auf Augustin zu Recht bestand oder nicht. Er hat das zunächst bestritten und versucht, Luther aus Augustin zu widerlegen. In den ihm dabei aufsteigenden Zweifeln veranlasste ihn dann eine Schrift Johannes' von Staupitz, vermutlich der 'Libellus de Executione eterne predestinationis', zum endgültigen Bruch mit seiner theologischen Vergangenheit." Kähler, *Karlstadt*, p. 4*. It is "...kennzeichnend für die Theologie K.s, dass er bei seiner Wendung zu Augustin nicht eigentlich den Gedankengängen Luthers nachgab, sondern der Autorität und dem Vorgang Staupitzens folgte." Kähler, *Karlstadt*, p. 7*. Karlstadt's dedication of his book to Staupitz is thus "...sicher mehr als eine der üblichen Dedikationen, sondern ein wirklicher Dank." Kähler, *Karlstadt*, p. 7*. In his discussion of Staupitz, however, Kähler follows Wolf. Staupitz and Karlstadt are "...beide anfänglich Thomisten..." and the Thomistic influences of Cologne are considered more important than the Scotistic-nominalistic influences of Tübingen. Kähler, *Karlstadt*, p. 5*. For further biographical information on Karlstadt, see George H. Williams, *The Radical Reformation*, pp. 39-44.

[2] Andreas Bodenstein von Karlstadt, "Pro Divinae gratiae defensione," ed. Kähler, *Karlstadt*, p. 27: "Levamus itaque ad predicatores aures opplendas, ad litteras oculos informandos, sed cor ad solum deum caeli et terrae creatorem, qui intrinsecus 'verax verbum' 'omnia opera' precedens inspirat et cor tangit." Cf. p. 84: "Vos autem modo tradiciunculam servate, quod non lege, non doctrina forinsecus insonanate, sed interna atque occulta, mirabili ac ineffabili deum potestate operari in cordibus bonas voluntates.

"works" of reading and listening.[1] The law, i.e., the external word of preaching or teaching, provides no help to man in gaining faith. The Spirit alone works faith in man. The original contrast between the ethical demand of the law and the fulfillment of that demand through the Spirit is transformed into a contrast between external preaching and teaching and inner illumination.[2]

B. *Law, Gospel and Augustine.* Staupitz's theology has affinities with both Augustine and Karlstadt, though Staupitz is more Christocentric than Augustine and less radical than Karlstadt. Like Augustine, Staupitz believes that the distinction between the letter and the Spirit is primarily a distinction between the moral demand of God and the indwelling Spirit who makes the fulfilment of that demand a possibility for man. Unlike Augustine, however, Staupitz uses the contrast between letter and Spirit as the contrast between Law and Gospel. Thus the distinction gains a hermeneutical dimension which is missing in Augustine. Staupitz agrees with Augustine that the moral demand of God condemns fallen man unless the Spirit gives him the power to fulfil that demand. He wishes to know, however, what is the relationship between this demand and Holy Scripture. The solution is Christological. Just as in the realm of grace and free will the letter is the demand of God without *Christus inhabitans,* so, too, in the realm of hermeneutics the letter is the text of Scripture divorced from its reference to *Christus revelatus.*[3]

The distinction between letter and spirit is not a distinction between the Old and the New Testaments. The error of Peter in the story of the Transfiguration is that he attempted to separate Jesus from the law and the prophets.[4] The Old Testament, however, cannot

---

[1] Kähler argues that the *omnia opera* which the *verax verbum* precedes should be understood as the "...Werk des äusseren Lesens und Hörens..." and not as "...das Werk als Erfüllung des Gesetzes." Kähler, *Karlstadt,* p. 42*.

[2] "In K.s Thesen ist nur noch die spiritualistische Tendenz wirksam: das Gesetz tötet nicht deshalb, weil es Gottes richtende Heiligkeit bezeugt, sondern weil es toter Buchstabe ist, der erst des belebenden Geistes bedarf, um zu seiner eigentlichen Bestimmung zu gelangen. Die dem Gesetz anhaftende Eigenschaft tödlicher Wirkung ist hier in seinem Geschriebensein begründet. Es geht also weder um den Gegensatz von Gesetz und Evangelium, noch um den von Gesetz und Gnade, sondern um den von Schrift und Geist." Kähler, *Karlstadt,* pp. 28*–29*.

[3] "Da ist kaine geschrift auf erdn dy so schedleich ist & also verdambt als das evangelum, so mans nach dem puechstabn liest...wer das evangelium liest & suecht den Christum nit & vindt jn nit darinen, dem ist dy höchst verdamnus." *Salzburger Predigten* (1523), No. 6, Aumüller, p. 129.

[4] "Syech Petrus, du abenteuer, Got mags nit leydn das du das gesetz & dy profetn von Christus wolts tailln. du hast doch wol gesechn das sy jm geleich klar

be separated from Christ.[1] It must be understood Christologically. The Old Testament contains figures which point ahead to a fulfilment in Jesus Christ.[2] Christ is, so to say, hidden in the law.[3] Or, to change the metaphor, the law is pregnant *(schwanger)* and bears Christ *(tregt Cristum)*.[4]

The New Testament is not unique in its proclamation of Jesus Christ. The Old Testament as well bears witness to Him. Job, for example, knew the incarnate Christ through divine revelation.[5] He pointed to the One who was yet to come. In this action he was not alone. The Hebrew law prefigures Christ (especially His sufferings) and the prophets promise His advent.[6]

If, however, both the Old and the New Testaments witness to Jesus Christ, then in what sense is the Old Testament "old" or the New Testament "new"? The answer is implied in what Staupitz has said already. The Old Testament is "old" because it offers Christ merely in prefigurement and in promise. It cannot offer the fulfilment of those prefigurements and promises. That is the proper task of the New Testament alone.

It is not, strictly speaking, the law which condemns man or which

---

habn muessen werdn. due hast auch gehört das sy nur von Christo allein habn geredt & nit vom gesetz oder andern sachn. sey dem Christo muest allain peleibn & nit pey Moysi & Helia." *Salzburger Predigten* (1523), No. 5, Aumüller, p. 126.

[1] "Da redt Sant Peter so narrisch als er dan oft ain narrisch red hat tan & sagt: ey mein lieber herr, lass nur alweg hie peleibn, ich wil drey tabernacl hie pauen, dir ain, Moysi ain & Helia ain. syech da wolt er das gesetz & dy profetn von Jesus taill. Ach es muess das gesetz gelesen werdn & dy profetn das al[le] auf den zaig, als sagt Moyses: das gesetz & ale sein figurn habent den bezeichnet; die ist dy warhait; & Sant Helias; syech was ich & dy andern profetn euch versprochn habn, das ist klar euch allen ins gesycht, ja & in dy hant gebn. Sy muessen gelesn werdn das sy klar mit Christo vergleicht werden." *Salzburger Predigten* (1523), No. 5, Aumüller, pp. 125–6.

[2] "Ach sagt mein got, es muess dy geschryft alle an mir erfüllt werden. Ich pin der, der alle geschrift von figur jn dy warhait so pringen. Ja mir muess nit ain tütel aus peleiben." Hs: b II 11, St. Peter (1523), Sermo 22, fol. 217ᵇ–218ᵃ.

[3] "Allein ist ein trost darbey, das unter dem buchstaben der geyst vorborgen ligt...Die disen geyst funden haben, und Christum ym gesetz verborgen erkenen, den ist die geschrifft zu nutzbarer lere und, alls Paulus sagt, zu troste kommen..." *Lieb gottes* (1518) Kn. 97.

[4] "...das allt gesetz schwanger ist und tregt Cristum..." *Lieb gottes* (1518) Kn. 97.

[5] "Sed dices Job Christi incarnacionem non vidisse, multis annis ante mortuus quam in carne visus est Cristus. Sed dicimus Job per divinam revelacionem Cristum futurum cognovisse, ut in processu libri manifestans patebit." *Hiob* (1497–8) 11.98.32–5.

[6] "...uns das alt gesetz dy leydn Christi gefigurirt; also habn jn uns dy profetn versprochen, aber das evangelij gibt uns jn jn dy hant." *Salzburger Predigten* (1523), No. 5, Aumüller, p. 125.

brings a knowledge of sin. There is a sense in which the law is itself gospel; i.e., to the extent that it bears witness to Jesus Christ.[1] It is not the law which condemns and kills; rather it is the letter of the law which brings man to his ruin. The demand which is not at the same time an offer is the *littera occidens*.

A merely external knowledge of the law cannot teach a man to love God supremely.[2] There must be a work of grace within him before he can devote his heart in love to God.[3] The letter of the law does bring man a fresh realization of his predicament. By teaching man the duty which he should fulfil, the letter of the law makes him aware of the sin which he has committed by not fulfilling that duty, jars him with the awareness that he is unable to fulfil it, and frightens him with the prospect of the eternal punishment which awaits him. More than this the law cannot do.[4]

The self-righteous man, however, places his reliance on the letter of the law.[5] He revels in his own knowledge of Holy Scripture and is haughty and audacious in his handling of the sacred text. But his knowledge does not profit him at all. He does not read Scripture according to the Spirit (i.e., he does not receive the truth in humility)

---

[1] "...das gesetz ain war zeugnus gibt dem Jesus jn alln fygurn..." *Salzburger Predigten* (1523), No. 5, Aumüller, p. 125.

[2] "Aber nie nichtz hat das gesetz tzum volkommen pracht, das ist eben tzu lieb gottes uber alle ding, die des menschens hochste volkommenheit ist." *Lieb gottes* (1518) Kn. 97.

[3] "Das die heilige geschrifft nit wircklichen seligen verstandt gewindt aus ausserer lernung zu erreichen die lieb gotes uber alle ding...Aus den augen muess christus ins hertz, aus dem fleisch in den geist geen, so er anderst seliglich erkennt werden. Darumb vertzeicht ehr sich selbst der frucht seiner ausseren lere, Wo die von der ynnern abgesundert unnd geteilt ist. In disem verstandt spricht Paulus, das seine und anderer aposteln lere nichtz sei, wo got nit selbst yns hertz lernt." *Lieb gottes* (1518) Kn. 99–100.

[4] "Dem nach gebiert der buchstaben des alten gesetz anders nichtz, den erkentnus der pflicht, das man die gepot halten muess, erkenntnus der sunde, das man sy ubertreten hat, erkentnus des unvermogens, das man sy nit halten vermog, erkentnus der ewigen pein, die man darumb leyden muess, darauss entspringet forcht, weyter vermag der buchstaben nichtz, deshalben todtet er als Paulus spricht, macht nit lebendig, zaigt die kranckheit, macht nit gesundt, offenbart die sund, macht schwerern." *Lieb gottes* (1518) Kn. 97.

[5] "Es sein zwayerlay menschen. Dy lerer sagen, juden und haiden. Ich sag frum und pös. Ja das ich vorstentlaicher red, dy sych frum halten, und sunder dy sych fur frum und gerecht halten, dy sein reich. Dan sy suechen all jren wolust jn der geschrift unnd zyechens wie sy wellen. Dye legen dye geschrift alle auf den puechstaben aus und predigen dan nur das Ewangelij auf verzweyfling und auf irr gewissen dy sy dem armen menschen machen..." Hs: b II 11, St. Peter (1523), Sermo 9, fol. 71ᵇ–72ᵃ.

but according to the letter.[1] Knowledge of the text apart from the renewing work of the divine Spirit cannot extricate a man from his predicament as a sinner. No one can keep the law unless he is in union with Jesus Christ. The letter kills; it does not impart life.

If there is a sense in which the Old Testament contains the gospel, there is also a sense in which the New Testament functions as law. If one understands the message of the New Testaments according to the letter—i.e., if one listens to the proclamation about Jesus Christ, but there is no accompanying work of the Spirit in one's heart—the "good news" of Jesus Christ, instead of bringing life, becomes the hardest law of all.[2] The reason for this is plain: the message about Jesus Christ the Redeemer is far more fully and clearly set forth in the New Testament than in the Old. The Old Testament prefigured Jesus Christ. His coming was prophesied and promised by the seers and sages of Israel. But His Person was only dimly seen; His work of redemption not yet accomplished.

The New Testament, however, witnesses to the fulfilment of the promises of the Old Testament. In Jesus Christ, God revealed the depths of His mercy. In the cross and resurrection, He acted to make that mercy effective for the redemption of fallen man. The more one knows of divine love, the more one has received from God's hand, the greater one's responsibility. Therefore, Staupitz insists that the letter of the New Testament is deadlier than the letter of the Old. Indeed, it is better not to read the gospel at all than to read it apart from the Spirit.[3]

---

[1] "Als geschriben ist, der puechstaben tödt, aber der geist macht lembtig [2 Cor. 3:6], sol verstanden werden, das kain swert so scharff ist, noch kain ding das den menschen als warlich und verdämleich tödt, und abschaid von der gnad gotz, als so von der ler und erkantnüs der heilig geschrift jn jm selber wirt erhebt und aufplät jn vermessenhait und hochfart." Hs: 23 E 16, Nonnberg, fol. 52^b. The spiritual understanding of Scripture is not merely the perception of the relationship of the sacred text to Jesus Christ (for the Old Testament, *Figur* and *Versprechung*; for the New, *Erfüllung*); it is the perception of this relationship in faith. "...man muess den Christus im Gelauben im gesetz lesn & findn..." *Salzburger Predigten* (1523), No. 5, Aumüller, p. 125. Cf. Hs: 23 E 16, Nonnberg, fol. 52^b–53^a: "Aber der geist macht lemtig, das ist so der puechstabn der warhait der heyling geschrift jn dyenmuetiger erkantnus wirt gelegt jn dy begir des hertzen."

[2] "Darumb ist das Evang. des allerhörtist gesetzt das ja gewesen ist dem der es nach dem puechstabn v'stet..." *Salzburger Predigten* (1523), No. 2, Aumüller, p. 56. Cf. *Lieb gottes* (1518) Kn. 97–8.

[3] "Ey sagt main got, ich gee vom tod ins lebn, vom fleisch in Geist, vom gesycht ins hertz; dan wan das evangelij nit gelesn wird zum lebn & zum geist so wär pesser man hiet es nye gesechn, noch gewist." *Salzburger Predigten* (1523), No. 6, Aumüller, p. 130.

Of course, Satan is eager to cloud the face of God in Holy Scripture.[1] One of the ways he does this is by the imposition of alien categories on the contents of the Bible. The New Testament witnesses to Jesus Christ as the God-man. The Aristotelians, however, who take their logical categories with far more seriousness than they do divine revelation, find the New Testament account of a *Gottmensch* an insurmountable obstacle.[2] He is either one or the other; He cannot be both. Thus the Aristotelians fail to understand a word of the gospel, because they do not approach divine revelation with humility.

The distinction between letter and spirit is not a distinction between the Old and the New Testaments. Both can be read according to the letter or understood according to the spirit. A spiritual understanding of the Old Testament is lifegiving; a merely literal understanding of the New Testament is deadly. To understand Scripture spiritually is to understand it in its relationship to Jesus Christ. That is not to say, however, that the spiritual understanding of Scripture is purely informational. To understand the New Testament according to the letter means that one has information about Jesus Christ, but no power to follow him in obedient discipleship. Information about Jesus Christ is not life-giving unless it is accompanied by an interior work of renewal, effected by the Holy Spirit in the heart of the believing man. A man understands Scripture spiritually when he per-

---

[1] "Facies, inquam, domini, i.e. aspectus divinitatis in praesenti ambulantibus adhuc in spe et fide in sola scriptura sacra ostenditur. Ideo Sathan egredi a facie domini nihil aliud est quam affectum a sacra leccione retrahere...Primo per scripturae falsum intellectum..." *Hiob* (1497–8) 31.239.13–20.

[2] "Aber dy juden geben yn [Christus] den hayden. Dy halten's für ain narrenwerch. Dann sy kynen's jn jrer vernunft nit begreiffen das er warer gott und mensch ist. Also ist es mit dem predigern dy den Aristotiles kynnen, dy maynen sy kynnen das gantz Ewangelij und wissen nit ain wart darumb. Ain gueter ainfaltiger man der got recht lieb hat, der redt von dem Ewangelij und es ist liebleich zu hören. Aber dy da fast wollen gelert sain, dy welons Ewangelij jnn Arestotilis ziechen, dy komen zum lesten darzue das sy amtweder Christum allain für got haben oder allain für ain menschen. got und mensch künnen sy nicht darynn vinden pey ainander." Hs: b II 11, St. Peter (1523), Sermo 8, fol. 66a-b. This is probably not so much an attack on Aristotelian philosophy as it is on learning without piety. Staupitz values piety more than learning, if he is forced to choose between them—though he would prefer to keep them united. See Hs: b V 8, St. Peter (1512), Sermo 8, fol. 35b: "Ain frumer ungelerter yst besser dann ain gelerter schalck...möcht es seyn, war mir lieber, er wär auch gelert und frum myt ain ander." In his sermons on Job of 1497–8, Staupitz cites Aristotle 57 times. On the other hand, one should not forget that university reform at Wittenberg aimed, among other things, at the displacement of Aristotle from the curriculum in favor of the Bible and St. Augustine. See *WAB* 1.99, No. 41.8–13 (18 May 1517). Cf. Gerhard Ebeling, *Luther, Einführung in sein Denken* (Tübingen, 1964), pp. 6–9.

ceives that the object to which the language of the Bible refers is Jesus
Christ and, renouncing all trust in his own ability to follow Christ,
enters into a living relationship with Him through the divine Spirit.

Staupitz divides the law into the law of nature, the law of Moses
and the law of Christ.[1] Of these three, the law of Christ *ad litteram* (i.e.,
without the power of the indwelling Spirit) is the most difficult to be
borne, because it demands of man a total abandonment of himself and
a total surrender to the will of God.[2] This is precisely what fallen man,
relying on his own natural powers, cannot do. The law as letter slays
him.

Conversion to Christ results in a change of affections.[3] The indwelling Spirit of God, diffusing love in the heart of man, lightens
the burden of the law and makes it possible for man to love God
super omnia.[4] Christ does not abolish the law for the Christian,[5] though
He abolishes the joyless legalism of the self-righteous Pharisee.[6] What
He changes is man's relationship to the law, giving him the power to
live in humble imitation of his Savior. Life under the cross is for
Staupitz life in the Spirit.

C. *Preaching, Illumination and Andreas Bodenstein von Karlstadt.* As we
have already seen in earlier discussions, the external word of Scripture
and preaching has an important role to play in the theology of Staupitz. He argues, for example, that the *facies domini* is revealed to the
viator in Scripture alone[7] and can insist that preaching is one of the
means which God uses to call men to the sacrament of penance.[8] Indeed, so highly does he value the preaching office that he spends con-
siderable time in his sermons to the Augustinian monks in Tübingen
commenting on the duties and qualifications of a preacher of the
gospel.

---

[1] "Dura est lex nature, durior Moysi, Christi durissima." *Libellus* (1517) 123.

[2] "Lex quoque Christi ad litteram durissima est, quia rapit totum hominem
sibimet et totaliter extra seipsum ponit." *Libellus* (1517) 126. "Ligatus itaque est
Christianus in omnibus, ita etiam ut semetipsum odisse debeat et perdere abnega-
reque ac cum cruce quotidie sequitur Christum." *Libellus* (1517) 127.

[3] "...qui diligit Christum, odit peccatum." *Libellus* (1517) 178.

[4] *Libellus* (1517) 122, 128–9; *Lieb gottes* (1518) Kn. 94, 115.

[5] "Ach Got wie sind das so ungeschickt lere, ketzerische erdichtung und ver-
blendung der warhait. Christus wil das gesetz verbracht haben, die narren wöllen
das gesetz vertilgen. Paulus lobt das gesetz, das es gut sey, die narren scheltens,
das es böss sey, darumb das sie nach dem fleysch wandern, unnd haben den ge-
schmack des geysts nicht." *Glauben* (1525) Kn. 132.

[6] *Lieb gottes* (1518) Kn. 114.

[7] See above, p. 177, footnote 1.

[8] *Hiob* (1497–8) 20.169.1–9.

No one, according to Staupitz, should preach unless he is called to do so by God.[1] There are far too many people who have Christ on their tongues and not in their hearts.[2] If he is called, he should love the truth which he is called to proclaim more than life itself.[3] It is God whom he is called to please, not the world.[4] He should not fear to rebuke princes for their faults, if it becomes necessary to do so.[5] He should discharge his office with zeal.

True zeal comes from the love of God.[6] It acts discreetly, knowing that while it is easy for the preacher to know something about Holy Scripture, it is difficult for him to have the grace to help men.[7] The zealous preacher edifies rather than destroys.[8] If he denounces sin, he is careful not to make it attractive.[9] And he never preaches about sin without showing the mercy of God which is available to the sinner.[10]

---

[1] "...ist ein fein ordnung in der kirchn das nyemant predign sol, er sey dan darzue erfadert & geweicht...ab Got fodert nit yederman. hör, er wirt dir wol ain recht warzaichn gebn, wil er das du sagst & lernst..." *Salzburger Predigten* (1523), No. 5, Aumüller, p. 127.

[2] "Also findestu auff disen tag, das vilmals die Christum am meisten auff der tzungen haben, finden ynn selten ym hertzenn... lernenn vil von ym reden, aber wenig lieben..." *Lieb gottes* (1518) Kn. 98.

[3] "Illius imitatores sunt praedicatores, qui magis timent deum quam homines et praeeligunt mori quam veritatis viam declinare." *Hiob* (1497–8) 21.175.30–1.

[4] "Primus ergo effectus, quo virtus praedicata confirmata persistat, est, quod praedicator studeat placere deo, non mundo. Parum namque curabit, si ista hominibus displiceant, quae deo veraciter placere non dubitat." *Hiob* (1497–8) 21.175. 1–4.

[5] "Ex illo principio habes, quod praedicatores debent vicia pastorum arguere, quod non solum de pastoribus spiritualibus, sed et principibus secularibus dictum intelligi debet, et hic modus est correctorius." *Hiob* (1497–8) 21.173.36–9.

[6] "Zelum hunc non habent praedicatores viciosi, quia producitur ab amore dei et intenso..." *Hiob* (1497–8) 20.164.6–7.

[7] "Es ist ein schlechte geringe kunst die heiligen schrifft zulesen Und dero vil Zuwissen, aber die gnad Zuhaben das sie Zu trost Und hilff der menschen appliart Und mer Zu ainer ergetzung dann Verzweifelung gepraucht werd, Wie selzam sein Und nit ainem yden mitgetailt werden." *Sentencien* (1517) Kn. 28.

[8] *Hiob* (1497–8) 20.166.32–6.

[9] "Videat ergo, videant, inquam, praedicatores, ne mundiciam cordium innocentem corrumpant, quando vicia aliorum impudice clamant. Hanc doctrinam eciam confessoribus scripsisse volo, quorum est ita inquirere peccata, un non doceant, quae ante fuerunt incognita." *Hiob* (1497–8) 20.168.10–14.

[10] "Ein gering ding ist es dem menschen taglich Vorzupredigen, das er vil sunden gethan hab, das solche sundt gross sein, das auch sovil sundt seyen, das sie tochtern, kinder, eniglein und Vrenigklein haben, Wie vil ungeschickter prediger pflegen zuthun. Aber was frucht und hilff Wirdet dem menschen domit mitgetailt...Es ist nit schwer ainen In ain Wasser zuwerffen, das ist aber nit gering Und vil grosser ainen Im wasser lebendig zubehalten und davon zuentledigen." *Sentencien* (1517) Kn. 27–8.

He is careful not to harm the faith of the simple[1] and, though he may long for reform in the Church, he knows that any reform which attacks the primacy of Rome is a false reform.[2] Real zeal is pastoral; it learns to bear patiently what it cannot change.[3]

The preacher of the gospel does not imitate the bad example of his superiors.[4] He knows that an evil life is a hindrance to the gospel,[5] and so he conforms his life to Christ rather than to the world.[6] Nevertheless, he knows that the authority of Scripture does not depend upon the authority of the preacher.[7] There is an anti-donatistic thrust in Staupitz's doctrine of preaching. The Word of God remains true, even if the preacher who proclaims it is evil.[8]

The preaching of the Gospel, however, must be accompanied by an inner illumination of the Spirit or the hearing of the gospel will be fruitless. The preacher can reach the ears; Christ alone can reach the heart.[9] The inner preaching of Christ does not dispense with the necessity for the outer proclamation of the Word. The inner work of

---

[1] *Hiob* (1497–8) 20.167.7–20.

[2] "Multos proinde invenimus hereticos, quos fefellit tales zelus tollendi scandala a domo dei indiscrete per hanc aut illam praedicacionis viam. Hinc hereses contra primatum Romanae ecclesiae, quod sine ea stat salus, contra religiosorum observanciam, quod sit contra libertatem legis Christi. Dum enim displicuerunt mores, suborti sunt errores." *Hiob* (1497–8) 20.165.1–6.

[3] "Verum itaque zelum elevate proprieque descripsit, qui dixit: illum comedit zelum domus dei, qui scandala, quae videt in ecclesia, tollere vult, sit potest. Si non potest, tollerat et gemit." *Hiob* (1497–8) 20.165.8–11.

[4] "Fac tantam diligenciam in re spirituali contempta vel non imitata negligencia tui superiores." *Hiob* (1497–8) 19.161.19–20. Cf. *Hiob* (1497–8) 19.157.27–33.

[5] "Et si manet difficultas in scandalo sacerdotum, quia, cuius vita despicitur, restat, ut eius praedicacio contempnatur, ut ait S. Gre. [Gregory the Great, *Moralia* 19.28, *PL* 76.121] Dedit dominus populo suo alios praedicatores, qui eciam huiusmodi vicia racionabiliter corrigere debent et populum diligenter informare." *Hiob* (1497–8) 19.162.10–14.

[6] *Hiob* (1497–8) 19.159.2–9.

[7] "Sed quia non meam, sed scripturae, sed Cristi sentenciam profero, qui sapiencia dei est et veritas, qui maculas iniquitatis non habuit. Innocens namque est sine dolo, sine falsitate, ideo ipse regula est omni viventi nec inventum est in eo, quod reprehensioni subiacet." *Hiob* (1497–8) 19.162.36–9.

[8] "...praedicatores, sint boni sive mali, verbum tamen dei, quod praedicant, verum est." *Hiob* (1497–8) 19.162.

[9] "aber uns leydt wenig dran ob der nit guet ist der predigt, wan ers nur recht predigt...er sey wie heilig er wil, so kan ers nit weyter dan in dy orn predign, Christus muess selbs ins herz predign, das muess auch seyn oder wir hörens nit saeligkleich." *Salzburger Predigten* (1523), No. 7, Aumüller, p. 132. Just as the *viator* cannot live a holy life without the Spirit at work in his own heart, so too the preacher cannot reach his listeners by the force of his own holiness, but must depend upon the work of the Spirit in their hearts. In preaching, as in life generally, man is absolutely dependent upon God.

Christ accompanies the outer Word, or, as Staupitz himself says
"...das muess *auch* seyn...." Unless Christ preaches, the sinner hears
the Word, but he does not hear it *saeligkleich*. The outer word is subordinate to the inner word, but it is not abolished by it.

On the other hand, the Spirit is not bound to the preaching of the
Word of God. Even though Staupitz is suspicious of visions, he does
teach that the Spirit of God speaks a Word of God to the heart of the
humble who wait in silence in His presence.[1] God is not circumscribed
or limited by Scripture. The Spirit who inspired the prophets can
speak directly to the heart of the justified in whom He dwells. And
Staupitz urges his listeners to refrain from their pious exercises and
to wait in silence for the voice of God.

Staupitz is willing to go part of the way with Karlstadt. He believes
that the external word is fruitless without the inner illumination of the
Spirit[2] and even loosens the bond between the Spirit and the preached
and written word.[3] But he does not abolish external means altogether.
God uses Scripture, preaching, and the institutions of monastic life to
bring men to life, even though He is not bound to them.[4] The law
slays man, not because it is written or preached, but because man as
sinner is impotent to fulfil its ethical demands. The Spirit vivifies man,
not merely by illuminating him concerning the will of God, but by
giving him the power to obey it.

---

[1] "dyr gehört nit mer zue dann das du gesweigst von innen & aussen & jm
stat gebst zu reden & last euch nit anfechten dy narren dye sagen, man bedürf
nichtz darzue than, es ist war & ich sag euch es ist nutz & noth darzue sweygen &
andre ordnung & sich gantz entschlachen von allen aussern dingen, auch von dem
aussern gesnürch & gebet. sweig und sitz pey euch selbst & sagt: ach mein frum
got, allerliebster vater, was wiltu doch mit mir reden? O red mein got, wan deine
word seint süess meinen oren, wiewol ich wais das ich daszuhören nit wurdig pin.
So weistu es auch wol das ich des aber gar nothdurftig pin. also pis gewis got
sweigt nit. Ach umb gots willen tuet euch eures aussern geswätz ab & hort auf
got damit er sein frewntlich gespräch jn euch müg haben." *Salzburger Predigten*
(1523), No. 1, Aumüller, pp. 52–3. Cf. *Nachfolgung* (1515) Kn. 83; *Lieb gottes* (1518)
Kn. 106, 108–9.
[2] *Salzburger Predigten* (1523), No. 7, Aumüller, p. 132.
[3] *Salzburger Predigten* (1523), No. 1, Aumüller, pp. 52–3; *Nachfolgung* (1515) Kn.
83; *Lieb gottes* (1518) Kn. 106, 108–9.
[4] *Hiob* (1497–8) 20.169.1–9.

CHAPTER SEVEN

CONCLUSION

The great themes of Staupitz's theology are thus interwoven in his doctrine of the Christian life. From the Scotistic-nominalistic tradition of theology Staupitz learned to envision God's relationship to the world as a covenantal relationship, in which the theme of the fidelity of God takes precedence over the Thomistic conception of the world as an organism. Like the nominalists, Staupitz emphasized uncreated over created grace, though unlike them he abandoned altogether the idea of grace as a *habitus*. To be justified is to be indwelt by the Spirit of Christ; and the life of discipleship is a life lived in union with Christ. In the midst of temptation and suffering, the Christian is confident of victory, not because he trusts his own natural powers—a nominalistic illusion of which he wants no part—but because he is sustained by the faithfulness of God, who has made conformity to Christ part of His covenanted mercies. All the gifts of God—vocation, justification, glorification—are the temporal fruition of the electing decree of God. Though no one can be certain apart from special revelation that he is elect, there are strong grounds for conjectural certitude. Justification makes man a co-worker with God, though man's cooperation is understood by Staupitz as always a fruit and never a presupposition of grace. Like the Virgin Mary, man's cooperation is little more than the uttering of a *fiat* to the Spirit of God.

Staupitz differs with the nominalists—not in their view of God as One who freely enters into covenant with man *de potentia ordinata*, but in their view of man as one who has the power *de puris naturalibus* to fulfil the law of God. The law slays; it does not give life. The fault, of course, does not lie in the law, but in the perverted will of fallen man. Man is impotent, not only to earn merits apart from grace (Thomas Aquinas is willing to assert that!), but even to act virtuously. Reliance on one's own natural powers is tantamount to a sentence of condemnation.

Staupitz advocates no technique for living life in the Spirit, but he elucidates how God lives with His elect. The sinner must abandon his pretensions and surrender his will to God. Since God will give the Christian both the desire and the ability to surrender himself to God,

detailed instructions on the proper way for doing this are both unnecessary and deceptive. God has promised to bring the elect into
conformity with Christ. And what He has promised, He has the
power to perform. That is all the Christian needs to know.

The theology of Staupitz moves easily from an explanation of the
works of God to a confession of His praise. The whole theology of
Staupitz is a confession of the fidelity of God, who seeks out men
when they do not seek Him and who preserves them from falling
when they despair of their own ability to remain faithful. It is the
same theme which is celebrated by Augustine in his *Confessions*[1] and
enunciated with a new force in the theology of the young Luther.[2]
New elements have entered the story as it is told by Staupitz, some
borrowed from other scholastics, some original with him. But the
theme itself is unchanged. Staupitz praises the fidelity of God who
seeks out men in their *miseria* and brings the elect back to fellowship
with God who is their true *origo et finis*.

---

[1] "One does not read far in the *Confessions* before he recognizes that the term
'confess' has a double range of meaning. On the one hand, it obviously refers to
the free acknowledgment, before God, of the truth one knows about oneself—and
this obviously meant, for Augustine, the 'confession of sins.' But, at the same time,
and more importantly, *confiteri* means to acknowledge, to God, the truth one
knows about God. To confess, then, is to praise and glorify God; it is an exercise
in selfknowledge and true humility in the atmosphere of grace and reconciliation."
Albert C. Outler, *Augustine: Confessions and Enchiridion, LCC* VII (Philadelphia:
The Westminster Press, 1955), p. 19.

[2] Heiko A. Oberman, "'Iustitia Christi' and 'Iustitia Dei', Luther and the
Scholastic Doctrines of Justification," *HTR* 59 (1966), pp. 25–6, footnote 52.

BIBLIOGRAPHY

I. *Periodicals*

ARG *Archiv für Reformationsgeschichte* (Leipzig und Gütersloh, 1903–   ).
HJ   *Historisches Jahrbuch* (Münster i.W., 1880–2; Munich, 1883–1930; Cologne, 1931–50; Munich and Freiburg i.Br., 1950–   ).
HTR *Harvard Theological Review* (Cambridge. Mass., 1908–   ).
JES *Journal of Ecumenical Studies* (Pittsburgh, 1964–   ).
NAK Nederlandsch Archief voor Kerkgeschiedenis (The Hague, 1900–   ).
ThQ *Theologische Quartalschrift* (Tübingen, 1831–1928; various places 1929–   ).
ThZ *Theologische Zeitschrift* (Basel, 1945–   ).
ZKG *Zeitschrift für Kirchengeschichte* (Gotha, 1877–1930, Stuttgart, 1931–   ).
ZKTh Zeitschrift für katholische Theologie (Innsbruck, 1877–1940; Vienna, 1947–   ).
ZThK Zeitschrift für Theologie und Kirche (Tübingen, 1891–   ).

II. *Collections, Editions, and Encyclopedias*

BB   *Beiträge zur Geschichte der Philosophie und Theologie des Mittelalters*, founded by Clemens Baeumker (Münster i.W., 1891–   ).
CSEL Corpus Scriptorum Ecclesiasticorum Latinorum (Vienna, 1866–   ).
Denz. Denzinger, H. *Enchiridion Symbolorum*, ed. Karl Rahner, S.J., 31 ed. (Freiburg i.Br., 1960).
DThC Dictionnaire de théologie catholique (Paris, 1909–50).
PG   *Patrologia Graeca*, ed. J. P. Migne (Paris, 1857–1912).
PL   *Patrologia Latina*, ed. J. P. Migne (Paris, 1844–1890).
RE   *Realencyklopädie für protestantische Theologie und Kirche*, 3 ed. (Leipzig. 1896–1913).
RGG Die Religion in Geschichte und Gegenwart, 3 ed. (Tübingen, 1957–   ).
DG   Seeberg, Reinhold, *Lehrbuch der Dogmengeschichte*. 5 ed. (Leipzig, 1953), 5 vols.
WA   D. Martin Luthers Werke: *Kritische Gesamtausgabe* (Weimar, 1883–   ).
WAB: Briefwechsel.
WATR: Tischreden.

III. *Primary Sources—General*

Abelard, Peter, *Ethica*, in *PL*, vol. 178.
Alexander of Hales, *Summa Theologica*, Quaracchi, 1924–48.
Altenstaig, Johannes, *Vocabularius theologie*, Hagenau, 1517.
Anselm of Canterbury, *Cur Deus Homo*, in *PL*, vol. 158.
Augustine, *Opera*, in *PL*, vols. 32–43, and in *CSEL*, vols. 25, 27–8, 33–4, 36, 40–44.
Bernard of Clairvaux, *De diligendo deo; Sermones*, in *PL*, vols. 182–3.
Biel, Gabriel, *Epithoma pariter et collectorium circa quattuor sententiarum libros*, Tübingen, 1501.
——, *Gabrielis Biel, Canonis Misse Expositio, Pars Prima*, ed. Heiko A. Oberman and William J. Courtenay, Wiesbaden, 1963.
——, *Sermones de festivitatibus christi*, Hagenau, 1510.
——, *Sermones dominicales de tempore*, Hagenau, 1510.
Bonaventura, *Opera Omnia*, Quaracchi, 1882–1902.

Bradwardine, Thomas, *De causa Dei contra Pelagium et de virtute causarum ad suos Mertonenses, libri tres*, ed. H. Saville, London, 1618.

Duns Scotus, John, *Opera omnia*, Vives ed. Paris, 1891–1895, vols. 8–15: *Opus Oxoniense—Quaestiones in IV Libros Sententiarum* [hereafter abbreviated as Ox.]; vol. 26: *Quaestiones quodlibetales;* vols. 22–3: *Opus Pariense—Reportatorum Pariensum libri IV* [hereafter abbreviated as Par.].

Eckhart, Meister, *Die deutschen Werke*, ed. J. Quint, vol. I: *Meister Eckharts Predigten*, Stuttgart, 1958.

——, *Die lateinischen Werke*, vol IV: *Magistri Echardi Sermones.*

Der Frankfurter, Eine deutsche Theologie, ed. Jos. Bernhart, Munich, 1947.

Gerson, Jean, *De Mystica Théologica*, ed. André Combes, Lugano, 1958.

——, *Oeuvres Complètes*, Vol. III. *L'Oeuvre Magistrale*, ed. Glorieux, Tournai, 1962.

Giles of Rome, "Aegidii Romani Impugnatio Doctrinae Petri Ioannis Olivi An. 1311–12," ed. P. Leo Amorós, O.F.M., *Archivum Franciscanum Historicum* 27 (1934), 399–451.

——, *De Ecclesiastica Potestate*, ed. Richard Scholz, Leipzig, 1929, Reprinted by Scientia Aalen, 1961.

——, *Errores Philosophorum*, ed. Josef Koch, trans. by John O. Riedl, Milwaukee: Marquette University Press, 1944.

——, *Primus Sententiarum*, Venice, 1521.

Gregory the Great, *Moralia super Iob*, in *PL*, vol. 75.

Gregory of Rimini, *Super Primum et Secundum Sententiarum*, St. Bonaventura, N.Y.: Franciscan Institute, 1955, A reprint of Venice edition, 1522.

Hus, Jan, *Documenta Mag. Joannis Hus*, ed. Frantisek Palacky, Prague, 1869.

——, *Opera Omnia*, vol. II ed. V. Flajšhans, Prague, 1905.

——, *Sermones de tempore*, ed. Anezka Schmidteva, Prague, 1959.

——, *Tractatus de ecclesia*, ed. S. Harrison Thomson, Cambridge, England, 1956.

John of Damascus, *De fide orthodoxa* in *PG*, vol. 94.

Karlstadt, Andreas Bodenstein von, "Pro Divinae gratiae defensione," ed. Ernst Kähler, in *Karlstadt und Augustin*, Halle, 1952.

Lombard, Peter, *Libri quattuor Sententiarum*, in PL, vol. 192.

Luther, Martin, *D. Martin Luthers Werke: Kritische Gesamtausgabe*, Weimar, 1883–

Ockham, William, *Quaestiones et decisiones in IV libros Sententiarum cum Centilogio theologico*, Lugduni, 1495.

——, *Quodlibeta septum una cum tractatu de sacramento altaris*, Strassburg, 1491.

Pseudo-Dionysius, *Oeuvres complètes du Pseudo-Denys l'Areopagite*, ed. M. de Gandillac, Paris, 1943.

Roth, R., *Urkunden zur Geschichte der Universität Tübingen aus den Jahren* 1476 *bis* 1550, Tübingen, 1877.

Tauler, Johannes, *Johannes Tauler, Predigten*, ed. Georg Hofmann, Freiburg i.Br. 1961.

Thomas Aquinas, *Opera omnia iussu impensaque Leonis XIII P.M. edita*, Rome, 1882–1948.

Thomas à Kempis, *De imitatione Christi*, ed. C. Hirsche, Berlin, 1874.

Wyclif, John, *Sermones*, ed. Johann Loserth, London, 1887–90.

IV. *Primary Sources—Works of Johannes von Staupitz*

A. Unprinted Works

Sermones, Codex Hs: b V 8, St. Peter, Library of the Benedictine Abbey, Salzburg, Austria.

Sermones, Codex Hs: b II 11, St. Peter, Library of the Benedictine Abbey, Salzburg, Austria.

Sermones, Codex Hs: 23 E 16, Nonnberg, Library of the Benedictine Abbey, Salzburg, Austria.

B. Printed Works

Const.	*Constitutiones Fratrum Heremitarum sancti Augustini ad apostolicorum privilegiorum formam pro Reformatione Alemanie*, Nuremberg, 1504.
Decisio	*Decisio questionis de audiencia misse in parrochiali ecclesia dominicis et festivis diebus.* Tübingen, 1500.
Hiob	Staupitz, *Tübinger Predigten, Quellen und Forschungen zur Reformationsgeschichte*, Vol. VIII. ed. Georg Buchwald and Ernst Wolf. Leipzig, 1927.
Kn.	Knaake, J. K. F., *Johannis Staupitii, opera quae reperiri poterunt omnia: Deutsche Schriften*, Vol. I. Potsdam, 1867.
Libellus	*Libellus de executione eterne predestinationis.* Nuremberg, 1517.
Salz. Pred.	Aumüller, H. "Die ungedruckten Staupitz-Predigten in Salzburg," *Jahrbuch der Gesellschaft für die Geschichte des Protestantismus in Oesterreich* 2 (Vienna, 1881), 49ff.; 11 (1890), 113ff. Sermo 24 is reprinted in Kolde, Th., *Die deutsche Augustiner-Congregation und Johann von Staupitz*. Gotha, 1879, pp. 454ff.

IV. *Secondary Sources*

Backes, Ignaz, "Die christologische Problematik der Hochscholastik und ihre Beziehung zu Chalkedon," in *Das Konzil von Chalkedon: Geschichte und Gegenwart*, Vol. II, *Entscheidung um Chalkedon*, ed. Aloys Grillmeier, S.J., and Heinrich Bacht, S.J., Würzburg, 1953, pp. 923–39.

Barth, Bernhard, O.S.B., "Ein neues Dokument zur Geschichte der frühscholastischen Christologie," *Theologische Quartalschrift* 100 (1919), 409–26; 101 (1920), 235–62.

Bernhart, Joseph, *Der Frankfurter: Eine Deutsche Theologie*, Munich, 1947.

Boehmer, Heinrich, *Luthers Romfahrt*, Leipzig, 1914.

——, *Martin Luther: Road to Reformation*, trans. by John W. Doberstein and Theodore G. Tappert, New York: Meridian Books, 1960.

Bonhoeffer, Thomas, *Die Gotteslehre des Thomas von Aquin als Sprachproblem, Beiträge zur historischen Theologie* 32, Tübingen, 1961.

Braun, W., *Die Bedeutung der Concupiscenz in Luthers Leben und Lehre*, Berlin, 1908.

Brecht, Martin, "Das Augustiner-Eremiten-Kloster zu Tübingen," *Mittelalterliches Erbe-Evangelische Verantwortung. Vorträge und Ansprachen zum Gedenken der Gründung des Tübinger Augustinerklosters* 1262, Tübingen, 1962.

Burnaby, John, *Augustine: Later Works, Library of Christian Classics*, vol. 8. Philadelphia: The Westminster Press, 1955.

Combes, André, "La doctrine mariale du chancelier Jean Gerson," *Maria: Etudes sur la sainte Vierge* 2 (Paris, 1952), 865–882.

Copleston, Frederick, S.J., *A History of Philosophy*, Vol. II, *Medieval Philosophy, Augustine to Scotus*, Westminster, Md.: The Newman Press, 1952.

Denifle, Heinrich, O.P., *Die deutschen Mystiker des* 14. *Jahrhunderts*, Freiburg i.d. Schweiz, 1951.

Dettloff, Werner, O.F.M., *Die Entwicklung der Akzeptations- und Verdienstlehre von Duns Scotus bis Luther*, Münster i.W., 1963.

———, *Die Lehre von der Acceptatio Divina bei Johannes Duns Scotus: mit besonderer Berücksichtigung der Rechtfertigungslehre*, Werl/Westf., 1954.

Dieckhoff, A. W., "Die Theologie des Johannes von Staupitz," *Zeitschrift für kirchliche Wissenschaft und kirchliches Leben* 8 (Leipzig, 1887), 169ff; 232ff.

Dublanchy, E., "Marie: Les privilèges essentiels de la Vierge Marie," *DThC*, vol. 9. Paris, 1927, cols. 2339–2409.

Ebeling, Gerhard, "Der hermeneutische Ort der Gotteslehre bei Petrus Lombardus und Thomas von Aquin," *Zeitschrift für Theologie und Kirche* 61 (1964), 283–326.

———, *Luther, Einführung in sein Denken*, Tübingen, 1964.

Ferdigg, Marcus, O.F.M., *De Vita et Operibus et Doctrina Joannis de Paltz, O.E.S.A.*, Unpublished dissertation, Pontificium Athenaeum Antonianum, Rome, 1961.

Garrigou-Lagrange, R., O.P., "Prémotion", *DThC*, vol. 13. Paris, 1936, cols. 31ff.

Geuder, A. D., *Vita Ioannis Staupitii*, Dissertation for the University of Göttingen, 1837.

Gilson, Etienne, *The Mystical Theology of Saint Bernard*, trans. by A. H. C. Downes, New York: Sheed and Ward, 1940.

Grabmann, Martin, *Mittelalterliches Geistesleben: Abhandlungen zur Geschichte der Scholastik und Mystik*, vols. I-III. Munich, 1936.

Graef, Hilda, *The Light and the Rainbow*, Westminster, Md.: The Newman Press, 1959.

Grane, Leif, *Contra Gabrielem, Luthers Auseinandersetzung mit Gabriel Biel in der Disputatio Contra Scholasticam Theologiam* 1517 (Gyldendal, 1962).

———, "Gabriel Biels Lehre von der Allmacht Gottes," *ZThK* 53 1956, 53–75.

Grimm, C. L. W., "De Ioanne Staupitio eiusque in sacrorum christianorum instaurationem meritis," *Zeitschrift für historische Theologie*, ed. Illgen, N.F. 1 (1837), 58–126.

Grunewald, Käte, *Studien zu Johannes Taulers Frömmigkeit*, Leipzig, 1930.

Hermelink, H., *Geschichte der Theologischen Fakultät in Tübingen vor der Reformation* 1477–1534, Tübingen, 1906.

Huempfner, W., O.E.S.A., "Äussere Geschichte der Augustiner-Eremiten in Deutschland," in the Festschrift, *St. Augustin*. Würzburg, 1930, pp. 147–96.

Iserloh, Erwin, *Gnade und Eucharistie in der philosophischen Theologie des Wilhelm von Ockham*, Wiesbaden, 1956.

Jedin, Hubert, *A History of the Council of Trent*, Vol. II, *The First Sessions at Trent*, trans. by Dom Ernest Graf, O.S.B. Edinburgh: Thomas Nelson and Sons Ltd., 1961.

———, "Die römischen Augustinerquellen zu Luthers Frühzeit," *Archiv für Reformationsgeschichte* 25 (1928), 256–70.

Jeremias, Alfred, *Johannes von Staupitz, Luthers Vater und Schüler*, Leipzig, 1926.

Kähler, Ernst, *Karlstadt und Augustin*, Halle, 1952.

Karrer, Otto, *Meister Eckehart*, Munich, 1926.

Keller, Ludwig, *Johann von Staupitz und die Anfänge der Reformation*, Leipzig, 1888.

Kolde, Th., *Die deutsche Augustiner-Congregation und Johann von Staupitz*, Gotha, 1879.

Lau, Franz, *Luther*, trans. by Robert H. Fischer, London: SCM Press, 1963.

———, "Père Reinoud und Luther: Bemerkungen zu Reinold Weijenborgs Lutherstudien," *Luther-Jahrbuch* 27 (1960), 64–122.

Laurentin, René, *Court Traité de Théologie Mariale*, Paris, 1953.

Le Bachelet, X. "Immaculee Conception," *DThC*, vol. 7. Paris, 1922, cols. 979–1218.

Leff, Gordon, *Bradwardine and the Pelagians*, Cambridge, England, 1957.

——, *Gregory of Rimini: Tradition and Innovation in Fourteenth Century Thought*, Manchester, 1961.

Locher, Gottfried W., "Die Prädestinationslehre Huldrych Zwinglis," *Theologische Zeitschrift* 12 (1956), 526–48.

Lohse, Bernhard, *Mönchtum und Reformation, Luthers Auseinandersetzung mit dem Mönchsideal des Mittelalters*, Göttingen, 1963.

Lorenz, R., "Die Herkunft des augustinischen Frui Deo," *Zeitschrift für Kirchengeschichte* 64 (1952/53), 54–60.

——, "Fruitio dei bei Augustin," *Zeitschrift für Kirchengeschichte* 63 (1950/51), 75–132.

Lossky, Vladimir., *The Mystical Theology of the Eastern Church*, London: James Clarke and Co., Ltd., 1957.

Lottin, Odon, O.S.B., "L'intellectualisme de la morale thomiste," *Xenia Thomistica* I (1925), 411–27.

——, *L'ordre morale et l'ordre logique d'après St. Thomas*, Louvain, 1924.

Martin, F. X., "Giles of Viterbo and the Monastery of Lecceto: the Making of a Reformer," *Analecta Augustiniana* 25 (1962), 225–53.

——, "The problem of Giles of Viterbo: a historiographical problem," *Augustiniana* 9 (1959), 357–79; 10 (1960), 43–60.

McIntyre, John, *St. Anselm and His Critics*, Edinburgh: Oliver and Boyd, 1954.

Minges, Parthenius, *Ioannes Duns Scoti doctrina philosophica et theologica*, 2 vols, Quaracchi, 1930.

Moeller, Bernd, "Frömmigkeit in Deutschland um 1500," *Archiv für Reformationsgeschichte* 56 (1965), 5–31.

——, "Tauler und Luther," in *La Mystique Rhénane, Colloque de Strasbourg* 16–19 *mai* 1961, Paris, 1963.

Müller, A. V., "Der Augustiner-Observantismus und die Kritik und Psychologie Luthers," *Archiv für Reformationsgeschichte* 18 (1921), 1–34.

——, *Luthers Theologische Quellen*, Giessen, 1912.

Oberman, Heiko A., *Archbishop Thomas Bradwardine: A Fourteenth-Century Augustinian*, Utrecht, 1958.

——, "Das tridentinische Rechtfertigungsdekret im Lichte spätmittelalterlicher Theologie," *Zeitschrift für Theologie und Kirche* 61 (1964), 251–82.

——, "*De Praedestinatione et Praescientia*: An anonymous fourteenth-century treatise on predestination and justification," *Nederlandsch Archief voor Kerkgeschiedenis*, n.s. 43 (1960), 195–220.

——, "'Facientibus Quod In Se Est Deus Non Denegat Gratiam.' Robert Holcot, O.P., and the Beginnings of Luther's Theology," *Harvard Theological Review* 55 (1962), 317–42.

——, "'Iustitia Christi' and 'Iustitia Dei', Luther and the Scholastic Doctrines of Justification," *Harvard Theological Review* 59 (1966), 1–26.

——, "Preaching and the Word in the Reformation," *Theology Today* 18 (1961), 16–29.

——, "Some Notes on the Theology of Nominalism with attention to its Relation to the Renaissance," *Harvard Theological Review* 53 (1960), 47–76.

——, *The Harvest of Medieval Theology, Gabriel Biel and Late Medieval Nominalism*, Cambridge, Mass.: Harvard University Press, 1963.

——, "The Virgin Mary in Evangelical Perspective," *Journal of Ecumenical Studies* 1 (1964), 271–98.

——, "Thomas Bradwardine: Un Précurseur de Luther?" *Revue d'Histoire et de Philosophie religieuses* 40 (1960), 146–151.

O'Malley, John, S.J., *Giles of Viterbo, on Church and Reform*, to be published in 1968 by E.J. Brill of Leiden.

Ott. Ludwig, "Das Konzil von Chalkedon in der Frühscholastik," in *Das Konzil von Chalkedon: Geschichte und Gegenwart*, Vol. II, *Entscheidung um Chalkedon*. ed. Aloys Grillmeier, S.J., and Heinrich Bacht, S.J., Würzburg, 1953, pp. 873–922.

Otto, Rudolph, *Mysticism East and West*, New York: Collier Books, 1962.

Outler, Albert C., *Augustine: Confessions and Enchiridion, Library of Christian Classics* 8, Philadelphia: The Westminster Press, 1955.

Pannenberg, Wolfhart, *Die Prädestinationslehre des Duns Skotus*, Göttingen, 1954.

Paulus, N., "Johannes von Staupitz, seine vorgebliche protestantische Gesinnung," *Historisches Jahrbuch* 12 (1891) 309–46; 773–777.

Reinhardt, Klaus, *Pedro Luis (1538–1602) und sein Verständnis der Kontingenz. Praescienz und Praedestination*, Münster i.W., 1965.

Ritschl, Albrecht, *A Critical History of the Christian Doctrine of Justification and Reconciliation*, Vol. I. trans. by John S. Black, Edinburgh: Edmonston and Douglas, 1872.

Robson, J. A., *Wyclif and the Oxford Schools*, Cambridge, England, 1961.

Rupp, Gordon, *Luther's Progress to the Diet of Worms*, New York: Harper Torchbooks, 1964.

——, *The Righteousness of God: Luther Studies*, London: Hodder and Stoughton, 1953.

——, "Word and Spirit in the First Years of the Reformation," *Archiv für Reformationsgeschichte* 49 (1958), 13–26.

Saarnivaara, U., *Luther Discovers the Gospel*, St. Louis: Concordia Publishing House, 1951.

Scheel, Otto, *Martin Luther, Von Katholizismus zur Reformation*, 3 and 4 eds. Tübingen, 1930.

Schüler, Martin, *Prädestination, Sünde und Freiheit bei Gregor von Rimini*, Stuttgart, 1934.

Schwarz, Reinhard, *Fides, Spes und Caritas beim jungen Luther*, *Arbeiten zur Kirchengeschichte* 34, Berlin, 1962.

Seeberg, Erich, *Luthers Theologie in ihren Grundzügen*, 2 ed. Stuttgart, 1950.

——, *Luthers Theologie: Motive und Ideen. I. Die Gottesanschauung*, Göttingen, 1929.

Seeberg, Reinhold, *Die Theologie des Johannes Duns Scotus*, Leipzig, 1900.

——, *Lehrbuch der Dogmengeschichte*, 5 ed. Leipzig, 1953.

Spykman, Gordon J., *Attrition and Contrition at the Council of Trent*, Kampen, 1955.

Stakemeier, Eduard, "De Beata Maria Virgine Eiusque Cultu Iuxta Reformatores," in *De Marologia et Oecumenismo*, Rome: Pontificia Academia Mariana Internationalis, 1962, pp. 424–77.

——, *Der Kampf um Augustin auf dem Tridentinum*, Paderborn, 1937.

Strohl, Henri, *Luther jusqu'en 1520*, 2 ed. revised, Paris, 1962.

Tierney, Brian, *The Crisis of Church and State* 1050–1300, Englewood Cliffs, N.J.: Prentice-Hall, Inc., 1964.

Toner, Nicolaus, O.E.S.A., "The doctrine of original sin according to Augustine of Rome (Favaroni)," *Augustiniana* 7 (1957), 100–17, 349–66, 515–30.

Trapp, Damasus, O.E.S.A., "Augustinian Theology of the 14th Century; Notes on Editions, Marginalia, Opinions and Booklore," *Augustiniana* 6 (1956), 147–265.

Ullmann, C., *Reformatoren vor der Reformation*, Vol. II., Hamburg, 1842.

Vignaux, Paul, *Justification et prédestination au XIVe siècle, Duns Scot, Pierre d'Auriole, Guillaume d'Occam. Grégoire de Rimini*, Paris, 1934.

——, *Luther, commentateur des Sentences*, Paris, 1935.

——, *Philosophy in the Middle Ages: An Introduction*, New York: Meridian Books, 1959.

Vooght, Paul de, *Hussiana*, Louvain, 1960.

——, *L'Hérésie de Jean Huss*, Louvain, 1960.

Weijenborg, Reinold, O.F.M., "Doctrina de Immaculata Conceptione apud Ioannem de Paltz, O.E.S.A., Magistrum Lutheri Novitii," *Virgo Immaculata*, Vol. XIV, *De Immaculata Conceptione apud varias Nationes*, Rome: Academia Mariana Internationalis, 1957, pp. 160–83.

——, "Neuentdeckte Dokumente im Zusammenhang mit Luthers Romreise," *Antonianum* 32 (1957), 147–202.

Weiler, A. G., *Heinrich von Gorkum (ob. 1431)*, *Seine Stellung in der Philosophie und der Theologie des Spätmittelalters*, Hilversum, 1962.

Werbeck, Wilfrid, *Jacobus Perez von Valencia, Untersuchungen zu seinem Psalmenkommentar, Beiträge zur historischen Theologie* 28, Tübingen, 1959.

Wilks, Michael J., *The Problem of Sovereignty in the Later Middle Ages*, Cambridge, England, 1963.

Williams, George H., *The Radical Reformation*, Philadelphia: The Westminster Press, 1962.

Wolf, Ernst, "Die Augustiner-Eremiten in Deutschland bis zur Reformation," *Mittelalterliches Erbe-Evangelische Verantwortung*. Tübingen, 1962.

——, "Johann von Staupitz und die theologischen Anfänge Luthers," *Luther-Jahrbuch* 9 (1929), 43–86.

——, *Staupitz und Luther, Ein Beitrag zur Theologie des Johannes von Staupitz und deren Bedeutung für Luthers theologischen Werdegang. Quellen und Forschungen zur Reformationsgeschichte*, Vol. 9. Leipzig, 1927.

Würsdörfer, J., *Erkennen und Wissen nach Gregor von Rimini, BB*, Vol. XX, Pt. 1. Münster i.W., 1917.

Wyser, Paul, O.P., "Taulers Terminologie vom Seelengrund," *Altdeutsche und Altniederländische Mystik*, ed. Kurt Ruh, *Wege der Forschung* 23, Darmstadt, 1964, pp. 324–52.

Ypma, Eelcko, *La formation des professeurs chez les ermites de Saint-Augustin* 1256 à 1324, Paris, 1956.

Zeller, Paul, "Johannes von Staupitz, seine religiösdogmatischen Anschauungen," *Theologische Studien und Kritiken* 52 (1879), 7–64.

Zumkeller, Adolar, O.E.S.A., "Das Ungenügen der menschlichen Werke bei den deutschen Predigern des Spätmittelalters," *Zeitschrift für katholische Theologie* 81 (1959), 265–305.

——, "Die Augustinerschule des Mittelalters: Vertreter und Philosophisch-Theologische Lehre," *Analecta Augustiniana* 27 (1964), 167–262.

——, *Dionysius de Montina: ein neuentdeckter Augustinertheologe des Spätmittelalters*, Würzburg, 1948.

——, "Hugolin von Orvieto über Prädestination, Rechtfertigung und Verdienst," *Augustiniana* 4 (1954), 109–56; 5 (1955), 5–51.

——, "Hugolin von Orvieto (ob. 1373) über Urstand und Erbsünde," *Augustiniana* 3 (1953), 35–62; 165–93; 4 (1954), 25–46.

——, *Hugolin von Orvieto und seine theologische Erkenntnislehre*, Würzburg, 1941.

INDEX OF NAMES

INDEX OF SUBJECTS